POPE FRANCIS AND THE FUTURE OF CATHOLICISM

Pope Francis and the Future of Catholicism is the first in-depth study of the most important teaching document from Pope Francis to date: *Evangelii Gaudium*. It explores the key components of his vision and agenda for the church – ecclesiological, social, and dialogical – drawing together a range of globally and disciplinary diverse voices from leading experts in the field. Contributions explore Francis's distinctive style of papacy as well as the substance of his ecclesial revolution and reforms. Chapters engage with the most pressing challenges for the church in today's world and Francis's debt to key influences from John XXIII and Vatican II to Liberation Theology. The global context and contributions to the dialogue of this papacy are assessed and discussed in-depth. The scope of the book will appeal to those interested in the Catholic Church in both contemporary and historical contexts and to those seeking to understand where the church is going today.

Gerard Mannion holds the Joseph and Winifred Amaturo Chair in Catholic Studies at Georgetown University, where he is also a Senior Research Fellow of the Berkley Center for Religion, Peace and World Affairs. He has authored, coauthored, and edited nineteen books and numerous other writings in the fields of ecclesiology, ethics and in ecumenical and interreligious dialogue, as well as in other aspects of systematic theology and philosophy. He serves as Chair of the Ecclesiological Investigations International Research Network.

Pope Francis and the Future of Catholicism

Evangelii Gaudium and the Papal Agenda

Edited by
GERARD MANNION

CAMBRIDGE
UNIVERSITY PRESS

CAMBRIDGE
UNIVERSITY PRESS

One Liberty Plaza, 20th Floor, New York, NY 10006, USA

Cambridge University Press is part of the University of Cambridge.

It furthers the University's mission by disseminating knowledge in the pursuit of education, learning, and research at the highest international levels of excellence.

www.cambridge.org
Information on this title: www.cambridge.org/9781107142541

© Cambridge University Press 2017

This publication is in copyright. Subject to statutory exception and to the provisions of relevant collective licensing agreements, no reproduction of any part may take place without the written permission of Cambridge University Press.

First published 2017

Printed in the United Kingdom by Clays, St Ives plc

A catalogue record for this publication is available from the British Library.
Library of Congress Cataloging-in-Publication Data
Names: Mannion, Gerard, 1970- editor.
Title: Pope Francis and the future of Catholicism: Evangelii Gaudium and the papal agenda / [edited by] Gerard Mannion.
Description: New York: Cambridge University Press, 2017. |
Includes bibliographical references and index.
Identifiers: LCCN 2016041861 | ISBN 9781107142541 (hard back)
Subjects: LCSH: Catholic Church. Pope (2013– : Francis). Evangelii Gaudium. | Francis, Pope, 1936– | Evangelistic work – Catholic Church. | Church work – Catholic Church. | Catholic Church – History – 21st century.
Classification: LCC BX2347.4.P67 2016 | DDC 266/.2–dc23
LC record available at https://lccn.loc.gov/2016041861

ISBN 978-1-107-14254-1 Hardback

Cambridge University Press has no responsibility for the persistence or accuracy of URLs for external or third-party Internet Web sites referred to in this publication and does not guarantee that any content on such Web sites is, or will remain, accurate or appropriate.

For my dear aunt and uncle,
Winnie and John Kelly
Two wonderful people who have embodied the Joy
of the Gospel for all who have encountered them
throughout their long and fruitful lives.
Rath Dé ort

Contents

Notes on Contributors   *page* ix

Foreword by David Hollenbach, S.J.   xv

Acknowledgments   xvii

Abbreviations and Works Frequently Cited   xix

1 Pope Francis's Agenda for the Church – *Evangelii Gaudium* as Papal Manifesto: Introduction 1
   Gerard Mannion

PART I A NEW VISION FOR THE CHURCH? *EVANGELII GAUDIUM* AND POPE FRANCIS'S ECCLESIOLOGY

2 Pope Francis's New Vision for the Church as Expressed in *Evangelii Gaudium* 23
   Dennis M. Doyle

3 *Evangelii Gaudium* as an Act of Reception of Vatican II. . . . 38
   Massimo Faggioli

4 "The Lord, your God, is in your Midst" (EG 4): *Evangelii Gaudium* – Francis's Call for a Kenotic Theology 55
   Judith Gruber

5 "An ecclesial renewal which cannot be deferred" (EG 27–33): Ecclesial Renewal and the Renewal of Ecclesial Structures 75
   Sandra Mazzolini

6 Francis's Ecclesiological Revolution: A New Way of Being Church, a New Way of Being Pope 93
   Gerard Mannion

PART II A CHURCH OF AND FOR THE POOR:
THE SOCIAL VISION OF EVANGELII GAUDIUM

7 The Social Vision of *The Joy of the Gospel*:
   Four Questions 125
   William Werpehowski

8 Taking on the "Smell of the Sheep": Racial Justice
   in the Missionary Key of *Evangelii Gaudium* 143
   Maureen O'Connell

9 A Church of and for the Poor: The Social Vision of
   Evangelii Gaudium through the Eyes of a
   Scholar-Practitioner 162
   Maryanne Loughry, AM, RSM

10 Evangelizing in an Economy of Death 179
    Mary Doak

PART III CHURCH AND WORLD IN THE TWENTY-FIRST
CENTURY: THE DIALOGICAL VISION OF EVANGELII GAUDIUM

11 The Global Vision of *Evangelii Gaudium*:
    Cultural Diversity as a Road to Peace 203
    Drew Christiansen, S.J.

12 The Dialogue of Fraternity: *Evangelii Gaudium* and the
    Renewal of Ecumenical and Interreligious Dialogue 221
    John Borelli

Index (compiled by Ted Dedon)   245

Notes on Contributors

John Borelli is Special Assistant for Interreligious Initiatives to President John J. DeGioia of Georgetown University. He also serves as the US Jesuit Conference's Coordinator for Interreligious Dialogue and Relations. Prior to these appointments in 2004, Dr. Borelli served as Associate Director of the Secretariat for Ecumenical and Interreligious Affairs at the US Conference of Catholic Bishops for more than sixteen years. Staffing the Bishops' Subcommittee on Interreligious Dialogue, he managed three ongoing dialogues with Muslims, one with Buddhists, one with Hindus, and other interreligious projects. He also staffed ecumenical dialogues with Orthodox Christians and with Anglicans. Dr. Borelli was a consultor to the Vatican's Pontifical Council for Interreligious Dialogue for seventeen years. In 1976, he received a doctorate in history of religions and theology from Fordham University, where he taught full time during his final year of graduate studies. He oversaw Religious Studies at the College of Mount St. Vincent for eleven years. He coauthored *Interfaith Dialogue: A Catholic View* with Archbishop Michael L. Fitzgerald (2006). He has edited *A Common Word and the Future of Christian-Muslim Relations* (2009) and *The Handbook for Interreligious Dialogue* (1988) and coedited *The Quest for Unity: Orthodox and Catholics in Dialogue* (1996) with John Erickson. He had published more than two hundred articles in the past forty years.

Drew Christiansen, S.J. is Distinguished Professor of Ethics and Global Human Development at Georgetown's School of Foreign Service and a senior fellow at the Berkley Center for Religion, Peace and World Affairs. He has served as editor in chief of *America*, the national Jesuit weekly, from 2005 to 2012, director of the Office of International Justice and Peace (1991–1998), and Counselor for International Affairs (1998–2004) of the United States Catholic Conference. Father Christiansen has taught social ethics at the Jesuit School of Theology at Berkeley (1980–1986) and theology and peace studies at the University of Notre Dame (1986–1990). He was also a member of the first team at Notre Dame's Kroc Center for International Peace Studies. Pope John Paul II named Father Christiansen an expert at the Synod for America (1997–1999), and he was an expert for the First Congress of Catholic Patriarchs and Bishops of the Middle East in Fatqa, Lebanon (1999). He is a coauthor of *Forgiveness: An Alternative Road to Peace* and coeditor of *Peacemaking: Moral and Political Challenges of the 90s*, *And God Saw It Was Good: Catholic Theology*, and *Environment and Faithful Witness: Michel Sabbah on Peace and Reconciliation in the Holy Land*.

Mary Doak is Associate Professor of theology at the University of San Diego, where she has taught courses in systematic theology for the past seven years. Before coming to San Diego, she taught in the Philosophy Department at North Park University and in the Theology Department of the University of Notre Dame. She holds an MA and a PhD in theology from the University of Chicago's Divinity School, and an Honors BA in theology and philosophy from Loyola University of Chicago. Her research interests include public theology, religious freedom, narrative, eschatology, and ecclesiology. She has published two books: *Translating Religion* (2013), coedited with Anita Houck; and *Reclaiming Narrative for Public Theology* (2004). She has also published numerous articles and book chapters on aspects of Christian theology and public life in the United States. She is currently writing a book on the Christian concept of the person in relation to community, as well as a book and articles on the specific challenges of the twenty-first century to the unifying mission of the church, especially the challenges raised by the global economy, climate change, and immigration (including human trafficking).

Dennis M. Doyle is a Catholic theologian who specializes in ecclesiology. He has taught at the University of Dayton for thirty years. He holds a BA in English from LaSalle University and an MA in English Language and Literature from Ohio University. He earned his doctorate in Religious Studies from the Catholic University of America. Doyle is the author of numerous articles and three books, *The Church Emerging from Vatican II* (updated 2002), *Communion Ecclesiology: Vision and Versions* (2000) and *What is Christianity? A Dynamic Introduction* (2016). He recently coedited *Ecclesiology and Exclusion: Boundaries of Being and Belonging in Postmodern Times* (2012). He spent the 2012–2013 academic year as a guest professor at the University of Augsburg.

Massimo Faggioli worked in the "John XXIII Foundation for Religious Studies" in Bologna between 1996 and 2008 and received his PhD from

Notes on Contributors

the University of Turin in 2002. He moved to the United States in 2008, where he was a Visiting Fellow at the Jesuit Institute at Boston College between 2008 and 2009. Dr. Faggioli then worked as assistant professor in the Theology Department of the University of St. Thomas in St. Paul (Minnesota) until 2016, when he became a full professor of systematic theology at Villanova University. He lives in the City of Brotherly Love with his wife and their two children. He writes regularly for Italian and American newspapers and journals on the Church, religion, and politics. Among his recent books are *Breve storia dei movimenti cattolici* (2008; Spanish translation 2011); *Vatican II: The Battle for Meaning* (2012; Italian translation and Portuguese translation, 2013); *True Reform: Liturgy and Ecclesiology in "Sacrosanctum Concilium"* (2012; Italian translation, 2013; German translation, 2015); *Nello spirito del concilio. Movimenti ecclesiali e recezione del Vaticano II* (2013); *John XXIII: The Medicine of Mercy* (2014); *Papa Francesco e la chiesa-mondo* (2014); and English trans, *Pope Francis: Tradition in Transition* (2015).

Judith Gruber received her PhD from the University of Salzburg (Austria) and is now Assistant Professor of Systematic Theology at Loyola University New Orleans. Her research focuses on epistemological and methodological issues in systematic theology, and to tackle these issues, she works in the interdisciplinary interface of theology and cultural studies. Currently, she works on an interpretation history of Melchio Cano's "De Locis Theologicis." She has published a number of articles in her research field, both in German and English. Her most recent publication is the monograph *Theologie nach dem Cultural Turn: Interkulturalitaet als theologische Ressource* (2013) (= *Theology after the Cultural Turn: Interculturality as a Theological Resource*).

David Hollenbach, S.J., is an American Jesuit and the Pedro Arrupe Distinguished Research Professor in Georgetown's School of Foreign Service as well as a Senior Fellow at the Berkley Center for Religion, Peace and World Affairs. Previously, he was the director of the Center for Human Rights and International Justice at Boston College, where he also held the University Chair in Human Rights and International Justice. A consultant for the Jesuit Refugee Service, he has also previously taught at the Weston Jesuit School of Theology in Cambridge, MA and at Georgetown once more earlier in his career. He has been Visiting Professor of Social Ethics at Hekima College of the Catholic University of Eastern Africa, Nairobi, Kenya; and at the Jesuit Philosophy Institute in Ho Chi Minh City, Vietnam. He assisted the National Conference of Catholic Bishops in drafting their 1986 pastoral letter, *Economic Justice for All: Catholic Social Teaching and the U.S. Economy*. In 1990 he conducted the annual Winter School of Theology in six cities in Southern Africa, sponsored by the Catholic Bishops Conference of Southern Africa.

Maryanne Loughry, AM is a Sister of Mercy and the Associate Director, Jesuit Refugee Service Australia. Dr. Loughry has been associated with the Jesuit Refugee Service (JRS) since 1986 and through JRS worked in the Indochinese refugee camps in the Philippines (1988) and the Vietnamese Detention Centres in Hong Kong (1990, 1992–1993) as a psychologist and trainer. Dr. Loughry is a Research Professor at Boston College, at the Centre for Human Rights and International Justice and the Graduate School of Social Work. She is a research associate of the Refugee Studies Centre, University of Oxford. Prior to this she was the Pedro Arrupe tutor at the University of Oxford Refugee Studies Centre for more than seven years (1997–2004) and Executive Officer of Mercy Works (2004–2006). Dr. Loughry is a member of the Australian government's Minister of Immigration's Advisory Council on Asylum Seekers and Detention and also serves on the Governing Committee of the International Catholic Migration Committee, Geneva. She has conducted research and program evaluation in numerous refugee and conflict settings including Banda Aceh, Indonesia, Gaza, Papua New Guinea, Syria, Rwanda, Uganda, and Sierra Leone. Dr. Loughry was awarded the Order of Australia for service to refugees and displaced persons.

Gerard Mannion holds the Joseph and Winifred Amaturo Chair in Catholic Studies in the Department of Theology at Georgetown University, where he is also a Senior Research Fellow of the Berkley Center for Religion, Peace and World Affairs and co-director of its Church and World Program. Educated at the Universities of Cambridge and Oxford, he is an Honorary Fellow of the Australian Catholic University and elected member of the American Theological Society. He has held visiting professorships and fellowships at the universities of Tübingen (Germany); the Dominican Institute of Theology/University of St. Michael's College, Toronto (Canada); the Institute of Religious Sciences, FBK, Trento, (Italy); the Katholieke Universiteit Leuven (Belgium), Chichester (UK); and, in 2004, was a Coolidge Fellow at Union Theological Seminary/Columbia University, New York City. Founding Chair of the Ecclesiological Investigations International Research Network, he is also editor of the Bloomsbury Series, "Ecclesiological Investigations," and coeditor (with Oxford University's Mark Chapman) of the Palgrave Macmillan "Pathways

Notes on Contributors

for Ecumenical and Interfaith Dialogue" series. He has authored, coauthored, and edited nineteen books and numerous articles and chapters elsewhere in the fields of ecclesiology, ethics, social justice, ecumenical and interreligious dialogue, as well as in other aspects of systematic theology and philosophy. He is an Irish citizen, passionate about social justice, rugby union, and music.

Sandra Mazzolini graduated from the History Department of the Faculty of Modern Literature and Philosophy of the "Università degli Studi" of Trieste (Italy). Her thesis, "Aspetti dell'azione dei Gesuiti in alcune parti dei territori asburgici alla fine del 1500," was directed by Giovanni Miccoli. In 1998, she completed her doctorate in dogmatic theology at the Gregorian University in Rome with a thesis entitled "La Chiesa è essenzialmente missionaria. Il rapporto 'natura della Chiesa' – 'missione della Chiesa' nell'iter della Costituzione 'De Ecclesia' (1959–1964)," directed by Angel Antón. She is presently Full (Ordinary) Professor and holder of the chair in "Church and Mission" in the Faculty of Missiology at the Pontifical Urbania University in Rome. She regularly collaborates with other academic institutions in Rome, as well as internationally. She has published various contributions in specialist journals, reviews, and collected works. Her most recent book is *Vaticano II in rete. IV. Una lunga preparazione andata in fumo?* (2012). See www.sandramazzolini.it.

Maureen O'Connell is Chair of the Department of Religion and Associate Professor of Religion at LaSalle University with expertise in Christian/Catholic social ethics, the arts and social justice, and racism and racial justice. Dr. O'Connell spent eight years in the Department of Theology at Fordham University in New York City before returning home to Philadelphia in the fall of 2013. She authored *Compassion: Loving Our Neighbor in an Age of Globalization* (2009) and *If These Walls Could Talk: Community Muralism and the Beauty of Justice* (2012), which explores the arts as source of ethical wisdom and catalyst for moral action and which won the College Theology Book of the Year Award in 2012, as well as the Catholic Press Association's first place for books in theology in 2012. Her current research project explores racial identity formation, racism, and racial justice on Catholic college campuses. She serves on the board of the Society for the Arts in Religious and Theological Studies and is the Vice President of the College Theology Society.

William Werpehowski holds the Robert L. McDevitt, K.S.G., K.C.H.S. and Catherine H. McDevitt L.C.H.S. Chair in Catholic Theology at

Georgetown University. He earned his baccalaureate degree at Princeton University and his PhD in Christian ethics at Yale University. He is the author of *Karl Barth and Christian Ethics: Living in Truth* (2014) and *American Protestant Ethics and the Legacy of H. Richard Niebuhr* (2002). He has also coedited (with Kathryn Getek Soltis) *Virtue and the Moral Life* (2014) and (with Gilbert Meilaender) *The Oxford Handbook of Theological Ethics* (2005). Prior to joining the Georgetown faculty, Professor Werpehowski worked for more than three decades at Villanova University, where he directed its Center for Peace and Justice Education from 1999 to 2010.

Foreword

The Joy of the Gospel: A Pastoral Message of Grace and Hope

David Hollenbach, S.J.

Some years ago I had a conversation with a Catholic layperson who held an important position in the administration of the US federal government. She told me that representatives of Catholic agencies had been among the most effective voices making the case that the government should take action better to assist poor and vulnerable people in the United States and globally. But she also commented that this lobbying produced less action than she hoped for because the decision makers knew that the Catholic agencies had only some of the people in the pews with them.

Pope Francis's apostolic exhortation *The Joy of the Gospel* (*Evangelii Gaudium*) and his joy-filled style of leadership has had an impact that could well lead many more people, both Catholics in the pew as well as members of other faith communities or none, to join in such efforts to overcome poverty and other forms of human suffering. The enthusiasm with which Francis's actions and writings are being received, both by those who are religious and those who see themselves as secular, shows that his style has captured the imaginations of many people. Such imaginative engagement with a Christian vision of how life can be lived is likely to help the Christian community have a considerably more effective impact when it seeks to assist those who are poor or suffering.

Christian doctrine has always told us that grace is the source of effective Christian action in all domains of life, including Christian efforts to empower the poor and marginalized. Effective social action in the church and the larger society rarely arises from guilt or from being told one is not doing one's duty. Francis's way of calling both the church and the secular community to work for the alleviation of poverty avoids negative and judgmental approaches. He presents a strongly positive message that greater justice for the poor is actually possible. Francis presents a message of grace that encourages rather than a message of blame that depresses. He knows that action is most likely to result from hope, from confidence that change is really possible, and from belief that action can make a difference.

Pope Francis's words and actions have been a genuine source of such hope and belief for many. He is showing us that even in the face of the enormous complexity of society today, God's gracious, healing, and redeeming love is present. Francis is surely not naïve about the magnitude of the problems we need to tackle in social life today or about the difficulties we must face in trying to address these problems. He knows full well that a kind indifference to human suffering is quite widespread today. But Francis's ministry exemplifies how God's love can make a real difference in public life, including in politics and economics. This ministry reveals something of the power of grace in both his actions and his words. Francis is a pastor making the good news of the gospel visible and credible to many, both inside the Catholic community and beyond its membership. His ministry can be seen as a manifestation of grace in action.

When *Evangelii Gaudium* was published, it set forth the agenda of Francis's pontificate for all to see. It shows that he wants to move the church forward in its service of the world by displaying how the Christian life can be filled with hope and joy. The essays in this book analyze how Francis is doing this. The authors who have contributed are much encouraged by the way Francis's style of leadership is revivifying the hope that marked Catholic life during and immediately following the Second Vatican Council. Some of the essays show how Francis is bringing new energy to the pastoral practice and inner life of the church. Others sketch how the pope's words and actions show real possibilities for effective response to major social challenges, such as racism, poverty, economic injustice, and war.

In addressing all these issues, Francis's central message is always one of hope. This book takes the same encouraging and hope-filled approach in its analyses of *Evangelii Gaudium*. The volume echoes Francis's truly pastoral message – a message that shows that the Good News can make a difference. Both Francis's words in *Evangelii Gaudium* and the discussions in this volume can help energize church life, enabling the Christian community to make a stronger contribution to a more just and peaceful world. We can be grateful both for Francis's contributions and also for the way this book helps us better understand these papal contributions. Both Francis's apostolic exhortation and the essays in this book carry messages touched by grace.

Acknowledgments

I wish to express my deep gratitude to several people who helped to make this volume come to fruition. First of all to Laura Morris who originally commissioned the volume for Cambridge University Press and also to the other fine people who I have worked with at the Press to bring this study into print including Martine Walsh, Beatrice Rehr, Marielle Poss, Mary Bongiovi, Fiona Allison and Sapphire Duveau. Sincere thanks also to Ramesh Karunakaran and all at NewGen for their professionalism in handling the different stages of production, and likewise to Christine Dunn for her copy-editing work at different stages. A very special word of thanks is due to Ted Dedon for compiling the index. A big thank-you, of course, to each and every one of our contributing scholars and to my colleague, David Hollenbach, for his generous Foreword. Finally a huge debt of gratitude is also due to all the staff and faculty colleagues at the Berkley Center for Religion, Peace and World Affairs who did so much to help us stage the event out of which the volume emerged and who work tirelessly to promote global peace, dialogue, understanding and harmony.

Abbreviations and Works Frequently Cited

AAS   *Acta Apostolica Sedis*
CDF   *Congregation for the Doctrine of the Faith*
ITC   *International Theological Commission*

N.B. Except where made explicitly clear in the text, all direct citations from official church documents from Rome are taken from the versions available publicly at vatican.va.

Pope Francis

EG   Pope Francis, *Evangelii Gaudium – The Joy of the Gospel: Apostolic Exhortation on the Proclamation of the Gospel in Today's World* (November 24, 2013), http://w2.vatican.va/content/francesco/en/apost_exhortations/documents/papa-francesco_esortazione-ap_20131124_evangelii-gaudium.html

LS   Pope Francis, *Laudato Si': On Care for Our Common Home* (May 24, 2015, released June 18, 2015), http://w2.vatican.va/content/francesco/en/encyclicals/documents/papa-francesco_20150524_enciclica-laudato-si.html

Documents of Vatican II

AA   *Apostolicam Actuositatem*, Decree on the Apostolate of the Laity (1965)
AG   *Ad Gentes*, Decree on the Mission Activity of the Church (1965)
CD   *Christus Dominus*, Decree Concerning the Pastoral Office of Bishop (1965)
DH   *Dignitatis Humanae*, Declaration on Religious Freedom (1965)

DV	*Dei Verbum*, Dogmatic Constitution on Divine Revelation (1965)
GE	*Gravissimum Educationis*, Declaration on Christian Education (1965)
GS	*Gaudium et Spes*, Pastoral Constitution on the Church in the Modern World (1965)
IM	*Inter Mirifica*, Decree on the Means of Social Communication (1963)
LG	*Lumen Gentium*, Dogmatic Constitution on the Church (1964)
NA	*Nostra Aetate*, Declaration on the Relation of the Church to Non-Christian Religions (1965)
OE	*Orientalium Ecclesiarum*, Decree on the Eastern Catholic Churches (1964)
OT	*Optatam Totius*, Decree on Priestly Training (1965)
PC	*Perfectae Caritatis*, Decree on Renewal of Religious Life (1965)
PO	*Presbyterorum Ordinis*, Decree on the Ministry and Life of Priests (1965)
SC	*Sacrosanctum Concilium*, Constitution on the Sacred Liturgy (1963)
UR	*Unitatis Redintegratio*, Decree on Ecumenism (1964)

Pope Paul VI

ES	*Ecclesiam Suam* (1964)
EN	*Evangelii Nuntiandi* (1975)

Pope John Paul II

RH	*Redemptor Hominis* (1979)
LE	*Laborem Exercens* (1981)
SRS	*Sollicitudo Rei Socialis* (1987)
RMi	*Redemptoris Missio* (1990)
CA	*Centesimus Annus* (1991)
UUS	*Ut Unum Sint* (1995)

CDF Documents

DI	*Dominus Iesus* (2000)
DVer	*Donum Veritatis* (1990)

CHAPTER 1

Pope Francis's Agenda for the Church – *Evangelii Gaudium* as Papal Manifesto

Introduction

Gerard Mannion

1. A Pope from the Ends of the Earth with a Name from the Heart of the Church

In February 2013, the Roman Catholic Church was suddenly thrown into a state of liminality – a phase of its long existence wherein it was caught between a troubled past all too familiar and a future as yet unknown. Therefore, this was a future anticipated to differing measures with hope, fear, and even trepidation: Sometimes these emotions were all felt by the same people within the church. Of course, this was not the first time the church had endured such a state of being. In many ways the church was born out of such experience of liminality as the first followers of Jesus strived to follow his radically transformative good news and actions.

What was, in many ways, distinctive about February 2013 was that when, without public warning, Pope Benedict XVI announced his resignation (although many had expected that one day this would happen), the church was forced not to fall back on ancient and quasi-ancient protocols, rituals, and realpolitik to determine its future, although that its main servant-pastors would revert to doing so was part of the very real fear that held many in its grip. It was rather that the church was offered the opportunity, however briefly, to take stock, to look around and see where the real priorities for the church lay. Many individuals and groups throughout the global church began to voice their perspectives on what the church for today and for the future most needed. Gradually some bishops and not a few of the cardinals, preparing to gather in conclave, took soundings from the wider church.

This, in itself was not distinctive – for example, one only has to go back to 1958 to see that the cardinals back then drew up what was, in effect, a job description for the new pope that the church *of those times* most needed. In many ways, it was, in effect, a description of a pope who would take the opposite approach to his predecessor on so many important issues. It was certainly, in effect, a description of a pope who would lead in a very different, more open and engaging style, and who would look out to the world and encourage dialogue with it rather than preaching down to it and turning the church inward on itself. Many believed that, in that 1958 conclave, only one cardinal fit the bill (and there were not too many to choose from of a realistic age – John XXIII was actually among the younger of their number).

Regardless of whether one believes that he was appointed merely to keep the seat warm for the then–Archbishop of Milan, who had been banished from the Roman curia and thus far denied the red hat for certain perceived progressive views, John XXIII was undoubtedly the pope the world needed at that time. His whole life and ministry had offered him a unique preparation for guiding the church through troubled yet also exciting and opportune times. He did not disappoint. What he set in motion for the church was nothing short of revolutionary, in particular the Second Vatican Council, which took place between 1962 and 1965, was one of the greatest historical events in the entire history of the church, and sought to bring the church up to date and to open the doors of engagement between the church and the wider world.

Angelo Roncalli, who became John XXIII, was the perfect man for a crisis. His career was wide and varied in experience: starting as a bishop's secretary in an age of troubled Italian and ecclesial politics alike, then as a seminary professor during the modernist crisis. He became a Vatican diplomat to countries with a minority Catholic population, then served in a wartime mission first in the Middle East – where he acted as a conduit for humanitarian dialogue on all sides, while channeling special efforts to rescue Jewish refugees from certain death- and onto a French society riven by internal scars and divisions as the war there came to a close. He then returned to Italy and to the social, economic, and ecclesiastical divides of the Patriarchate of Venice in postwar Veneto. Roncalli took to these challenges with gusto and transcended the divisions in the service of getting the focus back on what was most important – enhancing human community and well-being and overcoming what divides people. He achieved this by constantly stressing that what unites people is of far greater importance.

But, back to 2013, of course, the technological revolutions that have been visited upon the world in recent times made the scope of the global conversation about the next supreme pontiff unique in the history of the church. But even in the year 2005 and, to a much lesser extent, in 1978 and 1963, the eyes of the world were watching the Sistine Chapel and so many were venturing their own preferences and opinions. And yet, in 2013, as all too familiar factions jostled for preeminence and ultimately ecclesial power, something rather strange and unexpected happened.

At the time, despite those global soundings that identified many priorities for the church and world of these times alike, many in the church – and a majority of Vaticanologists and church historians affirmed them in such a view – did not expect anything especially radical to emerge on the balcony of St. Peter's Basilica whenever the cardinals had finally reached the required degree of agreement on which of their number would be the new universal shepherd to guide the Catholic Church into the twenty-first century proper.

They observed, quite rightly, how the cardinal electors had all been appointed by the two previous popes – forty-eight by John Paul II and sixty-seven in the much shorter pontificate of Benedict XVI. Indeed, Benedict had a hand in the nomination of many of the forty-eight, too, as his long prefectureship at the Congregation of the Doctrine of the Faith meant not only that could he single out bishops for elevation but that he could also veto appointments both to the red hat and even to the episcopacy. It is not at all controversial to say that we know for certain he exercised such a power.

Those appointed to serve as bishops and cardinals since the 1980s would increasingly be expected to remain in step with the line of thinking prevailing in the Vatican during this period of church history. The majority would oblige.

So, during that Roman springtime of 2013, the world weighed up the many candidates. Some cardinals dropped out or were ruled out through scandals or health concerns. The Italian bishops rather prematurely felt that the return of the papacy to their number was imminent. The odd US cardinal even appeared to be campaigning for such elevation for themselves. Book makers and journalists alike compiled tables of the favorites, the most *papabile* candidates.

As previously, many wondered whether this would be the moment for the papacy to return to African leadership for the first time since the sixth century? Or might Asia claim a pope from beyond its western regions, from which some of the popes in the early Christian centuries hailed? In previous conclaves, there had been great excitement that "*the* Catholic Continent," Latin America, would and should have a deep influence on the future direction of the church and its missionary priorities. But, when looking at the candidates in 2013, such enthusiasm had waned and few expected that this was Latin America's time for the papacy.

2. The Church's Dark Night

In many respects, the Roman Catholic Church has been through a period that can only be described as a "dark night" in recent decades. The turmoil, divisions, what some have called the "culture wars"; the battle for the soul and legacy of Vatican II; the very different ways in which Catholics in different cultures, countries, and continents refract the faith and its mission; the struggles between professional theologians and ecclesial offices and leaders; divisions among the theological community; conflict between religious orders, Rome, and episcopal conferences; oppression and marginalization within the church; exclusion from and exclusivity in the church; the tragic and deeply painful abuse crisis that continues to be a scandal crying out for justice; and the Vatileaks scandal that demonstrated the extent of the fault lines that the church was suffering from – stretching even to the higher echelons of its organizational leadership – were all pressing issues that demanded addressing.

Furthermore, the imperative of dialogue with other faiths, churches, and people of no faith also became an aspect of ecclesial life where divisions rose to the fore. Dialogical progress sadly stalled in far too many places as retrenched and revived forms of accentuating difference in a negative sense dominated too much ecclesial discourse. Even the liturgy, the celebration of communion, of unity, had become a battleground. These and many other issues have made it a very draining and often exhausting period of the church's history in which to be a Catholic.

In relation to the wider world, there were further challenges still, including the growing and glaring social challenges of this planet that cry out for action on the part of all people and communities of goodwill, and the desperate need to confront the environmental damage that human societies are inflicting upon our shared planet, building up ever more worrying crises that future generations will have to confront; so, also, is the ever-increasing extent and intensity of war and conflict among the human family. Many wanted the church to confront these challenges head-on.

There have been times in recent decades when Christians have despaired for various reasons. And often they would ask "Is there any hope?" Some would even have answered their own question with their feet or at least do so in existential terms as they become ever more detached from the church over divisive issues. Yet one of the great comforts Catholics should always take in the midst of such a dark night is the simple fact that, yes, there must be hope for the simple fact that when you consider the long and winding story of the church, our own age is but a blink of an eye in ecclesiastical history. The church has faced dark and challenging times before and come through them. It would surely do so again.

Of course, many in the church were also in great fear about who might emerge onto the balcony of St. Peter's following the conclave. It is easy to forget just how fearful many were. Some hoped for the best yet felt the worst was more likely.[1]

3. *Habemus Papam*: A New Pope, a New Style of Papacy

So, when, in the Italian evening of March 13, 2013, Cardinal Jean-Louis Tauran emerged to tell the waiting crowds and watching world the joyful news that "Habemus Papam," we have a pope, there was both anticipation and anxiousness around the Catholic world. In the media scrum it was not immediately obvious to everyone who was the cardinal who had actually been elected, but when Tauran announced his name, there was a gasp in so many places around the globe for the choice made by the new pope carried with it a very significant message, and so, also, for the new pope as well as for the church in general, a very challenging set of responsibilities: The church would now be shepherded forward into the future by *Papa Franciscus*. Pope Francis.

No previous pope had even dared try and live up to the responsibility of taking the name of Saint Francis of Assisi, the man who had been called by God to rebuild the church and who had sought to bring the church back to its radically transformative roots. So this choice of name was evocative of ecclesial renewal and reform.

The election of a pope who chose the name Francis signaled a church ready and, it seemed, also willing for change. A name that signifies humility, a dedication to the poor, to peace, to dialogue, to service, to the church getting back to gospel principles in all aspects of its life and therefore

---

[1] In these initial sections of the introduction, I draw upon and develop further some earlier reflections upon Pope Francis's election offered in Gerard Mannion, "Foreword: Crisis and Beyond: A New Dawn for the Catholic Church?," in the late Raymond Helmick's *The Crisis of Confidence in the Catholic Church* (New York and London: Bloomsbury, 2014), x–xix.

moving away from power and prestige toward simplicity, to following the gospel rather than human ambition. The name also signaled dialogue – both within and without the church – and concern for all creation. One doubted that any new pontiff could choose that name and not seriously try to live up to everything that it signals and evokes.

And yet Jorge Mario Bergoglio, the Cardinal Archbishop of Buenos Aries, from Argentina, from "the ends of the earth" as he joked himself that evening, did not shirk such a demanding challenge. Subsequently, he would confirm that he deliberately chose this Umbrian saint as his "guide and inspiration."[2] On that March evening of 2013, he came out onto the balcony and began his papacy as it has thus far continued: with humility, an engaging style, and dedication to the vision of St. Francis and to being open to dialogue with the world.

And if this new shepherd of Rome was really to follow Saint Francis, then by default he would need to be a listener and a "channel of peace" and so, as the pope is supposed to be, that true bridge builder, the "supreme pontiff." Above all else one dared to hope that this might really mark the beginning of the end of a very divisive era in the church. Regardless of whether one sees this as a positive thing or otherwise, the new pope instantly seemed totally different in style to his two predecessors.

As he emerged and introduced himself, he was dressed very simply, no elaborate papal paraphernalia whatsoever. The manner in which he greeted people and began with prayers was truly amazing – he asked the assembled crowd to pray both with him and for him. He especially asked for the blessing of the people before he was prepared to take the papal stole – which he removed before he said goodnight to them.

He made clear first and foremost that he is the bishop of Rome and one among other bishops and his duty was service – in charity – to the whole church. This was a sign of Vatican II collegiality coming to the fore, alongside ecumenical attentiveness and sensitivity. This was a message heard loud and clear and welcomed by members of other Christian churches. He asked for reconciliation and fraternity throughout the world. Here was a pope reaching out not just to the Catholics of the world but to all of its Christians. Not just the wider Christian Church either but sending a clear message to the watching world in its entirety. He evinced and embodied humility.

More was to follow. He renounced the right to live in the papal palace, choosing instead to live in simple rooms in the Casa Santa Marta, a

---

[2] In subsequent interviews and, most significantly, in his encyclical, *Laudato Si'* (June 2015), §10.

guesthouse beside St. Peter's. A pope from the global south living on the margins of the Vatican. Latin America had its first pope, after all. And very few people among the so-called experts had expected it to be this man. The Holy Spirit likes to keep people on their toes!

In the following months, his energy and vision helped usher in a period of tremendous excitement, hope, and now renewed anticipation. His key appointments, his daily homilies, his initial statements and teachings have all pointed toward a concerted effort to live up to that vision of Saint Francis. He made justice for the poor and wider questions of social justice both his own and the church's key priority.

He intervened to help promote peace and to denounce war and conflict, including holding a day for peace in Syria as the belligerents were pressing for an apocalyptic attack of devastation and destruction, which at least stalled the carnage that was to unfold in that nation for a significant period of time. He worked behind the scenes to help bring about a thawing in the relations between Cuba and the United States. He has given astoundingly frank, open, and revealing interviews. He has banished the exclusivistic attitudes that characterized too much of the church under his immediate predecessors.

Pope Francis, as many of our contributors also demonstrate, has resolutely set out to bring to full fruition the vision of the Second Vatican Council. In a short space of time, this pontificate has also given renewed energy to ecumenical and interfaith ventures in dialogue. For the first time in many decades, the church is being spoken about by Catholics and non-Catholics alike in increasingly positive, constructive, and hopeful terms – likewise his own office of the papacy.

He has denounced ecclesial factionism and clerical ambition. Francis has warned against a "spiritual worldliness" and how "to avoid it by making the Church constantly go out from herself, keeping her mission focused on Jesus Christ, and her commitment to the poor."[3] As many of our contributions remark, we can see so many remarkable parallels between the agenda of Pope Francis and that of John XXIII.

His priority of an unswerving commitment to the poor is another reason why he has equally made dialogue and relations between churches, faiths, and wider communities a priority too: We can fight better *together* against poverty, injustice, and the structures of social sin that present the world with the stark reality of there being more resources and wealth on the planet than ever before at the very same time as there being more poverty,

[3] EG, §97.

inequality, and injustice in our world. So, too, can we fight better to protect and care for our common home, the Earth – Francis has equally made ecology and the battle to save the environment for future generations a cornerstone policy of his papal ministry.

Like John XXIII again, Cardinal Bergoglio, it seems, has reflected at length upon his own mistakes in the past and the signs to date clearly suggest that he learned from them.

He has made curial reform and indeed reform of the Vatican's overall organizational practices and priorities another top priority. He appointed a committee of cardinals from the world's different continents to advise him on deciding upon priorities for the church's future. He instructed the nuncios and episcopal conferences of the world to elicit responses about questions concerning divorce, remarriage, and family life ahead of the Synod of Bishops in 2014 and again requested global consultations for its follow-up in 2015, thereby at once helping to try and make the process more truly synodal than has been the case hitherto.

He announced that there would be a year of mercy – beginning in December 2015 – and set the tone for this with a raft of measures stressing that priests and bishops should be more compassionate in their service to their flocks and this extended to the confessional, including for women caught in the tragedy of having to undergo an abortion. He became the first pope to address both houses of Congress when he visited the United States in September 2015, bringing with him a powerful message of justice, peace, mercy, and inclusion. He extended this message to still wider audiences with a moving address to the opening of the United Nations' historic 70th General Assembly, reminding that organization and the world's nations of their commonality and therefore joint responsibilities. His popularity during that visit was astonishing, with so much of the country – including millions who belong to other churches and faiths and those of no particular faith – gripped by Francis fever through his time there and well beyond.

These are just a few examples of how rapidly the Catholic Church has been changing in such a short space of time under its new shepherd. A pope "from the ends of the Earth," as he called himself, who took the name of the great servant of peace, Francis.

It goes without saying that it is hugely significant that this pope comes from Latin America – his worldview, his ecclesial view, by necessity, would be something dramatically different from that of his immediate and indeed any of his predecessors. This was a pope who would have to look at the world and the church in a very different way because he came out of a formative context that could not allow him to do otherwise. The centuries-old divisions within the European church, for example, look different when perceived from the other side of the world in a land where abject poverty is a more pressing and daily concern or where a ruthless dictatorship had left deep and lingering open wounds that equally demonstrated how the church should not align itself too closely with political power of any hue or cry. It was also hugely significant that he was the first Jesuit pope (and so the first SJ to owe obedience only to himself!). He is also the child of migrants (directly in the case of his father and one generation removed on his mother's side), so one hoped he would speak out of further important experiences there, and he would not disappoint.

The Global South is now the dominant arena for the future of religion, and the way the world seems in those different continents and so many different cultures, countries, and traditions is having its own extraordinary impact on the wider world.

Perhaps one obvious fact is being overlooked here that detracts not at all from the amazing and rapid achievements of Pope Francis: The ministry of this servant of the servants of God is as much (and probably to date, at least, still more) symptomatic rather than cause of the global changes in perspective among faith communities that has quietly been transforming our world. There are new social, economic, political, and intellectual perspectives emerging from the south that can help transform our one world so much for the better. Different generations are coming through with different experiences and ways of framing and so confronting the most divisive problems in the world and, indeed, in the church, too. And, as the pontificate of Francis began to unfold, one major question preoccupied so much of the discussion about this shepherd: What would be his agenda for the church? In what direction did he wish to steer Catholicism? In November, 2013, just eight months after being elected, Pope Francis gave a clear answer.

4. *Evangelii Gaudium* – A Key to Discerning Francis's Ecclesial Vision and Papal Agenda

This is a book about one single document. But what a profoundly significant document it is. Pope Francis's Apostolic Exhortation *Evangelii Gaudium – The Joy of the Gospel* – is the first major document to bear the distinctive stamp of his own vision for the church. This was released on November 24, 2013 and was, in theory, supposed to be the traditional papal document that would follow from a thematic meeting in Rome (in October 2012) of the (13th) Ordinary General Assembly Synod of Bishops.

Hence the focus was on evangelization, for the world's bishops had convened to discuss the topic most central to the pontificate of Pope Benedict XVI – that of the "new" evangelization for the transmission of the faith. But Pope Francis's document is about so much more and its understanding of evangelization, as we shall see, would emerge as something very different to that held by his predecessor.

In *Evangelii Gaudium*, Pope Francis, instead of simply addressing the topics and issues to emerge from the discussions of the bishops in 2012 (although he does indeed address many of those throughout the document), took the opportunity to set down in a more evocative and programmatic form his own sense of the key priorities for and challenges to the church in our times. This document immediately stood out and demanded attention and not just from those within the Catholic Church. Attracting the attention of the global media in a way that such documents had seldom previously ever done, it was immediately taken to be something of a papal manifesto and electrified the discourse about the church around the world.

In this volume we explore in more detail how Papa Francesco is transforming the church, considering at greater length some of his key priorities for both church and world.

Our collection does, of course, also engage other aspects of Pope Francis's ministry, teachings, and actions, but the primary focus is upon what insights this exhortation offers to the church and world about the priorities for the present and future of this supreme pontiff. *Evangelii Gaudium* is a document that engages the church-world relationship in multiple constructive ways, and our volume here will seek to do the same. This is a religious leader who has gripped the world's attention from the beginning of his ministry. It is only natural, therefore, that people will want to know more about the substance of his message and the thinking behind his actions. Our volume seeks to offer some detailed reflection, analysis, and evaluation of what insights into his vision for the church and papal agenda this groundbreaking document provides, as well as perspectives on the wider impact and trajectories of his pontificate thus far.

Although some criticized this document, some bishops and even cardinals, for example, spoke about it lacking a tight coherent structure, the vast majority of people, including those beyond the Roman Catholic Church and in the global media, saw it for what it was: A profoundly groundbreaking document that offered a radically transformative vision for the church of today and into the future.

Sources said that the pope composed it primarily on his own (in Spanish) and he confirms as much at the outset of the document, although he also admits having sought the wise counsel of others, too, reflecting his episcopal and now papal preference for a collaborative approach once more. Indeed, that collaborative approach becomes the preferred way forward to the church entire as the document makes clear throughout.

Nobody would wish to downplay that there are ambivalent sections to the document and mixed messages contained therein as we have heard from Francis in other contexts. But on a vital number of long-divisive ecclesiological issues the document is clear and unambiguous. Our volume will explore many of those issues.

This "Apostolic Exhortation on the Proclamation of the Gospel in Today's World" is divided into five distinct but interrelated sections. Following an introduction with particular reflections on the joy of the gospel, the exhortation is comprised of five chapters. The first explores "the Church's missionary transformation" and is groundbreaking in multiple ways in terms both of ecclesiological and pastoral focus. Chapter 2 explores "the crisis of communal commitment" and yet is equally groundbreaking in its focus upon social, political, and economic issues, especially inequality and social exclusion. It then strays into red-button questions such as inculturation and a variety of failings and temptations that may beset pastoral workers (including bishops and priests) and ends with reflections on spiritual worldliness, a plea to end "warring among ourselves" and a list of further ecclesial challenges for today's church to seek to overcome.

"The proclamation of the gospel" forms the focus of Chapter 3, and this builds upon the innovative perspectives already introduced in the preceding pages. A wider ecclesiological focus on the people of God leads the way to reflections on liturgy, preaching, and catechesis. Such reflections on evangelization are then widened further still to include the social dimension and implications of the kerygma and its proclamation in Chapter 4. Here Francis makes further important contributions to the church's social message and mission alike with an unswerving commitment of the church and its mission to the poor and excluded. The chapter also stresses how praxis must take precedence over ideas, and by implication, service and mission over doctrine – the latter serves the former not vice versa. Further incorporated into these reflections on "the social dimension of evangelization" are sections on the importance of dialogue – between faith, reason, and science, between differing churches, differing religions, and social dialogue in the context of religious freedom. Here Francis sets forth some of his most revolutionary ideas of all.

The fifth and final chapter speaks about "spirit-filled evangelizers," with sections on the reason why the renewal of the church's missionary priorities and methods is necessary, followed by more prayerful and spiritual reflections, ending with a homage to Mary as the "Mother of Evangelization."

Another welcome break with the tradition of some of his predecessors is his humor. Have we ever seen official magisterium exercised in an official document with so many wry jokes before? And even then, his more humorous messages were intended to communicate a very serious message, for example, Francis's reminder to priests that "that the confessional must not be a torture chamber but rather an encounter with the Lord's mercy which spurs us on to do our best."[4]

All in all, one may say that *Evangelii Gaudium* heralded not just an energizing vision toward a new way of being church, it also demonstrated that Francis would shepherd the church into the future through a new, very different and positive way of being pope. It represented not simply an indication of his agenda, but could even be described as something like a papal manifesto.

5. Assessing the Document: Three Areas of Focus

Evangelii Gaudium, then, provided the first substantial indication of Pope Francis's vision and agenda for the church. This book explores three thematic areas that reflect distinctive elements of the document's focus. The first part considers Francis's understanding of the church and his agenda for church reform and pastoral provision (*ecclesiological* dimensions). Part II appraises the *social justice* agenda of the document, while Part III explores the related *dialogical and global agenda* (peace, reconciliation and international affairs, ecumenical and interfaith dialogue).

This volume originated in a symposium gathered together at Georgetown University under the auspices of the Berkley Center for Religion, Peace and World Affairs in March 2014. This marked the inaugural event of the center's Church and World program, which is led by Fr Drew Christiansen SJ and myself. The very day that Francis released *Evangelii Gaudium*, it became obvious to me that this astonishing document should form the focus of the program's very first event because the entire document brings to the fore so many of the most important issues pertaining to the church and its relationship with the wider world.

The symposium gathered together a wonderfully talented range of voices to reflect upon this new document. And we explored numerous different aspects of the document and what it tells us about Francis's vision and

[4] EG, §44.

priorities for the church also clustered around the same three general thematic areas – ecclesiology, social justice, and the wider global and dialogical agenda for the church.

This event received national and international media coverage and the response from those attending was uniformly enthusiastic, helping to further demonstrate the desire among people from widely differing backgrounds to engage more deeply with the vision for the church that is being proposed by Pope Francis. All essays have been extensively further researched and considerably expanded and revised in the light of the discussions from the symposium and subsequent developments in the church and responses to *Evangelii Gaudium* from elsewhere.

This is the first major study of this most important document from Pope Francis (to date) to appear in English. And, to our knowledge, there is no other volume of this breadth and depth in existence at present in any language. There has been a whole raft of books published on Pope Francis in general already, although the majority of these that are presently most discussed either came out before the release of *Evangelii Gaudium* or do not offer detailed treatments of the document as such. So we believe this the first exhaustive and thematic scholarly treatment of the most extensive and original teaching document from Pope Francis to emerge to date – this notwithstanding the release in June 2015 of his encyclical *Laudato Si'*. For the latter is believed to have had at least some different sections heavily influenced and even drafted by experts from differing fields, whereas *Evangelii Gaudium* bears the imprint of Francis's own thinking both before and soon after his election as Bishop of Rome. And *Laudato Si'* builds heavily upon the vision and agenda for the church set down in *Evangelii Gaudium*, which soon became called the manifesto for the church of this new pope. *Laudato Si'* impressively and passionately develops further particular pressing issues, but *Evangelii Gaudium* draws together so many more issues, themes, challenges, and aspirations for the church as well.[5]

We think that both now and long into the future a snapshot of the initial impact, interpretation, and reception of the document will serve many within and without the church well. Some of the most fascinating reflections on Vatican II's documents, for example, are those written soon

---

[5] *Laudato Si'* appeared as this volume was in its final stages of completion. While many of our authors have included additional reflections in the light of that document, a conscious decision was made to retain the core focus of this volume on *Evangelii Gaudium* – not least of all because *Laudato Si'* deserves a comparable in-depth study all of its own and one could not do justice to both texts to the same degree in a single volume of this size.

after those documents were promulgated (and so they become valuable resources for future reflection).

The authors gathered together in this volume come from different disciplinary backgrounds, contexts, and continents. Our authors include pioneering and leading figures in their respective fields. There are essays by leading ecclesiologists and experts in other areas of systematic theology (such as missiology, contextual theology, and public theology), contributions from scholars with expertise in church history, moral theology, and ecumenical and interreligious dialogue, as well as conflict resolution and peace building. Questions of structural and pastoral reform are explored, as well as tensions between the vision of Pope Francis for the church and that of his immediate predecessors. The volume also includes contributions from the perspective of practitioners engaged in working for social justice. Therefore, topics and themes of both historical and ongoing relevance are treated, alongside pressing social, moral, and political issues, such as poverty, inequality, racism, the plight of migrants and refugees, as well as international affairs. All in all it draws together, within the confines of a single volume, a range of perspectives with international, disciplinary, and experiential breadth and depth.

So, following our inspiring foreword from Georgetown's new Pedro Arrupe Distinguished Research Professor, David Hollenbach, the first part of the volume explores "A New Vision for the Church? *Evangelii Gaudium* and Pope Francis's Ecclesiology." It opens the ecclesiological reflections with an essay from Dennis Doyle of the University of Dayton. He suggests the document offers a "synthesis" that blends a personal encounter with Christ together with an embodied engagement with the social problems of our times. Doyle explores some of the formative influences upon the vision we find there, particularly the notion of the people of God as fundamental ecclesiological motif and compares and contrasts it with the dominant ecclesiological ideas found in the teachings and visions for the church of Francis's immediate two predecessors. Doyle concurs with Cardinal Walter Kasper that in Pope Francis we see the church moving into a new phase in the reception of Vatican II.

This leads very well into Massimo Faggioli's contribution. The Italian church historian from Villanova University argues that *Evangelii Gaudium* can be read as an act of receiving Vatican II. Faggioli suggests that Francis now mirrors the council in focusing once more upon the wider world as well as upon internal church matters. This is reflected in his mission for the poor; his attentiveness to the relationship between the church, faith, and different cultures; and in his key eye for the significance of history. Faggioli, like others, also reflects upon the many parallels between John XXIII and Francis.

Austrian scholar, Judith Gruber (who is based at Loyola University, New Orleans), next explores the dogmatic implications of the social vision of Pope Francis, exploring in particular, what would the implications would be *for church doctrine* if the church were to become truly poor. She explores this via a close reading of two key aspects of Francis's overall vision in *Evangelii Gaudium*: first, that evangelization defines the mission of the church, and second, that evangelization also entails a form of kenosis. This entails a radical reframing of the church's relationship to and dependence upon the world, with implication for the formation of doctrine and theology alike. By taking Francis's call for a radically kenotic church practice to its theological conclusions, she argues that *Evangelii Gaudium* is not just a call for practical kenosis, but also for *doctrinal* kenosis. Therefore, the document is a call not only for a pastorally poor church, but also for a dogmatically poor church. And so, Gruber concludes, it is not just a critique of economic capitalism, but also of dogmatic capitalism.

Rome's Sandra Mazzolini (of the Pontifical University Urbaniana) picks up from the focus of each of the foregoing essays and surveys what *Evangelii Gaudium* tells us about Francis's priorities for much-needed ecclesial renewal, and especially for structural reform in the church. Although Francis draws on both Vatican II and some of the ideas of his predecessors in this document, there are also original and distinctive aspects to the reforming agenda set forth there. Chief among these are his emphasis upon the missionary nature of the church, along with the call for a pastoral conversion on the part of all within the church. These guide the proposed reforms and structural change. Mazzolini suggests that dynamism and decentralization are two further keywords that can help us better understand the priorities of Francis's renewal.

Our first section closes with my own contribution, which explores the fundamental ecclesiology of Pope Francis, particularly as set down in *Evangelii Gaudium*. This helps set a wider contextual background against which the themes introduced in the foregoing chapters can be further considered. I explore four particular themes. First, the issue of ecclesiological continuity or discontinuity between Francis and his immediate two predecessors. I suggest there is far more discontinuity than many anticipated and that this should, in fact, be both expected and welcomed. Second, I explore some of the key characteristics of Pope Francis's ecclesiology, particularly with regard to the most important insights into Pope Francis's vision and agenda for the church that the apostolic exhortation affords us.

These include the radical ecclesiological openness and inclusivity that *Evangelii Gaudium* embodies. Third, I survey some of the most formative influences upon the ecclesiology of Pope Francis, detailing two in particular: the specific *ecclesiological* legacy of Vatican II and the ecclesiological thinking behind the classical works and ministries of the founding pioneers of Latin American liberation theology. I then turn to consider another key characteristic we find in the document and this pontificate in general – a thoroughgoing ecclesiological *realism*. Fourth, I propose that the ecclesiological vision of *Evangelii Gaudium* is nothing short of revolutionary and therefore, Pope Francis's agenda for the church should be judged to be equally revolutionary – as multiple developments throughout the church since March 2013 confirm.

Our volume's second part focuses upon "A Church of and for the Poor: The Social Vision of *Evangelii Gaudium*." First among these reflections are four questions for that social vision, as laid out by my Georgetown University colleague, William Werpehowski. His starting point is Pope Francis's own caution that *The Joy of the Gospel* is "not a social document," by which he means a statement of the sort we find in the Roman Catholic social encyclicals from 1891's *Rerum Novarum* onward. Nevertheless, Francis does consider at least four closely related, even overlapping questions in *Evangelii Gaudium* that bear on Christian theological and social ethics. These are, in summary form, considerations of, first, what actually constitutes economic justice, in the light of Christian faith? What should be the religious and social priorities for Christians today? What helps shape and orient the Christian quest for justice today, especially for the poor? How do we foster collaboration among people of differing creeds and cultures, in the midst of the all too obvious divisions in today's world? Werpehowski explores these questions as well as the exhortation's answers, working toward a consideration of what in fact *is* "a social document," which also leads him to offer additional reflections along the way upon the pope's 2015 contribution to Catholic social teaching, *Laudato Si'*.

LaSalle University's Maureen O'Connell offers our eighth chapter, in which she unpacks the wider implications of Francis's famous call for pastors to take on the "smell of the sheep," through a focus on racial justice. She begins her reflections by stating that "*Evangelii Gaudium* might be the best document that we have to date in Catholic Social Teaching for animating racial justice work." In order to demonstrate why this is so, O'Connell painstakingly utilizes the structure and substance of *Evangelii Gaudium* to encourage Catholics to become more conscious of the hidden layers of racial prejudice and exclusion in our increasingly racialized societies. In particular, she believes the document can help unmask the historical role of religion in the racing of the Americas. Second, the culturally specific implications of the economy of exclusion and of alternatives to the same. Third, Francis's "emphasis on mercy as the proper response to individual and collective sinfulness provides a viable affective form of resistance to the 'acedia' of white supremacy."

Australian Sister of Mercy, Maryanne Loughry, who divides her time between the Jesuit Refugee Service in her native land and Boston College in the United States, explores what Francis might mean by his call for a church of and for the poor through the "lens of an observer," drawing upon her own decades of extensive experience working among the poor particularly in the form of refugees. Bringing her extensive years of experience as a scholar-practitioner to bear, she focuses upon some of the significant actions and events in the early pontificate of Francis and also offers reflections upon the significance of the fact that the document was released at the end of the 2012–2013 Year of Faith, declared by Benedict XVI. Loughry contrasts these two "bookends" of a very significant period of history for both the world and church alike. She concludes that the phrase "actions speak louder than words" might be a very good summary of Pope Francis's social agenda to date. This is a social agenda that is not especially novel to the church but Francis's approach is offering a social agenda that is simplified, more up to date, and more oriented toward praxis.

What does it mean to undertake evangelization in an "economy of death"? This is the stark question that forms the central focal point of our tenth essay, from Mary Doak of the University of San Diego. Doak analyzes the message of Francis about the idolatrous aspects of free market capitalism and explores Francis's vision of a countercultural ecclesial resistance directed against the economic practices (and idolatry) that lead to so much unnecessary suffering and death. She unpacks his alternative to individualism and competitiveness with a call to Christians to move beyond preoccupation with personal and ecclesial security and to foster universal solidarity, and to be dedicated to dialogic action with and for others. This radical message transcends Catholicism in a welcome and constructive fashion.

Our third and final section, "Church and World in the Twenty-First Century: The Dialogical Vision of *Evangelii Gaudium*," features contributions from two further Georgetown University professors. The first come from Drew Christiansen, SJ, former editor of *America*, veteran staffer of the United States Conference of Catholic Bishops (USCCB) and now Distinguished Professor of Ethics and Global Development at Georgetown University's School of Foreign Services. He explores how

Evangelii Gaudium affirms the diversity of cultures as being crucial for the task of evangelization in contrast with Pope Benedict XVI's attachment to western European culture and its cultural forms as the necessary carriers of the gospel message. Drew explicates Francis's insistence on the "transcultural" nature of the gospel in a fashion that recalls the missiological tradition of the sixteenth- and seventeenth-century Italian humanist Jesuits who attempted to spread the gospel in ways that showed respect and appreciation for Chinese culture. The apostolic exhortation, which emphasizes "diversity, plurality and multiplicity," therefore embraces diversity in a manner that opens up vast areas of the church's internal life, and also offers much hope for its future engagement in civilizational dialogue, peacemaking, and ecumenical and interreligious dialogue alike.

Our final chapter explores the implications of *Evangelii Gaudium* for the renewal of ecumenical and interfaith dialogue and is by John Borelli, another veteran of the USCCB and of multiple ecumenical and interfaith dialogue bodies, who has for many years been a special advisor to Jack DeGioia, President of Georgetown University on these and many other issues of greatest importance for today's church and society. He revisits highlights in the journey of these obligations in the past fifty years and (as with a number of our earlier chapters in relation to other themes) sees Vatican II, in particular, as a vital key to understanding the document's approach to these issues and that of Francis in practice, too. Although the document may be short on detailed policy, it nonetheless offers a message that is both simple yet profound at one and the same time. Borelli explores the importance of "fraternity" to Francis and explores his approach to dialogue prior to his election as Bishop of Rome. Further reinforcing parallels with John XXIII mentioned in our volume's first part, Borelli also points to how such parallels and the importance of Vatican II's own contribution to moving forward ecumenical and interfaith dialogue can help us understand the dialogical components of *Evangelii Gaudium* and so of Pope Francis ecclesial vision and agenda. Indeed, he suggests that in Francis we finally see a call to renew the dialogical initiatives of council in the spirit that the council intended them.

We know that *Evangelii Gaudium* offers the key to understanding the ecclesial vision and agenda of Pope Francis because in so many subsequent addresses, church documents, and actions, the words, themes, values, and virtues embodied in that document reoccur – sometimes explicitly so, sometimes implicitly. Therefore, in encouraging readers to enjoy a deeper engagement with and so understanding of *Evangelii Gaudium*, we hope that the essays in this book help enhance your own understanding and appreciation of Pope Francis and his hopes and aspirations for the church and world of today and tomorrow in general. In an address to the vigil gathered in St Peter's Square, Rome, on the eve of the 2014 Extraordinary Synod on the Family (October 4, 2014), Pope Francis further encapsulated the extraordinary openness of his vision and agenda, invoking the reforming spirit of Francis of Assisi and citing, *Lumen Gentium*, §8, "With the joy of the Gospel we will rediscover the way of a reconciled and merciful Church, poor and a friend of the poor; a Church 'given strength that it might, in patience and in love, overcome its sorrows and its challenges, both within itself and from without'" Further echoing the spirit of both John XXIII and *Gaudium et Spes*, also, he called for the bishops gathering for the synod to listen humbly to the "beat of this time", to "perceive the 'scent' of the people today" and encouraged them to engage in open and honest dialogue throughout their proceedings. He closed with a prayer that the spirit of Pentecost might "untie the knots which prevent people from encountering one another, heal the wounds that bleed, and rekindle much hope."[6] Pope Francis's vision and agenda for the church truly embody the essence of the sacramental character of the church's mission, a church called not simply to bear witness to the joy of the gospel, but also to strive to ensure that joy becomes a reality throughout the four corners of this wondrous world, our shared home.

---

[6] Address of His Holiness Pope Francis During the Meeting on The Family, Saint Peter's Square (Saturday, 4 October 2014), https://w2.vatican.va/content/francesco/en/speeches/2014/october/documents/papa-francesco_20141004_incontro-per-la-famiglia.html

PART I

A New Vision for the Church?
Evangelii Gaudium *and Pope Francis's Ecclesiology*

CHAPTER 2

Pope Francis's New Vision for the Church as Expressed in *Evangelii Gaudium*

Dennis M. Doyle

In the Apostolic Exhortation *Evangelii Gaudium*, Pope Francis lays out his reflections on the theme of the new evangelization in the aftermath of the 2012 Synod of Bishops held in Rome on that topic.[1] Francis writes with an evangelizing fervor that has touched me deeply each time I have read the document. He communicates not only as a pope addressing his flock, but also as a human being speaking from his heart to the heart of other human beings. He offers us what he calls his "synthesis." As I will explain, "synthesis" is a term that Francis uses in a very distinctive manner.

Does *Evangelii Gaudium* offer a new vision for the Church? Or has Francis changed only the style but not the substance of the agenda of his recent predecessors.[2] Those who claim the latter appear to limit the meaning of "substantial" to matters of defined doctrine. My own view is that Francis offers a new theological and pastoral synthesis. This shift is substantial. As with all things theological, though, this shift contains both *nova et vetera*, both the new and the old.

Let me start with what is old. When I consider individual points that Francis makes about the meaning of the Church, I have heard just about all of this before. Much of what Francis says about the Church I find in the theology of Jesuit theologians whose works were popular in the 1980s

---

[1] *Evangelii Gaudium* can be accessed at http://w2.vatican.va/content/francesco/en/apost_exhortations/documents/papa-francesco_esortazione-ap_20131124_evangelii-gaudium.html. Various documents related to the 2012 Synod of Bishops can be found at http://www.vatican.va/roman_curia/synod/.

[2] This characterization of "a change in style but not in substance" was offered by a university administrator in a brief welcoming address at a theology symposium that I attended. I prefer not to name the person or the event.

when this pope was engaging in graduate theological work in Argentina and Germany. When he speaks of a Church of the poor, I am reminded of Jon Sobrino.[3] When he speaks of a Church that is listening and learning as well as teaching, I think of Ladislas Orsy.[4] When he calls the Church a sacrament, I think of Otto Semmelroth and Karl Rahner.[5] When he talks about the need to keep up with the "epochal change [that] has been set in motion by the enormous qualitative, quantitative, rapid and cumulative advances occurring in the sciences and in technology, and by their instant application in different areas of nature and of life," (EG 52) I think of Pierre Teilhard de Chardin.[6] And when he speaks of the problem of spiritual worldliness, otherwise known as hypocrisy and inauthenticity, he explicitly cites Henri de Lubac's 1953 work, *The Splendor of the Church* (93n71).[7]

All of these points are also standard themes associated with the Second Vatican Council, as well as are yet other of Francis's teachings. When he speaks of the Church as the People of God that includes all of its members, and when he speaks of the Church as a Pilgrim on its journey, and when he speaks of the Church as a Leaven in the world, I associate these points directly with Vatican II.

I hear also other sources reflected in the teaching of Pope Francis. When Francis speaks of an approach that overcomes a negative overemphasis on a narrow range of doctrines, I hear the voice of Pope John XXIII.[8] When he speaks of a "missionary option" transforming everyone in the Church, I hear the voice of Pope Paul VI.[9] And when he calls us all beyond our excuses and rationalizations and hypocrisy to an authentic living out of the gospel, I am reminded of the Sermon on the Mount (Matt 5–7).

---

[3] Jon Sobrino, *The True Church and the Poor* (Maryknoll, NY: Orbis, 1985).
[4] Ladislas Orsy, *The Church: Learning and Teaching* (Wilmington, DE: Michael Glazier, 1987).
[5] Otto Semmelroth, *Church and Sacrament*, trans. Emily Schossberger (Notre Dame, IN: Fides, 1965 [German orig. 1960]); Karl Rahner, *The Church and the Sacraments*, trans. W. J. O'Hara (New York: Herder and Herder, 1963 [German orig. 1961]).
[6] Pierre Teilhard de Chardin, *The Future of Man*, trans. Norman Denny (New York: Doubleday/Image, 1964).
[7] Henri de Lubac, *The Splendor of the Church*, trans. Michael Mason (San Francisco: Ignatius, 1986 [French orig. 1953]).
[8] See *Gaudet Mater Ecclesia*, Pope John's Opening Speech to the Council, October 11, 1962, trans. Joseph A. Komonchak, accessed at http://jakomonchak.files.wordpress.com/2012/10/john-xxiii-opening-speech.pdf.
[9] *Evangelii Nuntiandi*, December 8, 1975, accessed at http://www.vatican.va/holy_father/paul_vi/apost_exhortations/documents/hf_p-vi_exh_19751208_evangelii-nuntiandi_en.html.

As I mentioned, a word that Francis uses frequently in the document is "synthesis" (*síntesis*). For Francis, a synthesis is what any Christian who has encountered the love of Christ can offer to any person in the world. What makes it a synthesis is that the Christian should not be reading off doctrines from a script but should be sharing what is in their heart. A synthesis is something that includes but goes beyond a set of intellectual ideas. It is something like an integrated and embodied personal presentation of the Christian faith.

Yet Francis's meaning of synthesis goes even beyond the reality of embodiment. He alludes to the Sermon on the Mount when he says, "[W]here your synthesis is, there lies your heart" (143). He is echoing Jesus's admonition: "[W]here your treasure is, there lies your heart" (Matt 6:21). So your synthesis is analogous to what Jesus calls your "treasure." And your treasure is what you place your ultimate value in. The goal is hopefully not riches that you can store on earth, but riches that you can, metaphorically, stockpile in the kingdom of heaven. Your treasure is what Jesus calls in a different passage in Matthew the pearl of great price. This is what Francis calls upon all Christians to offer in their work of evangelization: their own synthesis, their own expression of their treasure, of their encounter with the love of Christ. It is not simply a set of ideas, but the values expressed in how one lives one's life. And this is what Francis offers to us in this Exhortation: *his* own synthesis. It is a synthesis that brings a personal encounter with Christ together with an embodied engagement with the social problems of our times.

This is what is new in *Evangelii Gaudium*: Francis's synthesis. There is little new in the individual points that he offers about the meaning of the Church, but his own particular synthesis is new.

In comparison with John Paul II and Benedict XVI, Francis gives a renewed emphasis to the Church understood as the People of God. At the time of the Council, just about everyone thought that the Mystical Body of Christ would be the key image for ecclesial renewal.[10] Drawing upon Pius XII's 1943 *Mystici Corporis*, this image was used to put forth a personalist vision of the Church – that of all members united as one body with Christ as our head – in order to overcome an overly juridical understanding.[11] The initial draft of the document on the Church in 1962 used the Body of Christ image in a way that already contained many of the advances associated with the Council, such as a focus on all members of the church, on

---

[10] Raymond Brown, *The Churches the Apostles Left Behind* (New York: Paulist, 1984), 60 and 73–74.

[11] *Mystici Corporis*, June 29, 1943, accessed at http://www.vatican.va/holy_father/pius_xii/encyclicals/documents/hf_p-xii_enc_29061943_mystici-corporis-christi_en.html.

the special role of the laity in the world, and on other Christians as our separated brethren.[12]

In later drafts, however, the concepts of the People of God and the Pilgrim Church functioned in a way that was yet more radically inclusive and that added a focus on the historical and eschatological nature of the Church, a Church in many ways like Israel on a journey, a church as yet unfinished. For many, the Church understood as the People of God came to symbolize the progressive thrust of the Council and its self-awareness as being situated in history and needing to engage the modern world. When divisions arose, "People of God" served as the banner for the progressive side, whereas those opposed came to see it as the symbol of everything that went wrong in the years that followed the Council.

Some years after the Council, however, John Paul II and Benedict XVI prominently elevated the image of the Mystical Body of Christ over the image of the People of God.[13] They preferred the explicitly theological concept of the Body of Christ over what they judged to be merely sociological misuses of the less explicitly christological concept of the People of God. In doing so, they were reasserting the explicitly christological center of the Council, a center that they judged to be in danger of being lost. At the same time, though, they were slowing down the pace of change in the Church and re-emphasizing the distinctive identity of the Catholic Church in relation to other Christians, to those of other faiths, and to those of a secular mind-set.

In *Evangelii Gaudium*, Francis refers to the Church as either the People of God or God's People at least twenty-five times, almost always in order to reinforce the point that the evangelizing mission of the Church includes everyone, not just the clergy and the vowed religious. As Francis puts it:

> Evangelization is the task of the Church. The Church, as the agent of evangelization, is more than an organic and hierarchical institution; she is first and foremost a people advancing on its pilgrim way towards God.

---

[12] See an English translation by Joseph A. Komonchak, "Draft of a Dogmatic Constitution on the Church," found at https://jakomonchak.files.wordpress.com/2013/07/draft-of-de-ecclesia-chs-1-11.pdf.

[13] See, e.g., Joseph Cardinal Ratzinger with Vittorio Messori, *The Ratzinger Report: An Exclusive Interview on the State of the Church*, trans. Salvator Attanasio and Graham Harrison (San Francisco: Ignatius, 1985 [Italian edition, 1985], 47). See also John Paul II, *Christifideles Laici* (December 30 1980), http://w2.vatican.va/content/john-paul-ii/en/apost_exhortations/documents/hf_jp-ii_exh_30121988_christifideles-laici.html, #19, which highlights unreservedly the Body of Christ as it warns against sociological and psychological misunderstandings that can be associated with the People of God apart from its meaning as the "messianic people." See, also, Chapter 6 of this volume for a further comparative perspective on Francis and his predecessors.

She is certainly a mystery rooted in the Trinity, yet she exists concretely in history as a people of pilgrims and evangelizers, transcending any institutional expression, however necessary. (111)

Francis does not explicitly mention the Body of Christ even once, though there is one passage in which he clearly alludes to it (130). Now we should not thereby conclude that Francis has something against the image of the Church as the Body of Christ. For one thing, the document is not a theological treatise, it is an apostolic exhortation. Also, it is clear that Francis does indeed think that the Church can appropriately be called the Body of Christ. If the document were on a subject other than evangelization, it is quite possible that Pope Francis would have highlighted more the image of the Church as the Body of Christ. Still, in comparison with the ecclesial agenda of John Paul II and Benedict XVI that included explicit preference for the Church understood as the Body of Christ over the Church understood as the People of God, Francis's approach represents a difference in emphasis strong enough to be considered also a difference in kind.

Pope Francis's approach to the Church can be sharply contrasted with that found in the 1992 document of the Sacred Congregation for the Doctrine of the Faith (then headed by the future Pope Benedict; CDF), "Some Aspects of the Church Understood as a Communion."[14] This document included discussion of a range of dimensions of the Church but tended to be top-heavy in its emphases. It almost seemed as if it merely acknowledged the historical and social dimensions of the Church as it highlighted the mystical and divine elements. It put forth a rather centralized picture of the church as a communion in order to defend against "bottom-up" approaches that begin with local congregations or base communities. In 2000, I criticized what I perceived to be the lack of balance in "Some Aspects":

> The CDF is evidently more distressed at this time about theological positions that underplay the Church universal than those that underplay the local churches; about those that deny the transcendent dimensions of the church than those that deny its historical concreteness; about those that minimize the status of the Catholic Church in relation to other Christians than those that overemphasize it; and about those that threaten

[14] Congregation for the Doctrine of the Faith, *Communionis Notio*, "Letter to the Bishops of the Catholic Church on Some Aspects of the Church Understood as a Communion," May 28, 1992, accessed at http://www.vatican.va/roman_curia/congregations/cfaith/documents/rc_con_cfaith_doc_28051992_communionis-notio_en.html.

the internal structure of the church than those that stress its interrelation with the world.[15]

At that time, I was urging that a version of communion ecclesiology be developed that would place more emphasis upon the local churches as well as upon the need "to consult the faith of the entire church when making important decisions." Overall I called for emphasis on a wider range of the concerns expressed in the teachings of the Second Vatican Council.[16]

In comparison with "Some Aspects," Pope Francis's *Evangelii Gaudium* represents an about-face in ecclesiological emphasis. Francis's synthesis stresses the Church of the poor, the Church in the streets, the Pilgrim People that listens and dialogues, the People of God who struggle to remove barriers that unnecessarily exclude others. He stresses the Church as a sacrament, the Church in mission, the local churches, the movements, the Church as a Leaven in the world, the Church that basks in the glorious diversity of various cultures. He expressly supports decentralization of authority in favor of episcopal synods and individual bishops and, in contrast to his predecessors, puts in a strong word of endorsement for the authority of episcopal conferences.

1. Substantial Change Compatible with Substantial Continuity

So far I have made strong statements about Francis bringing about a significant change in direction. Still, I am in no way trying to put forth some kind of theory of ultimate discontinuity between the papacies of Francis and those of John Paul II and Benedict. One can recognize real and substantial change in Pope Francis's "synthesis" and at the same time also acknowledge significant continuity in many ways between him and his predecessors. I suspect that those who allow only for a stark choice – either Francis limits his changes to style or else he would be dangerously crossing boundary lines – tend to identify their own stances in the culture wars with the substance of the gospel.

Some of the themes most notably championed by Francis, such as his hard-hitting emphasis on Catholic social teaching laced with a corresponding stress on humility (emphasized further in *Laudato Si'*), can also be found also in his recent predecessors. In *Laborem Exercens*, John Paul II

---

[15] Dennis M. Doyle, *Communion Ecclesiology: Vision and Versions* (Maryknoll, NY: Orbis, 2000), 130.
[16] Ibid., 134. See also Christopher Ruddy, *The Local Church: Tillard and the Future of Catholic Ecclesiology* (New York: Crossroad, 2006).

teaches that everyone should think of oneself as a worker, and that the dignity of work comes from the fact that the worker is a human being. In *Sollicitudo Rei Socialis*, he scolds the people of the West for our materialism and consumerism. He explains his rationale by making a distinction between having and being. Having refers to possessions and the things by which we distinguish ourselves from others. Being has to do with being made in the image and likeness of God, and it is what all human beings share. John Paul II taught that having is not necessarily bad, and is even basically good, but that priority should be placed not upon having but upon being. What we share with others should be given priority over those things that distinguish us from each other. Materialism and consumerism are symptomatic of basing life upon the wrong priorities.

In *Deus Caritas Est*, Pope Benedict XVI said that it is the task of the laity to build a just society. He said that when we give service, we should not think of ourselves as better than those whom we serve. And in *Caritas In Veritate*, he discussed the importance of an economy of gift, a level of giving and receiving and sharing that goes deeper than the economy of market exchange. Those who want to stress the continuity between Francis and his predecessors have much solid evidence to which they can refer, although to take this point to an extreme would require an immoderate amount of selectivity.

Francis is not the first pope to implement a new agenda. John Paul II implemented a new agenda when he was installed as pope. He methodically slowed down the pace of internal change in the wake of Vatican II. For John Paul II, it was not the church and its traditions that needed to change but rather the culture of death at large in the world. On his watch, there would be no changes regarding Church teaching or policies regarding abortion. His "no-change" policy, however, meant that there would no women priests, and furthermore that there was to be no more talking about women priests as if they could be a real possibility. John Paul II systematically appointed notably conservative bishops throughout the world. Whether fairly or not, his political opponents within the Church called him a "restorationist."

No one would want to say that John Paul II brought change only in style, not in substance. He was too significant a figure for such a description, and the differences between his agenda and that of Paul VI were too obvious to ignore.[17] Paul VI was regarded as a kind of consensus builder

---

[17] John Paul I, of course, immediately preceded John Paul II. I have not included his brief papacy (August 26–September 28, 1978) in this discussion. Again, see Chapter 6 of this volume for further papal comparisons.

and compromiser. John Paul II's legend is a bit like that of Wyatt Earp's – he cleaned up the country, he made law and order prevail. Still, as pope he continued, as did his recent predecessors, to serve the tradition of the Church. He did not roll back the use of the vernacular in the Mass, nor did he push the altar back against the wall. In ways harmonious with his overall vision, he did foster the roles of laypeople and in particular women in the Church. He promoted and developed the Church's social teaching through his encyclicals and other speeches and writings.

It might be possible to argue, relatively speaking, that the changes brought in by Benedict XVI were more in style than in substance. He traveled somewhat less. He wrote encyclical letters at a slower pace. He took more concrete steps to reach out to traditionalists who had separated. Otherwise, however, his papal agenda was similar. Such was to be expected, though, because during John Paul II's papacy the two had already operated as a team. The former Cardinal Joseph Ratzinger had been one of the founders of the academic theological journal *Communio*, the task of which was to establish a new ecclesial balance in order to counter what they perceived to be an overly progressive agenda.

Pope Benedict XVI offered an alternative to those who wanted to limit the interpretation of Vatican II to a false dichotomy between continuity and discontinuity. Benedict indeed opposed what he labeled a "hermeneutics of rupture and discontinuity," but what he offered in its place was not a simplistic "hermeneutics of continuity." Instead, he described a "hermeneutics of reform" that recognized elements of discontinuity but that placed those elements within a framework of a deeper continuity. Benedict stated:

> It is precisely in this combination of continuity and discontinuity at different levels that the very nature of true reform consists. In this process of innovation in continuity we must learn to understand more practically than before that the Church's decisions on contingent matters – for example, certain practical forms of liberalism or a free interpretation of the Bible – should necessarily be contingent themselves, precisely because they refer to a specific reality that is changeable in itself. It was necessary to learn to recognize that in these decisions it is only the principles that express the permanent aspect, since they remain as an undercurrent, motivating decisions from within. On the other hand, not so permanent are the practical forms that depend on the historical situation and are therefore subject to change.[18]

---

[18] Address of His Holiness Benedict XVI to the Roman Curia Offering Them His Christmas Greetings," December 23, 2005, accessed at http://www.vatican.va/holy_father/benedict_xvi/speeches/2005/december/documents/hf_ben_xvi_spe_20051222_roman-curia_en.html.

Benedict gave the example of Vatican II's teaching on religious liberty. To teach that the dignity of the human person demands that no one be prevented from following their conscious in the choice of a religion went against some Catholic teaching of recent centuries, but it was also in harmony with the deeper tradition. The recognition of some degree of separation of church and state does not only acknowledge a modern idea, but also reflects the teaching of Jesus (Matt 22:21) and of the martyrs of the early church.

Pope Benedict thus offered a frame of reference regarding change and continuity that can easily apply both to John Paul II and to Francis. A substantial and evident change in direction does not at all imply radical discontinuity with tradition. Both John Paul II and Francis arrived in office with an ecclesial and theological agenda requiring a strong hand to guide the barque of Peter. Each in his own way has responded to the challenges posed to the Church by the modern world in ways that have been both innovative and in harmony with the deeper tradition.

2. A Balanced Range of References and a Dialectical Dance

In *Evangelii Gaudium*, Francis draws frequently, seriously, and positively from the writings and speeches of a range of his papal predecessors and cites them often amid his 217 endnotes. He cites John XXIII only once, but Paul VI twenty-one times. John Paul II appears in forty-eight endnotes. Benedict XVI appears as pope in only nineteen, but his prepapal work as Joseph Ratzinger is cited once, and the Congregation for the Doctrine of the Faith while he was the prefect is cited four times. The documents of Vatican II appear twenty times.

Francis's reliance upon the writings of John Paul II and Benedict XVI is anything but superficial. For example, when Francis states that the reservation of the priesthood to males only is "a question not open to discussion," he cites John Paul II's *Mulieris Dignatatem* in support of the point that sacramental power is in the realm of function rather than of dignity (§73). When he argues that the causes of poverty must be attacked on a structural basis (173), he cites a 2007 address by Benedict XVI.[19]

Pope Francis often makes balancing statements that sound as if they might have come from one of his recent predecessors:

> Just as the organic unity existing among the virtues means that no one of them can be excluded from the Christian ideal, so no truth may be

---

[19] "Address to the Diplomatic Corps," January 8, 2007, *Acta Apostolicae Sedes* 99 (2007), 73.

denied. The integrity of the Gospel message must not be deformed. What is more, each truth is better understood when related to the harmonious totality of the Christian message; in this context, all of the truths are important and illuminate one another. (§39)

Also from *Evangelii Gaudium* is this statement, which could possibly fool players in a trivia contest into guessing Pope Benedict as the author:

> We also evangelize when we attempt to confront the various challenges which can arise. On occasion these may take the form of … widespread indifference and relativism, linked to disillusionment and the crisis of ideologies which has come about as a reaction to anything which might appear totalitarian. This not only harms the Church but the fabric of society as a whole. We should recognize how in a culture where each person wants to be bearer of his or her own subjective truth, it becomes difficult for citizens to devise a common plan which transcends individual gain and personal ambitions. (§61)

Evangelii Gaudium, written in a dialectical style, is full of balancing statements.

Human thought is dialectical. Every yin calls forth its yang. Every pope must find a balance between continuity and change, between handing on the tradition and engaging the world in the present time. Usually when one holds two points in tension, one has a tendency to favor one of the two points and to make it the leading theme, even if only slightly. One way to describe Pope Francis's synthesis is to examine how his own balancing act appears to shift the leading role given to certain polar pairings. One might think of it as holding points in tension and then making them dance. As a kind of thought experiment, I noted the following themes when first working through *Evangelii Gaudium*, as indicated in the following chart:

The Dance of Ideas in Pope Francis' Synthesis	Leading Point	Following Point
	historical	metaphysical
	dynamic	static
	the new	memory
	learning	teaching
	inclusion	maintaining boundaries
	relationships	structures
	mission	community

I do not want to suggest that John Paul II and Benedict XVI represent diametrically the opposite of Pope Francis's synthesis, nor that the thought styles of these two popes were identical to each other. I do suggest, though, that the figure captures something of a thought dynamic that distinctively represents Francis.

As of this writing, Francis has yet to change anything that could be considered fundamental Church teaching. The absence of such change is probably what is on the mind of those people have who insist that anything new so far has been style rather than substance. Still, the question looms large as to whether the substantial change represented by Pope Francis's own synthesis will now issue in significant changes in doctrine or in long-standing church practices. Will the norm become that priests will be allowed to marry? Will there be changes in church teaching regarding the morality of homosexual activity?

It is not easy (and often unwise) to predict the future. On the one hand, there are two strong arguments against the likelihood of such changes. First, Francis demonstrates throughout *Evangelii Gaudium* a pattern of pushing the envelope without actually making such changes happen. Second, historically, when changes in doctrine or in long-standing practices have occurred, the change is usually played out over the course of more than one papacy. It is difficult for a current pope to simply change things that his predecessors had been strongly emphasizing. It is more usual for a pope to become relatively silent about certain matters so that one of his own successors can more readily make changes.

On the other hand, I can think of two strong arguments in the other direction. First, Pope Francis has been full of surprises. Second, Francis's synthesis includes a strong push toward decentralization. His approach has been to set wheels in motion, to create an atmosphere that encourages consultation and participation by a wide range of Catholics. If serious changes in teaching and practice do take place, they will have emerged from within the context of consultative and participatory processes. As Francis shifts the way in which the Church makes decisions, other changes are likely to follow. All of these factors were given further evidence in the concluding Synod of the Family in October 2015.

3. A New Phase in the Reception of Vatican II

I like the way Cardinal Walter Kasper has named the Pope Francis shift: What we have here is a new phase in the reception of Vatican II.[20] Kasper contrasts the approach of Benedict XVI, which he calls "renewal in continuity," with that of Francis's "prophetic interpretation of the

---

[20] See also, especially, Chapters 3, 5, and 6 of this volume on Francis and Vatican II.

council."[21] Calling this shift "a new phase" helps to highlight how Pope Francis vision fits into a larger trajectory that presupposes earlier phases. It does not simply discard or replace the earlier phases so much as it incorporates (or sublates) them as it moves forward into new territory.

Although Francis does not refer explicitly to his own vision as something new, he uses the word "new" 121 times in *Evangelii Gaudium* (206 times if one includes variations such as "anew," "newness," "renewal," etc.). In the very first passage of the document, Francis directly connects the joy of the gospel with newness: "With Christ joy is constantly born anew" (§1). He writes explicitly about "a new phase of evangelization, one marked by enthusiasm and vitality" (§17). Moreover, he quotes Vatican II's *Unitatis Redintegratio* in order to highlight the relationship between renewal and continuity: "Every renewal of the Church essentially consists in an increase of fidelity to her own calling.... Christ summons the Church as she goes her pilgrim way ... to that continual reformation of which she always has need, in so far as she is a human institution here on earth" (UR §6; as quoted in EG §26). Thus what Kasper identifies as the main theme of the approach of Benedict XVI, "renewal in continuity," continues as a major subtheme throughout *Evangelii Gaudium*.

Pope Francis grounds his extensive use of John Paul II and Benedict XVI within a retrieval of some key aspects of Vatican II and of the emphases of Paul VI. It is perhaps no accident that *Evangelii Gaudium* combines in its title the initial word from two famous documents: Vatican II's 1965 *Gaudium et Spes* and Paul VI's 1976 encyclical, *Evangelii Nuntiandi* (see as indicated in the following chart).

Gaudium et Spes	+	Evangelii Nuntiandi	=	Evangelii Gaudium
Joys and Hopes		Proclamation of the Gospel		Joy of the Gospel

Gaudium et Spes called for dialogue and engagement with the world in the quest for justice and peace. *Evangelii Nuntiandi* put evangelization at the core of Christian life and mission. Both of these documents are directly connected with the universal call to holiness that formed the central chapter of *Lumen Gentium*. After *Lumen Gentium*, there was to be no more talking about the Church without placing spirituality at the center of the discussion. After *Gaudium et Spes*, there was to be no more talking about

---

[21] From an article by Walter Kasper appearing in *L'Osservatore Romano* April 11, 2013, as reported by John Thavis, accessed at http://www.johnthavis.com/cardinal-kasper-pope-francis-has-launched-new-phase-on-vatican-ii#.U1XGXVfDVcU.

spirituality without integrating social, cultural, and political dimensions. After *Evangelii Nuntiandi*, there was to be no more talking about spirituality and politics without realizing that evangelization remains always the core mission of each Christian and of all Christians. *Evangelii Gaudium* is a document whose title matches its content with a precision fit. "The Joy of the Gospel" teases out an important thread from *Evangelii Nuntiandi*, the joy that is inextricably bound up with evangelization. The document then demonstrates how to weave that thread together with "the joys and the hopes, the griefs and the anxieties of the people of this age, especially those who are poor or in any way afflicted" (*Gaudium et Spes* §1).

What Kasper identifies as the "prophetic" approach of *Evangelii Gaudium* can be found in many examples. Pope Francis calls out those of us living in the contemporary world for our willingness to tolerate everyday blatant injustices. He resoundingly exhorts Christians to say *no* to an economy of exclusion; to the idolatry of money; to a financial system that rules rather than serves; and to the inequality that spawns violence (§53–§60). He hopes that Christians will be moved by the fear of remaining shut up within structures that give us a false sense of security, within rules that make us harsh judges, within habits that make us feel safe, while at our door people are starving, and Jesus does not tire of saying to us: "Give them something to eat" (MK 6:37) (EG §49). Francis asks, "How can it be that it is not a news item when an elderly homeless person dies of exposure, but it is news when the stock market loses two points?" (§53). He speaks of "the dictatorship of an impersonal economy" that reduces human beings to being nothing more than consumers (§55). He states that "the socioeconomic system is unjust as its root" (§59). He even calls out laypeople who "fear that they may be asked to undertake some apostolic work and they seek to avoid any responsibility that may take away from their free time." He includes as well "priests who are obsessed with their own free time" (§81). When he speaks of the "option for the poor" he goes so far as to declare that "we need to let ourselves be evangelized by them" (§198).

Anyone who grasps the prophetic dynamics of newness and continuity in *Evangelii Gaudium* can easily see this dynamic still at work in Francis's 2015 encyclical *Laudato Si'*.[22] A key theme of *Laudato Si'* is already present in *Evangelii Gaudium*: "The thirst for power and possessions knows no limits. In this system, which tends to devour everything which stands in the way of increased profits, whatever is fragile, like the environment,

---

[22] *Laudato Si'* can be accessed at http://w2.vatican.va/content/francesco/en/encyclicals/documents/papa-francesco_20150524_enciclica-laudato-si.html.

is defenseless before the interests of a deified market, which become the only rule" (*EG* §56; see also §§215–216). In *Laudato Si'* Francis places his focus more directly on our fragile, threatened environment. He expands the call to love God and each other to include not only the poor but also all of creation. Many times in various wordings Francis emphasizes that everything – to repeat, everything – is interrelated and interconnected (something again further emphasized in *Laudato Si'*). Francis explains that reason and faith, philosophy and theology, and science and tradition have often in the past combined to offer syntheses for addressing the problems that human beings face. He points to Catholic social teaching as an example of such a synthesis. Then he emphasizes that the new ecological challenges of today call for yet a new synthesis (*LS* §§63; 112; 121).[23]

Francis's prophetic emphasis is bold and new. No one can read either *Evangelii Gaudium* or *Laudato Si'* and not be struck immediately and deeply by these characteristics. These traits are not done justice by simply calling them Francis's "style." Yet even on this point, the *nova et vetera*, the new and the old, form a kind of synthesis. One can find significant examples of both John Paul II and Benedict XVI being unmistakably prophetic in their proclamation of Catholic social teaching. The prophetic innovation of Pope Francis in *Evangelii Gaudium* includes the renewal in continuity associated with his recent predecessors, even as he moves the Church into a new phase of the reception and implementation of Vatican II. In *Laudato Si'*, Francis connects his own teaching not only with that of his Petrine predecessors, but also and especially with the teachings of bishops in many episcopal conferences from throughout the word. He draws much inspiration from St. Francis of Assisi. In this encyclical, though, when Pope Francis speaks of the "church," he most often is speaking about the official teaching church, without even mentioning the People of God or the Church in the streets. This usage reflects his deep concern to explain to his audience how what he is saying and doing in this encyclical is indeed in continuity with the great tradition of the Catholic Church.

One can argue, along with my colleague, William Portier, that in 1978, when John Paul II was installed as pope, the Church was more in need of a John Paul II than a Francis. Portier claims further that John Paul II and Benedict combined to leave behind a Church that is now ready for

---

[23] In *Laudato Si'*, Francis' use of the word *synthesis* is closer to the usage found in Vatican II's *Gaudium et Spes* than in his own *Evangelii Gaudium* in that it is a blending of reason and faith to address present-day challenges more than the personal synthesis in one's heart that allows one to share the gospel.

Pope Francis's new direction.[24] In this evaluation of the phases of the reception of Vatican II, the situation in 1978 called for a firm hand that would steer the Church away from the confusion and fragmentation that marked the first decade after the Council. Now, after three and a half decades of slowing the pace of change and sharpening the christological focus of Catholic teaching, a more secure framework is in place to support a leader who in more radical ways can reap the fruits of Vatican II.

Weaving together and embodying the trajectory of Vatican II in a way that is both old and new, Pope Francis offers us his synthesis. He is calling forth each Catholic to share their own synthesis, a synthesis of their treasure, of the joy of the gospel, as we work together to address the urgent social problems of our times.

---

[24] See William L. Portier, "Jesus and the World of Grace, 1968–2014: Reading the Signs of the Times Then and Now," paper given June 7, 2014 at the Annual Convention of the Catholic Theological Society of America conference in San Diego, June 2014. Subsequently published as 'Jesus and the World of Grace, 1968–2016: An Idiosyncratic Theological Memoir', *Horizons*, 43 (2) (December 2016): 374–396.

CHAPTER 3

Evangelii Gaudium as an Act of Reception of Vatican II

Massimo Faggioli

1. Vatican II in *"Evangelii Gaudium"*

Pope Francis's apostolic exhortation *Evangelii Gaudium* is a document remarkably inspired by Vatican II.[1] With the very title of the exhortation *Evangelii Gaudium*, Pope Francis is reclaiming and integrating the legacy of the last document approved by Vatican II (the pastoral constitution *Gaudium et Spes*, December 7, 1965) and the highest moment in the immediate post–Vatican II history in terms of theological and pastoral reflection on the evangelization in the modern world (Paul VI's apostolic exhortation *Evangelii Nuntiandi*, published exactly ten years after the conclusion of Vatican II on December 8, 1975).

With this exhortation Francis presents himself as a pope who tries to recapture Vatican II not only in its letter but also in its spirit, being both letter and spirit necessary for the reception of the council (as we read in the *Final Report* of the Extraordinary Synod of the Bishops of 1985).[2] Pope Francis's apostolic exhortation, which has the value of a programmatic document for Pope Francis's pontificate, does not talk about "the spirit of Vatican II," but quotes the documents of Vatican II twenty times.[3]

The most quoted document is the constitution on the Church *Lumen Gentium* in these particular passages: paragraph 36 on the laity, paragraph

---

[1] See also Chapters 5 and 6 of this volume, which also consider aspects of *Evangelii Gaudium* in relation to Vatican II.
[2] See *The Final Report of the 1985 Extraordinary Synod* (Washington, DC: National Conference of Catholic Bishops, 1986).
[3] EG 32 mentions the "collegial spirit" of the episcopal conferences, quoting *Lumen Gentium*, par. 23.

1 on the Church as a mystery and sacrament, paragraph 9 on the people of God, paragraph 12 on Church and *sensus fidei*, paragraph 16 on nonbelievers, and paragraphs 52–69 on the Virgin Mary. Three quotations come from the decree on ecumenism *Unitatis Redintegratio*: paragraph 6 on ecumenism and Church renewal, paragraph 4 on ecumenism and unity of the Church, and paragraph 11 on the "hierarchy of truths." The third most quoted document is the constitution on divine revelation *Dei Verbum*: paragraph 12 on the task of exegetes, and paragraphs 21–22 on scripture in the life of the Church. Two quotations come from the pastoral constitution on the Church in the modern world *Gaudium et Spes*: paragraph 22 on salvation proclaimed to everyone, and paragraph 36 on the legitimate autonomy of culture. One quotation each come from the decree on the pastoral ministry of bishops *Christus Dominus* at paragraph 11 on the "particular Church" as the place of evangelization; from the decree on the missionary activity of the Church *Ad Gentes* at paragraph 9 about the relationship between mission and interreligious dialogue; and the decree on the mass media *Inter Mirifica* at paragraph 6 on catechesis and the "way of beauty."

2. John XXIII and Francis: "*Gaudet Mater Ecclesia*" and "*Pacem in Terris*"

Of all these twenty quotations from conciliar documents, the most important quotation from Vatican II in *Evangelii Gaudium* is at paragraph 41 on the relationship between the deposit of faith and the way to express it. Here Pope Francis quotes from John XXIII's opening speech of the council, *Gaudet Mater Ecclesia*:

> At the same time, today's vast and rapid cultural changes demand that we constantly seek ways of expressing unchanging truths in a language which brings out their abiding newness. "The deposit of the faith is one thing … the way it is expressed is another" [John XXIII, *Gaudet Mater Ecclesia*, October 11, 1962]. There are times when the faithful, in listening to completely orthodox language, take away something alien to the authentic Gospel of Jesus Christ, because that language is alien to their own way of speaking to and understanding one another. With the holy intent of communicating the truth about God and humanity, we sometimes give them a false god or a human ideal which is not really Christian. In this way, we hold fast to a formulation while failing to convey its substance. This is the greatest danger. Let us never forget that 'the expression of truth can take different forms. The renewal of these forms of expression

becomes necessary for the sake of transmitting to the people of today the Gospel message in its unchanging meaning.' [John Paul II, encyclical *Ut Unum Sint* (1995) par. 19]

The other most important quotation of *Gaudet Mater Ecclesia* though is in *Evangelii Gaudium* 84 about the challenges to evangelization and the lack of hope that is typical of our times:

> The joy of the Gospel is such that it cannot be taken away from us by anyone or anything (cf. *Jn* 16:22). The evils of our world – and those of the Church – must not be excuses for diminishing our commitment and our fervor. Let us look upon them as challenges which can help us to grow. With the eyes of faith, we can see the light which the Holy Spirit always radiates in the midst of darkness, never forgetting that "where sin increased, grace has abounded all the more" (*Rom* 5:20). Our faith is challenged to discern how wine can come from water and how wheat can grow in the midst of weeds. Fifty years after the Second Vatican Council, we are distressed by the troubles of our age and far from naïve optimism; yet the fact that we are more realistic must not mean that we are any less trusting in the Spirit or less generous. In this sense, we can once again listen to the words of Blessed John XXIII on the memorable day of 11 October 1962: "At times we have to listen, much to our regret, to the voices of people who, though burning with zeal, lack a sense of discretion and measure. In this modern age they can see nothing but prevarication and ruin.... We feel that we must disagree with those prophets of doom who are always forecasting disaster, as though the end of the world were at hand. In our times, divine Providence is leading us to a new order of human relations which, by human effort and even beyond all expectations, are directed to the fulfillment of God's superior and inscrutable designs, in which everything, even human setbacks, leads to the greater good of the Church."

In this section of *Evangelii Gaudium*, with this quotation, Pope Francis is re-enacting Pope John XXII's reorientation of the Church's message, thus showing many parallels between the Church at the end of Pius XII's pontificate and at the beginning of Pope Francis.[4] It is interesting to see that Vatican II is very present in the final document of the Aparecida conference of 2007, but in that document (largely the fruit of Bergoglio's crucial role at that conference of CELAM) John XXIII is not mentioned. Bergoglio's

---

[4] About the impact of John XXIII's *Gaudet Mater Ecclesia* on Vatican II, see John W. O'Malley, *What Happened at Vatican II* (Cambridge, MA: Belknap Press of Harvard University Press, 2008), 93–96; Andrea Riccardi, "The Tumultuous Opening Days of the Council," in *History of Vatican II*, dir. Giuseppe Alberigo, English ed. Joseph A. Komonchak, vol. 2 (Leuven, Peeters, and Maryknoll, NY: Orbis, 1997), 14–19.

closeness to Roncalli seemed to have been made activated, if not caused, by the conclave of 2013. Like John XXIII, the election of Francis took place during difficult times for the Church not because of external circumstances, but also in relation to the unstated but clear sense of exhaustion of a given theological-cultural paradigm and the need to reframe and rephrase the message of the Church in a new paradigm. It is no surprise then that the resistance and fear of change met by John XXIII at the time of the council is similar to the reception of Pope Francis in some quarters of the Catholic Church of today.

Francis has continued to stress the parallels between John XXIII and himself also after *Evangelii Gaudium*. The bull of indiction of the extraordinary jubilee of mercy *Misericordiae Vultus* (April 11, 2015) quotes once again from John XXIII's opening speech of Vatican II, *Gaudet Mater Ecclesia*:

> I have chosen the date of 8 December because of its rich meaning in the recent history of the Church. In fact, I will open the Holy Door on the fiftieth anniversary of the closing of the Second Vatican Ecumenical Council. The Church feels a great need to keep this event alive. With the Council, the Church entered a new phase of her history. The Council Fathers strongly perceived, as a true breath of the Holy Spirit, a need to talk about God to men and women of their time in a more accessible way. The walls which for too long had made the Church a kind of fortress were torn down and the time had come to proclaim the Gospel in a new way. It was a new phase of the same evangelization that had existed from the beginning. It was a fresh undertaking for all Christians to bear witness to their faith with greater enthusiasm and conviction. The Church sensed a responsibility to be a living sign of the Father's love in the world. We recall the poignant words of Saint John XXIII when, opening the Council, he indicated the path to follow: "Now the Bride of Christ wishes to use the medicine of mercy rather than taking up arms of severity.... The Catholic Church, as she holds high the torch of Catholic truth at this Ecumenical Council, wants to show herself a loving mother to all; patient, kind, moved by compassion and goodness toward her separated children."[5]

In a similar way, Francis quotes John XXIII's theological testament and last encyclical, *Pacem in Terris* (April 11, 1963), in the beginning of the encyclical "on our common home" *Laudato Si'*:

> More than fifty years ago, with the world teetering on the brink of nuclear crisis, Pope Saint John XXIII wrote an Encyclical which not only rejected

---

[5] Pope Francis, *Misericordiae Vultus* (April 11, 2015), par. 4, http://w2.vatican.va/content/francesco/en/apost_letters/documents/papa-francesco_bolla_20150411_misericordiae-vultus.html.

war but offered a proposal for peace. He addressed his message *Pacem in Terris* to the entire "Catholic world" and indeed "to all men and women of good will". Now, faced as we are with global environmental deterioration, I wish to address every person living on this planet.[6]

3. Pope Francis's Conciliar Ecclesiology in "Evangelii Gaudium"

Pope Francis' ecclesiology in *Evangelii Gaudium* cannot be easily framed as a progressive or liberal ecclesiology, but rather a missionary ecclesiology faithful to the message of Vatican II: "renewal/renewed" is used twenty-nine times against the five times of "reform/reformation." But it is not an ecclesiology complacent with the institutional status quo.

Evangelii Gaudium 26 opens by remembering Paul VI's call to the renewal of the Church in his first encyclical *Ecclesiam Suam* and concludes the paragraph with a quotation from the decree on ecumenism *Unitatis Redintegratio* par. 6: "The Second Vatican Council presented ecclesial conversion as openness to a constant self-renewal born of fidelity to Jesus Christ: 'Every renewal of the Church essentially consists in an increase of fidelity to her own calling.... Christ summons the Church as she goes her pilgrim way ... to that continual reformation of which she always has need, in so far as she is a human institution here on earth.'" The ecclesiology of Pope Francis here is a Vatican II ecclesiology in the sense of a Church ecumenical because on the path of reform: But this passage is only one of the many instances, since his election in March 2013, when Pope Francis is reclaiming the almost forgotten legacy of Paul VI.[7]

In *Evangelii Gaudium* 30 there is also an interesting quote from the council's document on the pastoral ministry of the bishops that reveals other elements of Francis's ecclesiology, and in particular his view of the relationship between the universal and local dimension of the Church: "Each particular Church, as a portion of the Catholic Church under the leadership of its bishop, is likewise called to missionary conversion. It is the primary subject of evangelization, since it is the concrete manifestation of the one Church in one specific place, and in it 'the one, holy, catholic, and apostolic Church of Christ is truly present and operative'" [citing *Christus Dominus* par. 11]. The choice of this passage about "the primary subject of evangelization" is interesting because *Christus Dominus* is the decree that

---

[6] Pope Francis, encyclical *Laudato Si'* (May 24, 2015), par. 3, http://w2.vatican.va/content/francesco/en/encyclicals/documents/papa-francesco_20150524_enciclica-laudato-si.html.

[7] The relationship between Jorge Mario Bergoglio-Francis and Paul VI deserves a separate and more comprehensive analysis.

not only actualizes for the "local/particular Churches" the ecclesiological framework of *Lumen Gentium*, but it also strengthens (if compared with *Lumen Gentium*) the importance of the local level of the Church vis-à-vis the universal level.[8]

The connection between reform ecclesiology and local ecclesiology leads in *Evangelii Gaudium* to a paragraph on the reform of the Petrine ministry, which Pope Francis words as "conversion of the papacy." Francis admits that little progress has been made since Vatican II and since John Paul II's encyclical *Ut Unum Sint*:

> Since I am called to put into practice what I ask of others, I too must think about a conversion of the papacy. It is my duty, as the Bishop of Rome, to be open to suggestions which can help make the exercise of my ministry more faithful to the meaning which Jesus Christ wished to give it and to the present needs of evangelization. Pope John Paul II asked for help in finding "a way of exercising the primacy which, while in no way renouncing what is essential to its mission, is nonetheless open to a new situation" [citing of John Paul II, encyclical *Ut Unum Sint* 1995, par. 95]. We have made little progress in this regard. The papacy and the central structures of the universal Church also need to hear the call to pastoral conversion.[9]

Another crucial part of Francis's reclaim of Vatican II is the role of the bishops conferences as an integral element for a Church that is on its way to reform and conversion, again in *Evangelii Gaudium* 32:

> The Second Vatican Council stated that, like the ancient patriarchal Churches, episcopal conferences are in a position "to contribute in many and fruitful ways to the concrete realization of the collegial spirit" [citing *Lumen Gentium*, paragraph 23]. Yet this desire has not been fully realized, since a juridical status of episcopal conferences which would see them as subjects of specific attributions, including genuine doctrinal authority, has not yet been sufficiently elaborated [citing John Paul II, motu proprio *Apostolos Suos*, May 21, 1998]. Excessive centralization, rather than proving helpful, complicates the Church's life and her missionary outreach.

Institutional centralization in the Church is a major concern for Francis in *Evangelii Gaudium*. So, also, in a similar way, should dogmatic absolutism be a concern for a truly missionary Church. In *Evangelii Gaudium* 36 Francis mentions explicitly one of the key achievements of Vatican II for method in theology: "In this sense, the Second Vatican Council explained,

---

[8] See Massimo Faggioli, *Il vescovo e il concilio. Modello episcopale e aggiornamento al Vaticano II* (Bologna: Il Mulino, 2005).
[9] *EG* 32.

'in Catholic doctrine there exists an order or a "hierarchy" of truths, since they vary in their relation to the foundation of the Christian faith' [citing *Unitatis Redintegratio*, par. 11]. This holds true as much for the dogmas of faith as for the whole corpus of the Church's teaching, including her moral teaching." The quotation of the council's decree on ecumenism is a key principle in Francis's theology that is evident throughout his work.[10] For Francis the missionary activity makes of the Church "a missionary disciple; she needs to grow in her interpretation of the revealed word and in her understanding of truth. It is the task of exegetes and theologians to help 'the judgment of the Church to mature.'" Here in *Evangelii Gaudium* 40, the quotation of *Dei Verbum* paragraph 12 signifies an inclusive role for exegetes and theologians, which in previous and recently published official documents (such as the postsynodal exhortation *Verbum Domini* of September 30, 2010) seemed to have been perceived as a threat to the Church.

The image of the Church in *Evangelii Gaudium* is conciliar because without neglecting the problems of the institution is less concerned with the institutional element and more centered on the sacramental element: "The Church is sent by Jesus Christ as the sacrament of the salvation offered by God [citing *Lumen Gentium*, par. 1]. Through her evangelizing activity, she cooperates as an instrument of that divine grace which works unceasingly and inscrutably" (*EG* 112).

But Francis is not uninterested in the relevance of the institutional element and especially of relationship between the center and the periphery of the Church, for this relationship affects the way the Church assesses reality and constructs its teaching. The quotations from bishops conferences' documents are integral and essential part of *Evangelii Gaudium* and even more in *Laudato Si'*. These two major documents of Francis show Francis's idea that papal teaching builds largely on the recent teaching of bishops conferences, and not only on the tradition of papal documents or of the ancient tradition.

4. Church, Culture, and Community in Evangelizing

This sacramental and invisible element of the Church – essential in Pope Francis's ecclesiology – is noticeable also in the following paragraph of *Evangelii Gaudium* about God's universal will of salvation through a quotation from the two ecclesiological constitutions of Vatican II:

---

[10] About the role of *Unitatis Redintegratio* 11 and the "hierarchy of truths" in Francis, see book-interview conducted by Paolo Rodari with Víctor Manuel Fernández, one of the closest advisors to Jorge Mario Bergoglio, *Il progetto di Francesco. Dove vuole portare la chiesa* (Bologna: EMI, 2014).

> The salvation which God has wrought, and the Church joyfully proclaims, is for everyone [reference to *Gaudium et Spes* 22]. God has found a way to unite himself to every human being in every age. He has chosen to call them together as a people and not as isolated individuals [reference to *Lumen Gentium* 9]. No one is saved by himself or herself, individually, or by his or her own efforts. God attracts us by taking into account the complex interweaving of personal relationships entailed in the life of a human community. This people which God has chosen and called is the Church. Jesus did not tell the apostles to form an exclusive and elite group. (113)

The quotation of *Gaudium et Spes* paragraph 22 ("Christ, the New Man") is very interesting, this paragraph being one of the most commented of the whole pastoral constitution,[11] regarded as "the focal point of the entire theological argument formulated by *Gaudium et Spes*."[12]

Also the following quotation, from *Gaudium et Spes* paragraph 36, shows a full and unembarrassed reception of the pastoral constitution of Vatican II by Pope Francis:

> The People of God is incarnate in the peoples of the earth, each of which has its own culture. The concept of culture is valuable for grasping the various expressions of the Christian life present in God's people. It has to do with the lifestyle of a given society, the specific way in which its members relate to one another, to other creatures and to God. Understood in this way, culture embraces the totality of a people's life [reference to *Gaudium et Spes* 36]. Each people in the course of its history develop its culture with legitimate autonomy. (115)

Gaudium et Spes paragraph 36 is focused on the "autonomy of the earthly realities."[13] It is not an accident that in the footnote to *Gaudium et Spes* paragraph 36 there is an indirect reference to the case of Galileo Galilei

---

[11] "In regard to the whole article it may be observed that, despite less satisfactory elements, it represents an advance over *Lumen Gentium* [which is] too focused on man's activity": Joseph Ratzinger, commentary on *Gaudium et Spes*, part I, chapter I, in *Commentary on the Documents of Vatican II*, general editor Herbert Vorgrimler, vol. 5 (New York: Herder and Herder, 1969), 162.

[12] Hans-Joachim Sander, "Theologischer Kommentar zur Pastoralkonstitution über die Kirche in der Welt von heute," in *Herders Theologischer Kommentar zum Zweiten Vatikanischen Konzil*, ed. Hans Jochen Hilberath and Peter Hünermann, vol. 5 (Freiburg: Herder, 2005), 739.

[13] Francis's quotations of the pastoral constitution in *Laudato Si'* are from *Gaudium et Spes* par. 26 (the idea of common good), par. 36 (the rightful autonomy of earthly affairs), and par. 63 on anthropocentrism ("man is the source, the focus and the aim of all economic and social life").

when the text talks about the compatibility between faith and science.[14] The claim of Pope Francis about the Church in the modern world is also visible from the quotation of *Lumen Gentium* 12, at paragraph 119 of *Evangelii Gaudium*:

> In all the baptized, from first to last, the sanctifying power of the Spirit is at work, impelling us to evangelization. The people of God is holy thanks to this anointing, which makes it infallible *in credendo*. This means that it does not err in faith, even though it may not find words to explain that faith. The Spirit guides it in truth and leads it to salvation [reference to *Lumen Gentium*, par. 12]. As part of his mysterious love for humanity, God furnishes the totality of the faithful with an instinct of faith – *sensus fidei* – which helps them to discern what is truly of God. The presence of the Spirit gives Christians a certain connaturality with divine realities, and a wisdom which enables them to grasp those realities intuitively, even when they lack the wherewithal to give them precise expression.

This passage about the *sensus fidei* is even more remarkable because *Evangelii Gaudium* 119 is the only passage of the exhortation that talks about infallibility, and it does that in terms of infallibility *in credendo* of the people of God. The ecclesiological constitution of Vatican II *Lumen Gentium* paragraph 12 is quoted also a few lines after in §130:

> The Holy Spirit also enriches the entire evangelizing Church with different charisms. These gifts are meant to renew and build up the Church. [reference to *Lumen Gentium*, par. 12]

Lumen Gentium paragraph 12 plays an important role in the exhortation: It is clear the intent to rephrase once again the infallibility of the magisterium as based on the infallibility of the people of God. This key element of Catholic ecclesiology builds in *Lumen Gentium* paragraph 12 a connection between infallibility and charismatic structure of the Church: Charisms are not extraordinary and exceptional in the Church, but they are common, diverse, universal, and not limited to a group of people. The Church is all-charismatic, and the value of every charism must be measured against the good of the people of God.

The ecclesiology of *Evangelii Gaudium* is committed to a dynamic idea of the structures of the Church, and this has deep repercussions in the way

---

[14] The reference in the footnote of *Gaudium et Spes* is to the book by Pio Paschini, *Vita e opere di Galileo Galilei*, 2 vols. (Pontificia Accademia delle Scienze, Città del Vaticano 1964). About this see Alberto Melloni, "Galileo al Vaticano II. Storia d'una citazione e della sua ombra," *Cristianesimo nella Storia*, XXXI (1) (2010): 131–164.

the exhortation envisions ecumenism. In the fourth chapter on the social dimension of evangelization, Pope Francis talks about ecumenism quoting the conciliar decree on ecumenism *Unitatis Redintegratio*, paragraph 4:

> Commitment to ecumenism responds to the prayer of the Lord Jesus that "they may all be one" (Jn 17:21). The credibility of the Christian message would be much greater if Christians could overcome their divisions and the Church could realize "the fullness of catholicity proper to her in those of her children who, though joined to her by baptism, are yet separated from full communion with her." (EG 244)

The correlation between different poles of Catholic ecclesiology is visible in both the intra-Christian sphere and in the inter-religious dialogue. *Evangelii Gaudium* 244 reflects upon Catholicity and ecumenism, citing *Unitatis Redintegratio* paragraph 4, being aware of the historical centrality of the Catholic Church in the history of the Christian theological tradition – at least, a centrality in the mind of the fathers and theologians of Vatican II. In a similar way, *Evangelii Gaudium* 251 does not see a contradiction between dialogue and proclamation thanks to a reference in the footnote from the decree on the missionary activity of the Church, *Ad Gentes*, paragraph 9:

> In this dialogue, ever friendly and sincere, attention must always be paid to the essential bond between dialogue and proclamation, which leads the Church to maintain and intensify her relationship with non-Christians. A facile syncretism would ultimately be a totalitarian gesture on the part of those who would ignore greater values of which they are not the masters.... Evangelization and interreligious dialogue, far from being opposed, mutually support and nourish one another. (EG 251)

This reference to *Ad Gentes* is particularly important, in the context of the "new evangelization," because in the last few years before the election of Francis the ecclesial debate on evangelization tried to avoid references to Vatican II in general, but also because *Ad Gentes* plays an important role in Paul VI's *Evangelii Nuntiandi*.[15]

These last references to Vatican II come in *Evangelii Gaudium* in part III of chapter IV, "The Common Good and Peace in Society." Here, in paragraphs 222–233, we have a condensed summary of Vatican II in four axioms: "Time is greater than space," "Unity prevails over conflict,"

---

[15] See Stephen B. Bevans, "Decree on the Church's Missionary Activity," in Stephen B. Bevans and Jeffrey Gros, *Evangelization and Religious Freedom: Ad Gentes, Dignitatis humanae* (New York and Mahwah, NJ: Paulist Press, 2009), 3–148.

"Realities are more important than ideas," and "The whole is greater than the part."[16] These are titles of short sections of *Evangelii Gaudium* where Vatican II is not directly quoted or referenced, but it is present indirectly. "Giving priority to time means being concerned about initiating processes rather than possessing spaces" (*EG* 223) is a reception of the new awareness expressed by Vatican II about historicity. In *Evangelii Gaudium* 233 we read: "Realities are greater than ideas. This principle has to do with incarnation of the word and its being put into practice." This is most close to the theological culture of Vatican II, and especially to the core of *Gaudium et Spes*' existential-ontological thesis: Also in the realm of concrete spiritual decisions, the particular and individual element cannot, despite the real validity of general principles, be simply drawn general principles. "Time is greater than space" embodies the shift from a purely metaphysical approach to God's revelation to the "history of salvation." "Realities are more important than ideas" embodies the shift from the deductive to the inductive method.

5. Pope Francis, the First Postconciliar Pope

Pope Francis's use of Vatican II is mostly ecclesiological, and not without interesting absences. Very visible absences from *Evangelii Gaudium* are the constitution on the liturgy *Sacrosanctum Concilium* (despite the long section on the homily, *EG* 135–144), the declaration *Nostra Aetate* on non-Christian religions (despite the section on Judaism and other religions, *EG* 247–254), and the declaration on religious liberty *Dignitatis Humanae* (despite the paragraphs on dialogue and religious freedom, *EG* 255–258). But in these paragraphs, and others where we do not find quotations from Vatican II, we have quotes from post–Vatican II documents that received Vatican II: pastoral documents from national or continental bishops conferences, such as the bishops of India, the Philippines, the United States, CELAM in Latin America, Brazil, of France, and the European continent.

The lack of emphasis on the liturgical constitution in Francis signals not a lack of attention on the issue of the liturgical reform, but the intention to de-escalate the intra-Catholic debate on the liturgy. Liturgy is evangelizing, and not part of a power struggle in the Church, or a way to express an exclusive ecclesiology, or to use the gospel to ignore the deep solidarity between the Church and the world:

---

[16] See Drew Christiansen, S.J., "The Church Encounters the World," *America*, January 6–13, 2014, 20–21.

Evangelii Gaudium as an Act of Reception of Vatican II

This insidious worldliness is evident in a number of attitudes which appear opposed, yet all have the same pretence of "taking over the space of the Church". In some people we see an ostentatious preoccupation for the liturgy, for doctrine and for the Church's prestige, but without any concern that the Gospel have a real impact on God's faithful people and the concrete needs of the present time. In this way, the life of the Church turns into a museum piece or something which is the property of a select few. (*EG* 95)

By contrast, Francis's celebration of the fifty years from the first Mass in vernacular Italian, on March 7, 2015, in the parish of Ognissanti in the city of Rome left no doubt on Bergoglio's reception of the liturgical reform.[17]

In *Evangelii Gaudium* the balance between the quotes from magisterial documents (encyclicals and apostolic exhortations) and from local episcopates is carefully maintained. The relationship between Pope Francis and theologians after the pontificate of the "pope theologian" Benedict XVI is one of the many facets of this pontificate on which *Evangelii Gaudium* casts a light that is not yet exhaustive of the whole issue. But in *Evangelii Gaudium*, Thomas Aquinas, Augustine, John Henry Newman, Georges Bernanos, Romano Guardini, and Henri de Lubac – authors that have been part of the competitive narratives about Vatican II in these last fifty years – are utilized for a document that is undoubtedly seeing Vatican II as firm ground for the Catholic tradition.

Evangelii Gaudium is important in order to understand the pontificate of Pope Francis, but it is important also to understand this particular moment of the reception of Vatican II in the history of the Catholic Church. Francis represents a new beginning also for the reception of Vatican II: "With the election of Bergoglio we see a departure from a fifty-year-old tradition: the popes who succeeded John XXIII, from Paul VI to Benedict XVI, felt committed to qualify their position with respect to Vatican II.... For the first time since the election of Paul VI that took place half a century before, the new pope has not held a real programmatic speech after his election and, therefore, he did not feel the need to state his positioning with respect to Vatican II."[18]

Unlike his predecessor, Francis has not addressed programmatically, in this document or in other acts of his pontificate, the issue of the correct "interpretation" or "hermeneutics" of Vatican II. Francis's reception

---

[17] See http://www.news.va/it/news/papa-chiede-sintonia-tra-liturgia-e-vita-a-50-anni (March 7, 2015).

[18] Enrico Galavotti, "Il concilio di papa Francesco," in *Il conclave e papa Francesco*, ed. Alberto Melloni (Roma: Istituto della Enciclopedia Italiana Treccani, 2013), 37–39.

of Vatican II is the reception of the council by a post–Vatican II Catholic who takes Vatican II as both accomplished and to be implemented. It is therefore clear why the importance of Vatican II in *Evangelii Gaudium* extends well beyond the paragraphs where the documents of Vatican II are quoted or referenced. The very title of the exhortation is also a rescuing of *Gaudium et Spes*, the most original of all the documents of Vatican II, after a decade of ecclesial amnesia about it. *Evangelii Gaudium* is a further evidence of the fact that the pontificate and the teaching of Pope Francis cannot be understood without making reference to Vatican II. Pope Francis is not an academic who devoted studies to the interpretation of Vatican II, nor he was a participant at Vatican II (in this, different from his four predecessors). The pope has made thus far few explicit references to the council and has carefully avoided taking part in the debate on the hermeneutics of Vatican II:[19] but this is indeed indicative of a full reception of Vatican II. Francis is a postconciliar pope with an unproblematic relationship with Vatican II.

Thanks to the work done in these last twenty years of scholarship on Vatican II, we know now much more about the council, and especially about the four key elements for understanding it. The first element is Vatican II as an historical event that needs to be put in context and part of a developing tradition.[20] The second, the importance of the "invitational style" of Vatican II for the message of the council about what kind of Church the Catholic Church wants to be.[21] The third element is about the "constitutional value" of Vatican II, or, in other words, about the particular hierarchy of truths that Vatican II acknowledges and the particular role of Vatican II in defining this hierarchy.[22] The fourth element is the pastoral character of the doctrine of Vatican II as a moment of fundamental reframing (*recadrage*) of the tradition in light of the gospel.[23]

It is clear that Pope Francis is embodying all these acquisitions (and many more) of Vatican II in a way that is, not only for biographical reasons, different from the way his predecessors embodied it. It can be said that

---

[19] In relation to these debates, see, e.g., Massimo Faggioli, *Vatican II: The Battle for Meaning* (New York: Paulist Press, 2012).

[20] See *History of Vatican II*, 5 volumes, ed. Giuseppe Alberigo (Bologna: Il Mulino, 1995–2001), English translation, ed. Joseph A. Komonchak (Maryknoll, NY: Orbis, 1995–2006).

[21] See John O'Malley, *What Happened at Vatican II* (Cambridge, MA: Belknap Press of Harvard University Press, 2008).

[22] See *Theologisches Kommentar zum Zweiten Vatikanischen Konzils*, 5 vols., ed. Peter Hünermann and Hans-Jochen Hilberath (Freiburg: Herder, 2004–2005).

[23] See Christoph Theobald, *Le christianisme comme style. Une manière de faire de la théologie en post-modernité*, 2 vols. (Paris: Cerf, 2007).

Evangelii Gaudium as an Act of Reception of Vatican II

Pope Francis is the first pope of the post–Vatican II in a proper sense, as a cleric (ordained priest in 1969) who served the Church when Vatican II had already ended and was already being received. Pope Francis is the first pope coming from the global Church, that is, the Church that for the first time at Vatican II was given a voice in the conciliar tradition.[24]

The conclave in 2013 and the election of Francis have returned the Catholic Church to its global dimension – in a sense, trying to restore the promise made at Vatican II. The conclave has restored to the Catholic Church an image of itself that is much closer to that of Vatican II than it has been in recent years. The Church realigned itself to a more "world Church" dimension, just as it was in that council: from *urbs* to the *orbis terrarum*, the *oikumene*. According to the most important theologian of Vatican II, Yves Congar, at the council "the *orbis* had almost taken possession of the *urbs*."[25]

This acknowledgment of the reversal of positions between the *urbs* and the *orbis* in Catholicism has been clear from the very beginning of Francis's pontificate, with the strong emphasis on the *poor* and on *mercy* – both key words also for the pontificate of John XXIII. Pope Francis and his non-European and non-Western origins are overturning a paradigm that is at once geopolitical and cultural, along with other European and Western paradigms that are typical of Catholicism in the northwestern part of the globe, such as the "Tridentine paradigm," which sees the Council of Trent (1545–1563) as the event that defined once and for all the relationship between Catholicism and historicity.[26] The pope coming from Latin America shows that he has an awareness of the relationship between Church, historicity, and existential dimension, and between history and theology that clearly comes under the heading of "inculturation" of the gospel – with *cultures* in the plural. Pope Francis shows that he can do so in a new way: The postconciliar Church saw inculturation as an attempt to embody Christianity in non-European cultures as it had been enunciated by Vatican II and Paul VI, and while it had been expressed more in a "performative" way by John Paul II, it was not expressed in written magisterial form. The apostolic exhortation (with the value of a real encyclical) *Evangelii Gaudium* represents in this sense a beginning. The encyclical

---

[24] About this see Massimo Faggioli, *Pope Francis: Tradition in Transition* (New York: Paulist Press, 2015. Original Italian: Rome: Armando Editore, 2014).
[25] See Yves Congar, *Le Concile de Vatican II. Son Église, Peuple de Dieu et Corps du Christ* (Paris: Cerf, 1984), 54.
[26] See Paolo Prodi, *Il paradigma tridentino. Un'epoca della storia della Chiesa* (Brescia: Morcelliana, 2010).

Laudato Si' of May 24, 2015 has continued this path with its emphasis on a "contextual ecology" and "human ecology" that comes from the humanization project of Vatican II.

This new tone by Pope Francis is therefore also an ecclesiological turn, that is very clear with *Evangelii Gaudium*. Pope Francis's *Evangelii Gaudium* embodies a reception of the historical ecclesiology of Vatican II on many levels as evidenced in the following examples:

- The reform of a Roman Catholicism whose theological and cultural shape goes "beyond Rome," beyond Europe and the West, requires a rethinking of a number of theological and cultural issues, even before the institutional issues: "It is not advisable for the Pope to take the place of local Bishops in the discernment of every issue which arises in their territory. In this sense, I am conscious of the need to promote a sound 'decentralization'" (EG 16). In fact, one can speak of a "Tridentine paradigm" due in large part to the monocultural, or European, character of the Catholic Church between the sixteenth and nineteenth centuries. The "world Church" turn of Francis is visible also in the encyclical *Laudato Si'* and especially in the ecumenical, interreligious, and global appeal.
- *Ressourcement* as a return to the sources and to the consequent relativization of other Church norms. Liturgy is a prime source for theology. In the words of *Sacrosanctum Concilium*: "This sacred Council has several aims in view: it desires to impart an ever increasing vigor to the Christian life of the faithful." The passages of *EG* on the homily (esp. 137–138) are a clear reception of the liturgical reform of Vatican II even without quoting the liturgical constitution.[27] In all of Francis's pontificate there is a careful balance between full reception of the liturgical reform and preservation of popular devotions – something that is expressive not only of the Latin American identity of Bergoglio, but also of his theological center of gravity.
- A dynamic interchange between scripture, tradition and teaching, and a recovery of the *sensus fidei* are part of a conciliar Church – a requirement for a missionary Church. Francis presents clearly the complexity of the work of theologians for a Church in state of mission: "The Church is herself a missionary disciple; she needs to grow in her interpretation of the revealed word and in her understanding of truth. It

---

[27] Second Vatican Council, constitution on the liturgy *Sacrosanctum Concilium*, no. 1: see Massimo Faggioli, *True Reform: Liturgy and Ecclesiology in Sacrosanctum Concilium* (Collegeville, MN: Liturgical Press, 2012).

is the task of exegetes and theologians to help 'the judgment of the Church to mature'. The other sciences also help to accomplish this, each in its own way." (EG 40)
- The inculturation of Catholicism aimed at making it truly universal: "It is imperative to evangelize cultures in order to inculturate the Gospel. In countries of Catholic tradition, this means encouraging, fostering and reinforcing a richness that already exists. In countries of other religious traditions, or profoundly secularized countries, it will mean sparking new processes for evangelizing culture, even though these will demand long-term planning. We must keep in mind, however, that we are constantly being called to grow. Each culture and social group needs purification and growth." (EG 69)
- A detachment from preassumed sociocultural models, because "time is greater than space": "People live poised between each individual moment and the greater, brighter horizon of the utopian future as the final cause which draws us to itself. Here we see a first principle for progress in building a people: time is greater than space. This principle enables us to work slowly but surely, without being obsessed with immediate results. It helps us patiently to endure difficult and adverse situations, or inevitable changes in our plans. It invites us to accept the tension between fullness and limitation, and to give a priority to time." (EG 222–223)
- The pastoral nature of the doctrine of Vatican II that entails a reception of its message that "necessarily takes the form of a conversion"[28]: "In her ongoing discernment, the Church can also come to see that certain customs not directly connected to the heart of the Gospel, even some which have deep historical roots, are no longer properly understood and appreciated. Some of these customs may be beautiful, but they no longer serve as means of communicating the Gospel. We should not be afraid to re-examine them. At the same time, the Church has rules or precepts which may have been quite effective in their time, but no longer have the same usefulness for directing and shaping people's lives." (EG 43)

All these statements signify a vast program in Pope Francis that has also clear social and political implications, as we can see from chapter IV of *Evangelii Gaudium* (and even more in *Laudato Si'*). It is clear that Francis's pontificate is also a declaration of a truce on the battlefront of the so-called

---

[28] See Christoph Theobald, *La réception du concile Vatican II. I. Accéder à la source* (Paris: Cerf, 2009), 409.

culture wars. The truce declared by Francis on this and other fronts involves a reshuffling of entrenched positions within Western Catholicism. In fact, overcoming the Roman Tridentine and European paradigm has very importance implications, not from a "progressive" or "liberal" point of view (which are Euro-western categories), but from a perspective of theological *ressourcement*, a "return to the sources" that it intends to make the largest church in the world a church that is more faithful to the original message than to the social, political, and cultural aspects of more recent times. Pope Francis shows awareness of the needs of the Eurocentric paradigm through his gestures rather than his words, and of the urgency of this missionary perspective.

In this sense, there is a clear parallel between John XXIII and Pope Francis: just as John XXIII in the encyclical *Pacem in terris* (1963) disengaged Catholic theology from the ideological role assigned to it by the West in the Cold War, so Francis is trying to disengage Catholicism from the "culture wars" – and the reactions are not very different fifty years after.[29] The objections (or worse than objections) against both popes arrive from the ones who see their attempt as "appeasement." The election of Bergoglio to the papacy is an unprecedented step toward the fulfillment of what the German Jesuit theologian Karl Rahner called the "world Church," that is a third macroperiod of its history (after the Judeo-Christianity of its origins, and the church of Hellenism and Greek-Latin culture) with the self-realization of the Catholic Church as a Church in the global dimension through the incarnation of Catholicism in different cultures.[30] If the Second Vatican Council was the first council of the world Church, and Pope John XXIII was the first Pope of a Church that was conceived as global in nature, then the pontificate of Pope Francis is the first pontificate of a bishop coming from the world Church.

The clear "no to a sterile pessimism" proclaimed in *Evangelii Gaudium* 84 is a further clear and explicit reference to John XXIII's opening speech of Vatican II (October 11, 1962), *Gaudet Mater Ecclesia*. No wonder Pope Francis is redefining the dimensions of the Church, making it practicable again, after it had been taken away because of the undue pervasiveness of ecclesiastical power from the people who are the Church.

---

[29] See Massimo Faggioli, *John XXIII: The Medicine of Mercy* (Collegeville, MN: Liturgical Press, 2014).

[30] See Karl Rahner, "Basic Theological Interpretation of the Second Vatican Council," in Karl Rahner, *Theological Investigations*, vol. 20: *Concern for the Church* (New York: Crossroads, 1981), 77–90.

CHAPTER 4

"The Lord, your God, is in your Midst" (EG 4)

Evangelii Gaudium – Francis's Call for a Kenotic Theology

Judith Gruber

Pope Francis took the church – and the world – by surprise. From the very first moment of his public appearance on the balcony above St. Peter's Square, clad in a modest white gown, with a humble smile on his face, and a simple "buena sera" on his lips, he has performed his office in ways distinctly different from established ecclesial and papal practices – and it is these practices that have stirred up global attention. A pope who takes public transport, a pope who does not wear Prada, a pope who is not to judge is not just new(s) to Catholics; he even makes the cover page of the *Rolling Stone Magazine*. In his headline, "The Times They Are A-Changin,'" journalist Mark Binelli captures well the unsettling spirit of aggiornamento that has had the church in its grip since Francis's inauguration, and his cover story documents the "scandal of normality" that marks Francis's papacy and shows how, with the "simplest of gestures," the "celebrity pope" "revolutionizes" the church.[1]

Yet, it has not taken long for questions to arise as to the scope of Francis's revolution. Within its journalistic means, the *Rolling Stone* article sketches the question that is at stake – and that has been widely and controversially discussed in both progressive and conservative camps in the church: Do the pope's "radical changes" in church practice initiate a change in doctrine? Intriguingly, a majority of Catholics from *both* camps seem to negate this question – while progressive Catholics deplore the pope's reluctance to translate his rearrangements of the church practice

[1] Mark Binelli, "The Times, They Are A-Changin': Inside the Pope's Gentle Revolution," *Rolling Stone* (January 28, 2014).

into a readjustment of church doctrine,[2] conservatives hold on to the claim that the deposit of faith cannot be changed, no matter what the pope does.[3] In his *Rolling Stone* article, Binelli, too, answers to the negative – "The pope's tonal changes don't necessarily signal a wild swing from tradition." In quoting from an interview with Thomas Reese, he does indicate, though, that theologically, the relation between church practice and church doctrine is more intricate: "In the Catholic Church, style is substance," Reese says in this interview, "We are a church of symbols. That's what we call the sacraments: symbols that give us grace. These things really matter. So Francis is already changing the church in real ways through his words and symbolic gestures."[4]

Thus, with Reese, we can trace the dispute over Francis's practice and its impact on church teaching back to the very core of the Catholic creed: Founded on the belief in incarnation and its christological reflections, Catholic theology does not allow for an easy separation between form and substance, between practice and teaching. To believe that Jesus the Christ was fully divine and fully human, in no separation and no division, configures Catholic theology in a very distinct way: It undermines a binary opposition between the divine and the human, between the transcendent and the immanent and instead maps immanence as the place where God can be found. The *world* is the foundational *locus theologicus*. Its relations to the world, therefore, are constitutive for the church to find its knowledge of God – *it is in the pastoral activities of the church that ecclesial doctrine takes its shape*. In its ressourcement of the constitutive parameters of Catholic tradition, the Second Vatican Council laid out these theologico-epistemological implications of the belief in incarnation and codified them as the normative framework for Catholic theology. This can be exemplified in three crucial passages of the conciliar texts:

(1) It is widely acknowledged that the Second Vatican Council was the first council of the Church particularly dedicated to questions about the church itself: In times of intensifying secularization and

---

[2] "Substantive Structural and Doctrinal Issues Do Not Evaporate Just Because the Pope Does Not Wear Prada," Mary Hunt, "The Trouble with Francis: Three Things That Worry Me," *Religion Dispatches* (January 6, 2014), http://religiondispatches.org/the-trouble-with-francis-three-things-that-worry-me/.

[3] Mark Shea: "The Pope is not going to alter essential doctrines. He's just not going to. He can't. It is a guarantee of the Faith,' Mark Shea, "'A Reader with Jitters about Pope Francis Writes ... ," http://www.ncregister.com/blog/mark-shea/a-reader-with-jitters-about-pope-francis-writes.

[4] Binelli, '"The Times, They Are A-Changin."

due to the shortcomings of preconciliar neoscholastic theology, the church had lost its self-confidence and was challenged to explicate its ecclesiological self-understanding. The council set out to tackle this task. Yet, in the endeavor to outline the identity of the Catholic church, it soon became evident that in order to describe the church, one perspective "ad intra" does not suffice. It is in need of a complementary perspective "ad extra"[5] – the original draft "De Ecclesia" was replaced by *two* ecclesiological constitutions, *Lumen Gentium*, the doctrinal constitution on the church and *Gaudium et Spes*, the pastoral constitution on the church: the church can only be defined in the interplay of a pastoral and a doctrinal approach.

(2) Within *Gaudium et Spes*, this performative moment of entangling pastoral and doctrine is revisited and translated into a theological hermeneutics: "To carry out its [defining] task, the Church has always had the duty to scrutinize the signs of the times and of interpreting them in the light of the Gospel" (GS 4). The signs of the times allow the church to find "language intelligible to each generation" (GS 4); the church's proclamation takes its shape in an engagement with the signs of the times. In the world, the church finds language adequate for the communication of God. Its relation to the world, therefore, is constitutive for the formulation of theology. Pastoral, then, is not the application of the given doctrine of the church, but allows for the formation of church teaching. There is a *mutual* hermeneutics between the signs of the times and the gospel – not only are the signs of the times discerned and shaped by the gospel, but they give the gospel its shape (or, more precisely, its many shapes).

(3) *Lumen Gentium*, in turn, draws the ecclesiological conclusions from this entanglement of pastoral and doctrine and ties it back to its christological foundation: "In no weak analogy ... to the mystery of the incarnate word" (LG 8), the church and its teaching represent God in the world not in a clear delineation between the divine

---

[5] "[T]o use the unfortunate division commonly invoked at the time," Joseph Komonchak, "The Redaction and Reception of Gaudium et Spes. Tensions within the Majority at Vatican II," 21, https://jakomonchak.files.wordpress.com/2013/04/jak-views-of-gaudium-et-spes.pdf, (first published as "Le valutazioni sulla Gaudium et spes: Chenu, Dossetti, Ratzinger," in *Volti di fine Concilio: Studi di storia e teologia sulla conclusione del Vaticano II*, eds. Joseph Doré and Alberto Melloni (Bologna: Il Mulino, 2000) 115–153; a shorter English version appeared as "Augustine, Aquinas or the Gospel sine glossa: Divisions over Gaudium et Spes," in *Unfinished Journey: The Church 40 Years after Vatican II. Essays for John Wilkins*, ed. Austen Ivereigh (New York: Continuum, 2003), 102–118.

and the secular, but is always and irresolvable both, "a society ... with hierarchical organs and the Mystical Body of Christ," "a visible assembly and the spiritual community," an "earthly Church and the Church enriched with heavenly things," "holy and in need of purification" (LG 8). In short, the church takes its shape in an entanglement of the transcendent and the immanent, in no confusion and no separation.

In anchoring ecclesiology in the belief in incarnation, the conciliar texts defy a binarization of church and world – and if the world is constitutive for the God-talk of the church, then Catholic theology cannot be neatly separated into doctrine as a given deposit within the church and pastoral as its application in the world. In acknowledging this interrelation as the foundation of ecclesial identity and theology, the council reclaims a theological principle that is at the heart of the Jewish-Christian tradition but that has always remained dangerous and endangered knowledge: the knowledge that the story of God with God's people unfolds *in* history, the knowledge that God has a human body.

The dualistic epistemology of its hellenistic heritage has always tempted the church to break up this entanglement of the divine into the world into two separate spheres, and to thereby undermine the core of the Christian creed – the creed that Jesus the Christ is fully human and fully divine, in no confusion and no separation; and the creed that the church also takes its shape in this irresolvable enmeshment of the divine and the human/secular. Yet, it is not just the intellectual difficulties of dualistic thinking that all too often have cut short endeavors to take the belief in incarnation to its unsettling theological conclusions. Rather, these epistemological difficulties have to do with a dynamics of power that lies at the heart of the production of knowledge. The authority of the church is rooted in its knowledge of God. It finds its very definition in the claim that it embodies the truth given from God to all humanity – and to acknowledge that this knowledge is entangled into the world massively complicates the authority of the church in its claim to represent divine truth in the world.

The constitutive relation of theology to the world seems to relativize the authoritative position of the church in the world. It is for these political implications that it has always been a theological challenge for the church to fully acknowledge the world as its principle theological locus. The interpretation history of the Second Vatican Council is a case in point. Wolfgang Beinert shows that one of the most contentious issues in its reception has been the question whether its documents are dogmatically binding or solely pastoral statements – the schism/heresy of the Society of St. Pius X is only the most radical expression of this intense debate.[6] However, as Beinert points out, even posing the question in this way already runs counter to the theologico-epistemological presuppositions of the council. It relies on a split between doctrine and pastoral and succumbs to the binarization of church and world, which the council aimed at overcoming in its explicit shift from neoscholastism. This allows for a clearer definition (literally: a demarcation) of the church vis-à-vis the world, but it does not live up to the belief in incarnation as its theologico-epistemological foundation. Even after Vatican II, an understanding of doctrine split from the pastoral has remained a constant temptation to Catholic theology.[7]

By privileging pastoral over explicitly doctrinal matters, Francis's papacy raises the issue of their theological relation with renewed urgency. The pope's focus on orthopractice does not leave the question of orthodoxy unaffected. Precisely because he practices church in distinctly new ways, the definitions of Church doctrine need to be theologically revisited. The focal point of this papacy, therefore, is anything but "'just pastoral." On the contrary, it forces the church to again think through the foundational parameters of ecclesial teaching and Catholic theology.

Francis has begun to tackle this task. His first apostolic exhortation, *Evangelii Gaudium*, is dedicated not only to outlining his pastoral visions for the church in today's world; beyond that, it can be read as an endeavor to develop a theological framework that anchors the orthopractical emphases of his papacy firmly within the Catholic tradition. In this article I argue that this reflection of ecclesial practice necessarily takes him right to the theologico-epistemological foundations of ecclesial teaching and has an unsettling impact on a theological understanding of church doctrine: In a close reading of the document, I first extract its two core arguments: (1) evangelization is the defining mission of the church, and (2) evangelization is kenosis. A second step shows how these two arguments come together to promote a kenotic dogmatics that defies the heterodox currents of "dogmatic capitalism" in the tradition of the Catholic church.

---

[6] Wolfgang Beinert, „"Nur pastoral oder dogmatisch verpflichtend? Zur Verbindlichkeit des zweiten Vatikanischen Konzils," *Stimmen der Zeit*, 2010, 3–15.

[7] This tendency found a culmination in Pope Benedict's 2011 call for a "desecularization" of the church. Benedict XVI, "Meeting with Catholics Engaged in the Life of the Church and Society. Address of his Holiness Benedict XI. Concert Hall, Freiburg im Breisgau" (Sunday, 25 September 2011).

1. Two Core Arguments in *Evangelii Gaudium*

First and foremost, *Evangelii Gaudium* is a passionate call for a radically different church *practice*. Pope Francis exhorts all Catholics to "adopt a definite style of evangelization ... in every activity [we] undertake" (EG 18). He calls on the church to "put all things in a missionary key" (EG 34) so that the first and principal proclamation can "ring out over and over: 'Jesus Christ loves you'; he gave his life to save you; and now he is living at your side every day to enlighten, strengthen and free you'" (EG 164). Again and again, he drives his core message home: *It is the church's raison d'etre to proclaim the gospel*. For Francis, this means that the church has to *live* the gospel – for him, the proclamation of the gospel takes its shape in the way we treat others, in the way we live with and, more particularly, for others: "The kerygma has a clear social content: at the very heart of the gospel is life in community and engagement with others. The content of the first proclamation has an immediate moral implication centered on charity" (EG 177). As a social practice of living for others, *evangelization has a kenotic dimension*. Even though the term *kenosis* never appears explicitly in the document, Francis relies on verbal paraphrases of its core meaning to offer his definition of evangelization – according to the pope, to evangelize means for the church to give itself fully up to the world: "An evangelizing community is willing to abase itself if necessary.... It take[s] on the 'smell of the sheep' ... and ... is ready to put [its] whole life on the line, even to accepting martyrdom" (EG 24). Rendered as a practice, kenosis is the theological key metaphor for evangelization in *Evangelii Gaudium*.

Two core arguments can thus be extracted from the pope's first apostolic exhortation: First, he proposes that evangelization is the defining mission of the church and, second, he outlines evangelization as kenosis. These two core arguments do not remain isolated from each other but have a significant overlap with far-reaching ecclesiological implications: If kenotic "missionary outreach is paradigmatic for all the church's activities" (EG 15), then *being church is practicing kenosis*. We will explore this overlap further in the following text.

In order to facilitate the evangelizing practice of his church, the pope gives a detailed analysis of the economic, cultural, and social conditions of our globalized society, and he outlines how he believes the church should act in relation to these specific challenges. Still, he insists that *"this is not a social document"* (EG 184; emphasis added). Instead, he argues that these practices are *theo-logical* in the literal sense of the word: They are "God-talk," they make the gospel heard in the world: "Being a disciple means being constantly ready to bring the love of Jesus to others, and this can happen unexpectedly and in any place.... This communication takes place in so many different ways that it would be impossible to describe or catalogue them all, and God's people, with all their many gestures and signs, are its collective subject" (EG 128.129). Francis thus firmly roots the methodological framework of his call for evangelization within the theologico-epistemological tradition of the Second Vatican Council. His description of the "context in which we all have to live and work" (EG 50) is not confined to, or more precisely, is not intended to be a "purely sociological analysis ... employing an allegedly neutral and clinical method" (EG 50). Instead, he unfolds this passage within the framework of a theological hermeneutics, "an evangelical discernment" (EG 50) – he offers a reading of the signs of the times in light of the gospel as the indispensable starting point for the church to fulfill its defining mission, evangelization. The proclamation of the gospel depends on deciphering the signs of the times. They are the basis of the God-talk of the church; they are the principle of its theo-logy. An "analysis of contemporary reality" (51), therefore, is a genuinely *theological* task.

Theologically, this methodological approach can be accounted for in a number of ways. Among others, incarnation, creation, or pneumatology offer thought patterns that allow to anchor theological discernment within the complexities of human/worldly reality. In *Evangelii Gaudium*, it finds its theological justification in the key metaphor that the pope uses for the proclamation of the gospel – kenosis. The kenotic framework that Francis develops for his call for evangelization gives theological support to the argument that an analysis of the world is necessarily the starting point of theology; this, in turn, establishes a normative form for theology: It shows that the God-talk of the church emerges from the pastoral activities of the church. Ultimately, then, Francis's call for a kenotic church practice also has implications for an understanding of Catholic doctrine. It exposes that ecclesial doctrine has always already taken its shape in the relations of the church to the world. These implications come into sharper relief through a closer analysis of Francis's two interrelated core arguments in *Evangelii Gaudium*:

1.1. Evangelization Is the Defining Mission of the Church

Evangelization, the pope first proposes, is the defining mission of the church. Its all-encompassing task is to share the εὐαγγέλιον, the good news that "the kingdom of God is at hand" (Mk 1:14). With Jesus and as the body of Christ, the church proclaims this as the "gospel of God" (Mk 1:14). Its key role, then, is to spread the Word of God; literally, *the task of the church is to do theology, God-talk*. It has always understood this to be a multidimensional endeavor – from its earliest beginnings, ecclesial theology has functioned as kerygma, leiturgia, and diakonia. In performing these multiple functions, several distinct genres have developed; among others, ecclesial theology can take the shape of intellectual reflection, liturgical worship, or magisterial definitions. Clear demarcations between these genres, however, were established only gradually. The etymological kinship of "doxa" and "dogma" points to this shared origin of now-distinct genres within ecclesial theology – both the worshipping and the definitory dimension of the God-talk of the church have their roots in a common, more broadly conceived discourse of theology. While through the history of theology a clear distinction between doctrinal language and other theological genres has been forged, this differentiation did not yet inform the conciliar definitions of the early church. On the contrary, the council fathers made a deliberate (if not thoroughly successful) attempt to draw on language that was not "aristotelice" but "piscatore"[8] – their goal was to define the faith of the church not through the specialized, and hence exclusionary, discourse of "philosophers" but in the idiom of "fishermen" (and, we can extend, "shepherds"), who epitomize the vast majority of the early church in terms of its socioeconomic structure. In other words, the dogmatic definitions of ecclesial theology arise from piscatorial/pastoral contexts; theologically, the dogma of the church was and is to reflect the doxa of the believers – it is a declaration of the *sensus fidelium*.

This, of course, is not to say that a historical-critical analysis of ecclesial theology does not expose less consensual and more profane forces at play in the formation of doctrine. Decades of historical research have thrown a spotlight on the contingent constellations out of which the definitions of the faith emerged – and they have exposed the politics of ecclesial theology. A Foucauldian discourse analysis, in particular, shows that the normative corpus of the church has been consolidated in interplay of power and knowledge. Its theological demarcations have been forged in processes of simultaneous inclusion and exclusion; they emerge from negotiations in which those in power have the ability to define ecclesial knowledge in a way that reinforces their power.[9] The orthodox doctrine of the church has

---

[8] Alois Grillmeier, *Mit ihm und in ihm: Christologische Forschungen und Perspektiven* (Freiburg: Herder, 1975), 283–300.

[9] Bart Ehrman gives an account of the interplay between theological debates and political relations between the Roman church and other local churches across the Roman

taken its shape in the definition of heresies[10] – it depends on alternative theologies that have been anathematized and excluded. What remains as the tradition of the church rests on a host of excluded stories and silenced voices.

Both the theological and the historical-critical approach to the formation of doctrine highlight, each in their own way, that the doctrinal formulations of the church do not precede ecclesial theology. Even though the doctrines have, through powerful negotiations, become the normative cornerstones of the God-talk of the church, they do not come before other theological genres but emerge from a wider discourse of theology. When, as Francis says, the defining task of the church is the practice of theology, then ecclesial doctrine does not offer an independent foundation for, but is shaped in and through this mission; in other words, the formulation of the doctrine of the church is not absolute (literally: detached) from, but contingent on the theological practice of the church.

Overwhelming historical evidence, mounting since the Reformation and Enlightenment, but particularly through the historical-critical research of the nineteenth and twentieth century, has made it inevitable for the church to acknowledge this contingency of its teaching and to accommodate it into its understanding of theology. While first met with considerable and forceful resistance, the "development"[11] or "'history'"[12] of dogma has now become widely accepted in Catholic theology and was canonized by the Second Vatican Council (*DV* 8). By highlighting that God's revelation in the world is mediated by, and therefore cannot but be conditioned and limited by human experience,[13] the "development of doctrine" can account for the perceivable transformations and modifications in the teaching of the church throughout its tradition.[14] With the concept of the "development of

> Empire in the emergence of orthodoxy. Bart D. Ehrman, *Lost Christianites: The Battles for Scripture and the Faiths We Never Knew* ([Place of publication not identified]: OUP Inc USA, 2005), 74–80.

[10] Cf. the groundbreaking study by Walter Bauer, *Orthodoxy and Heresy in Earliest Christianity* (Sigler Press ed., Mifflintown, PA: Sigler Press, 1996 [first published in German, 1934]).

[11] John Henry Newman, *An Essay on the Development of Christian Doctrine*, 6th ed. (Notre Dame, IN: University of Notre Dame Press, 1989).

[12] Adolf von Harnack, *Lehrbuch der Dogmengeschichte*. 3 vols. (Mainz, 1886–1890).

[13] Cf. 1Tim 2: 5: "For there is one God, and one *mediator* between God and men, the man Jesus Christ" (emphasis added).

[14] "Since God speaks in Sacred Scripture through men in human fashion, the interpreter of Sacred Scripture, in order to see clearly what God wanted to communicate to us, should carefully investigate what meaning the sacred writers really intended, and what God wanted to manifest by means of their words [DV12]. "For there is a growth in the understanding of the realities and the words which have been handed down. This happens

doctrine," Catholic theology embraces the contingency of ecclesial teaching as a theological resource: Registering the "'growth" (*DV* 8) in doctrine throughout tradition allows the church to reflect the eschatological proviso that conditions all mediations of the body of Christ – it expresses the Christian hope for "complete fulfillment" (*DV* 8) at the end of times. How, though, does this relate to the Catholic belief that Christ is the "fullness of all revelation" (*DV* 2) and "what was handed on by the Apostles includes everything which contributes toward the holiness of life and increase in faith of the peoples of God" (*DV* 8) so that "we now await no further new public revelation before the glorious manifestation of our Lord Jesus Christ" (*DV* 4)? How, in short, does ecclesial doctrine relate to the "sure gift of truth" (*DV* 8) given to the church in revelation – or, even shorter, how does ecclesial theology relate to revelation? In other words, how does the God-talk of the church (theo-logy in *genetivus objectivus*) relate to the God-talk of revelation (theo-logy in *genetivus subjectivus*)?

One well-paved way of interpreting the "ever deeper understanding of revelation" (*DV* 5) through the development of ecclesial doctrine is in terms of its ever further "unfolding."[15] Framing the development of doctrine as the "unfolding" of given revelation accounts for the conditionality of doctrinal formulations throughout tradition and thereby highlights the eschatological incompleteness of ecclesial theology in its mediations of God's revelation – the God-talk of the church cannot simply be equated/nor confused with the God-talk of revelation. The metaphor of "'unfolding" does not, however, take the contingency of ecclesial theology *radically* enough – it does not trace it back down to its very roots and origins; instead,

---

through the contemplation and study made by believers, who treasure these things in their hearts (see Luke 2:19, 51) through a penetrating understanding of the spiritual realities which they experience, and through the preaching of those who have received through Episcopal succession the sure gift of truth. For as the centuries succeed one another, the Church constantly moves forward toward the fullness of divine truth until the words of God reach their complete fulfillment in her" [DV8)],

[15] Wolfgang Beinert, e.g., in the article quoted in the preceding text, draws on this metaphor to give theological substance to his argument that there is a mutual dependence between pastoral and dogmatics: It is "grounded in the fact that, on the one hand, with the Christ event, revelation is materially completed in its written records; on the other hand, however, it is conceptually inexhaustible. According to the Gospel of John, the spirit of God has the task to introduce [the church] ever further into the truth already given ... (John 16:13). A terminus ad quem or post quem is not mentioned. The tradition of revelation, therefore, is an incomplete and incompletable process.... It is part of the unfolding of [given] revelation." Beinert, "Nur pastoral oder dogmatisch verpflichtend? Zur Verbindlichkeit des zweiten Vatikanischen Konzils" (see n. 6), 11f. Translation by the present author.

"The Lord, your God, is in your Midst" (EG 4)

it is still prone to the idea of revelation as an absolute deposit of truth given within the church that precedes and informs its contingent ecclesial mediation, and that comes to "'full bloom" through the tradition of the church. It relies on a *separation* between an absolute deposit of the divine logos and the theo-logy of the church. Ultimately, then, framing the contingency of doctrine as an "unfolding" runs counter to the Chalcedonenian christological prefiguration of ecclesial theology as stipulated by the Second Vatican Council (*LG* 8): Cutting short the contingency of doctrinal formulations by positing an absolute foundation for ecclesial theology does reflect the axiom that there is "'no confusion" between the divine and the human/secular in the (ecclesial) body of Christ, but it falls short of the indispensably complementary "no separation" in the mediation of God in the world. Positing the presence of revelation as a deposit detached from the theological practices of the church cannot fully conceive of the human/secular as the locus of God-talk, but splits the Word of God from its mediations into the world – it makes for a docetic misconception of the ecclesial body of Christ.

1.2. *Evangelization Is Kenosis*

At this point, Francis's second core argument in *Evangelii Gaudium* comes into play: evangelization is kenosis. The thought pattern of kenosis was introduced into the theological discourse in resistance to such an absolutization of the Word of God from its mediation in the world – kenosis defies a truncation of radical contingency in Christian God-talk and, instead, embraces God's relation to the world as both medium and content of revelation: As the belief that, in Jesus the Christ, God revealed God-self gradually took its shape through the earliest stages of ecclesial theology, it led to irritations of established theologies. One major point of contention, especially as early Christological titles fluctuated between Jewish and hellenistic contexts, was the relation of the divine and the human in Jesus the Christ. Against docetic approaches, which stressed Christ's divinity at the expense of his humanity, the discourse of ecclesial theology always held on to his full humanness:[16] It proclaims that he

---

[16] As John Macquarrie has observed, the importance of the teaching of kenosis lies in its insistence on the material, the historical, and the embodied. It offers a "safeguard against those docetic tendencies which seem to have dogged the classical Christology through the centuries," John Macquarrie, *Jesus Christ in Modern Thought* (London and Philadelphia: SCM Press; Trinity Press International, 1990), 245.

was "fully human, fully divine, in no confusion and no separation" (DS 148). The concept of kenosis is one christological device (among others) to bring both, the divine and the human, to the fore as constitutive for the Christ-event – within the essentialist framework of hellenistic metaphysics, it holds on the nonseparation between divine and human in Jesus the Christ by way of a "self-limitation" of God – kenosis is the mode of God's revelation as a human being: The word was fully divine, but did not hold on to its divinity. This relinquishment, however, did not diminish the divinity in Jesus the Christ, on the contrary, through this abasement, Christ transcends "every name" (Phil 2:6–11).[17] This is proclaimed as God's *self*-revelation – kenosis, then, is not only mode, but also content of revelation: In kenosis, God reveals God-self as a God who gives everything to be in relation to the world.[18] This interpretation of the Christ-event brought ecclesial theology into conflict with established notions of God[19] – the proclamation of a God who does not hold on to being God in order to be in relation with the world triggered major theological shifts and, eventually, developed into the Trinitarian creed, embracing relationality as the appropriate framework for Christian God-talk.[20] A relation to the world is constitutive of God's revelation in the world; it is mode and content of God-talk in *genetivus subjectivus*.

---

[17] For a nuanced analysis of the relation of the human and the divine in a kenotic Christology, cf. Graham Ward's critique of the kenoticists of the nineteenth century: "Kenosis is … a doctrine of divine representation.… [Jesus Christ] existed in the form of God (en morphé theou) but in the emptying Christ became the form of a slave (morphén doulou).… In this morphology he took on the likeness (homoiómati) of human beings and was found in human form (schémati).… Christ's kenosis is his incarnation (and death) – that is the point. Christ's kenosis is not the abandonment of his divine attributes (as those nineteenth-century kenoticists would have it)." Graham Ward, "Kenosis and Naming: Beyond Analogy and toward Allegoria Amoris," in *Religion, Modernity, and Postmodernity*, ed. Paul Heelas, David Martin, and Paul Morris (Oxford and Malden, MA: Blackwell Publishers, 1998), 233–257.

[18] "If the Incarnation is indeed our best window into the nature of God, then it makes sense that a kenotic Christology should lead to a kenotic theism, in which the self-giving love shown in Christ is seen as central to God's very nature," C. Stephen Evans, "Introduction: Understanding Jesus the Christ as Human and Divine," in *Exploring Kenotic Christology: The Self-emptying of God*, ed. C. Stephen Evans (Vancouver, BC: Regent College Publishers, 2010), 1–24. For an exploration of such a kenotic understanding of God, see the essays in J. C. Polkinghorne (ed.), *The Work of Love: Creation as Kenosis* (Grand Rapids, MI: W. B. Eerdmans, 2001).

[19] "a stumbling block to Jews, and foolishness to Gentiles" (1Cor 1:23).

[20] Thomas Thompson and Cornelius Plantinga, Jr, "Trinity and Kenosis," in *Exploring Kenotic Christology: The Self-emptying of God*, ed. C. Stephen Evans (Vancouver, BC: Regent College Publishers, 2010), 165–190.

2. Toward a Kenotic Theology

It is this relationality that implicitly makes kenosis the key metaphor for evangelization in *Evangelii Gaudium*. The pastoral practices that Francis describes as paradigmatic for the proclamation of the gospel all relate the church to the world – in practicing evangelization, the church gives itself fully to the world in order to relate (the gospel) to the world. Evangelization takes place in the pastoral relations of the church to the world. Yet, in Francis's argument, kenosis does not remain a metaphor just for the pastoral practice of the church. There is an overlap in his two core arguments that exposes that the kenotic definition of revelation has a profound impact on the definition of theology: When the defining mission of the church is evangelization, and when evangelization is kenosis, then *being church is practicing kenosis*. And, when being church is the proclamation of the gospel of God – evangelization, or in more technical terms, when being church is doing theology, and when being church is practicing kenosis, then *theology is the practice of kenosis* – the overlap in Francis's two core arguments claims kenosis not only as the mode of God-talk in *genetivus subjectivus* but also as the appropriate mode for God-talk in *genetivus objectivus*. In a christological theology of revelation, the concept of kenosis resists a docetic truncation of God's mediation in the world, and through the interplay of its two main arguments, *Evangelii Gaudium* retrieves this as a constitutive factor for theology, too. For both, revelation and theology, a relation to the world is constitutive. By describing evangelization as a kenotic practice, Francis makes the argument that the church depends on the world to perform its defining task – it depends on the world to do theology. It is in the world that the church develops its God-talk. The world, in short, is a *locus theologicus*.[21]

Francis repeatedly points to this theological quality of the world: "[I]n today's world" (*EG* 86), he says, "God dwells among" us and must be found (*EG* 71). Amidst the death-dealing mechanisms of global capitalism, "signs of resurrection suddenly spring up" (*EG* 276). "Resurrection is already secretly woven into the fabric of this history" (*EG* 278). With these statements, the pope underlines the significance of the world for the theology of the church: The world is the place where the church finds God. Yet, in Francis's mapping, the world remains an ambiguous place. His description

---

[21] During the conciliar debates on the *Gaudium et Spes*, Joseph Ratzinger pointed to the complexities and problems of defining the world as a locus theologicus: Joseph Ratzinger, "Angesichts der Welt von heute: Überlegungen zur Konfrontation mitder Kirche im Schema XIII," *Wort und Wahrheit*, 1965, 493–504.

does not share the optimism that characterized *Gaudium et Spes* in its approach to the world and instead offers a stinging critique of the systemic injustices that mark our world and make it a deathbound place for many. It is only "with the eyes of faith" (EG 68) that signs of resurrection – traces of a life-giving God – become visible there "where all seems dead" (EG 276). As the locus of God's kenotic revelation, the world remains a profoundly ambivalent place: When God reveals God-self by relinquishing God-self to the world, then the life given by God – which cannot be confused with the death-dealing structures of the world – is not clearly and ostensibly separated from the deathbound ways of the world.[22] It is the church's hope for God overcoming death; it is the ecclesial gospel of resurrection that allows us to see life amidst hopeless deathbound-ness. It is the faith of the church that allows for (a discernment of) God's revelation in the world; it is ecclesial theology that turns the world into a place where God can be found. God's kenotic revelation in the world cannot be seen independently and, therefore, as independent from ecclesial theology. A kenotic mode of revelation, hence, has far-reaching and unsettling implications for theological epistemology – it is intimately tied to a kenotic theology.

In *Evangelii Gaudium*, the pope does not make these implications directly explicit, but he does hint at them – using negativa, in a critique of pastoral relativism (*the* Catholic buzzword for an inadequate theological position), and he does so by simultaneously underscoring the primacy of pastoral in the formulation of doctrine: "Pastoral ... relativism proves even more dangerous than doctrinal relativism.... This practical relativism consists in acting as if God did not exist, making decisions as if the poor did not exist, setting goals as if others did not exist" (EG 80). When we recall that Francis considers his exhortation not as a social but a "programmatically" (EG 25) ecclesiological document, and when we recall that the pastoral practice of kenotic evangelization always has theological and, more narrowly, dogmatic implications (i.e., *being church is the kenotic practice of theology. The doctrine of the church does not precede its other theological practices*), we can rephrase this critique of pastoral relativism into a critique of doctrinal relativism: It consists in *believing* as if the poor did not exist, as if others did not exist – in short, doctrinal relativism consists in believing as if the world in all its complexity did not exist. In order not to succumb to pastoral relativism, the pope calls on the church to pursue "a [kenotic]

---

[22] Paradigmatically, this irresolvable tension of presence and absence in God's revelation in the world is captured in the christological reflections of the early church. It found its normative expression in the formula of Chalcedon – Jesus the Christ is divine and human in no separation and no confusion.

lifestyle of ... giving [our] lives to others" (EG 80). In order not to succumb to doctrinal relativism, then, the church has to pursue a *kenotic dogmatics* in which it gives itself up to the world. Pastoral and doctrinal relativism are combatted by relating the church to the world, or, to put this into positive terms: The church's orthodox teaching emerges from its relations to the world. It is only in its kenosis into the world that the church can come to an orthodox proclamation of the gospel.

The kenosis of revelation (God-talk in *Genetivus singular*), therefore, gives ecclesial doctrine (God-talk in *Genetivus objectivus*) a kenotic shape. When revelation is kenosis, then it can never be safely contained in the teachings of the church. "The Church has to accept this unruly freedom of the word, which accomplishes what it wills in ways that *surpass our calculations and ways of thinking*" (EG 22; emphasis added). Only by getting lost in the world can the church get a grasp on revelation – and so become an adequate proclaimer of the gospel. *Evangelii Gaudium* 11 clearly outlines these theologico-epistemological implications of God's kenotic revelation: When ecclesial theology takes its foundation in God's kenotic incarnation in Jesus the Christ, it can never rest on a stock of given theology, but has to always again relinquish itself to the world and cannot but be continuously renewed: "The heart of the message will always be the same: the God who revealed his immense love in the crucified and risen Christ.... Christ is the 'eternal Gospel' (Rev 14:6); he 'is the same yesterday and today and forever' (Heb 13:8), yet his riches and beauty are inexhaustible. He is for ever young and a constant source of newness.... Whenever we make the effort to return to the source and to recover the original freshness of the Gospel, new avenues arise, new paths of creativity open up, with different forms of expression, more eloquent signs and words with new meaning for today's world. *Every form of authentic evangelization is always 'new'*" (emphasis added). Ecclesial doctrine is found and formulated by the church in its kenotic movement into the world and it represents God's revelation only by way of this kenosis – the doctrine of the church is revelatory only insofar as the church can fully let go of it. The church, therefore, cannot build up a safe deposit of secure knowledge of God, but has to shed its dogmatic wealth.

A kenotic theology, of course, has precarious ecclesiological implications. When the church acknowledges the world as its prime *locus theologicus*, it becomes inextricably entangled into the world. It finds its definition only in relation to the world – it cannot take its shape without the world. Francis recognizes this constitutive role of the world for the formation of the church – "communion and mission are profoundly interconnected. In fidelity to the example of the Master, it is *vitally important* for the Church today to go forth and preach the Gospel to all" (*EG* 23; emphasis added). This reflects the "bipolar" ecclesiology of the Second Vatican Council and its two ecclesiological constitutions – the communio of the church *ad intra* cannot be defined under omission of the mission of the church *ad extra*. It is only in relating (the gospel) to the world that the church is constituted as a community in discipleship of Jesus the Christ. In order to be fully church, the church has to "go forth" out of itself.

Its mission in the world is the precondition for the formation of its communion. Kenotic theology (in *Genetivus subjectivus* and *objectivus*), therefore, does not allow for clear-cut definitions of church and world, but makes for blurred, leaking, and shifting borders between them. God's kenotic revelation, in short, results in an instable church – and it results in an internally heterogeneous church: Taking its shape by relating the gospel to changing worlds, a kenotic church cannot but be *many*; kenosis makes for a plurality of theologies. In their shared and yet competing claim to all be authentic representation of the Word of God, they bear the mark of fragmentation rather than wholeness, of loss rather than possession. The plurality of ecclesial theologies, then, is sign and instrument – it is a *sacrament* (cf. LG 1) – of revelation as kenosis: The discrepancies between these theologies reveal that the church does not simply and purely have God's word at its disposal – its evangelizations differ because each of them is inseparately entangled into the world in relation to which it has found its shape.

Key ecclesiological passages in *Evangelii Gaudium* speak toward such a kenotic church that needs the world to find itself. In choosing to describe the church as a pilgrim people on its way toward God (*EG* 111), as leaven in the midst of humanity (*EG* 114), Francis zeroes in on the constitutional relations of the church to the world – both metaphors resist the idea of a church as self-contained, independent, autonomous body in clear delineation from the world, and instead imagine a church open in terms of both time and space; they picture a church in the midst of the world. This is substantiated when the pope gives a more personal account of his vision for a kenotically evangelizing church: "A Church which 'goes forth' is a Church whose doors are open.... Let us go forth, then, let us go forth to offer everyone the life of Jesus Christ. Here I repeat for the entire Church what I have often said to the priests and laity of Buenos Aires: I prefer a Church which is bruised, hurting and dirty because it has been out on the streets, rather than a Church which is unhealthy from being confined and from clinging to its own security.... More than by fear of going astray,

"The Lord, your God, is in your Midst" (EG 4)

my hope is that we will be moved by the fear of remaining shut up within structures which give us a false sense of security" (EG 46.49).

In *Evangelii Gaudium*, then, the pope strongly argues for a church that finds its mission – its very identity – in the midst of the world. Yet, he also brings other interpretations of church teaching into play that run counter to these images and conflict with a consistently kenotic understanding of the church.

This becomes first tangible in the way Francis sketches the relation between evangelization and inculturation. In a kenotic church, founded on God's self-revelatory incarnation in Jesus the Christ, the gospel has always already taken its shape *in* relation to the world. Evangelization and inculturation cannot be two separate operations performed one after the other because the gospel does not exist apart from its inculturation; it is always already in the world. Francis, however, repeatedly describes this as a two-step-process – first evangelization, then inculturation (EG 69, 122-23). This understanding introduces a separation between the gospel and its mediations into the world; it makes the gospel appear to be detached from its relations to the world; it is no longer considered to emerge from the relation of the church to the world, but is claimed as a deposit within the church, which the church then passes on to the world at its own discretion. A quote from John XXIII puts this assumed split between the gospel and its inculturations into a nutshell: "The deposit of faith is one thing ... the way it is expressed another" (EG 41).

This absolutization of ecclesial theology from its constitutional relations to the world is made more explicit when Francis quotes his immediate predecessor Benedict: "We do not ... wait for [God] to speak to us first, for 'God has already spoken, and there is nothing further that we need to know, which has not been revealed to us'" (EG 75). Revelation is understood here as the complete "treasure of the revealed word" (EG 175), to be safeguarded by the church. It takes the shape of an eternally unchanging, clearly defined deposit of a set of truths to which the church has immediate and full access. This understanding does not sufficiently take into account that revelation takes place as God's kenotic self-relinquishment to the world and is, therefore, inextricably tied to the world – the kenosis of the Logos makes the world an irreducibly ambivalent theological locus. Neither does this understanding of revelation make visible that, in order to find "which has ... been revealed to us," the church has to mimic God's kenotic movement into the world – the theology of the church is revelatory only insofar it follows the Logos in its self-relinquishment to the world. In short, this understanding of revelation conceals that God-talk (both in

Genetivus subjectivus and *Genetivus objectivus*) takes it shape in relation to the world. Instead, it absolutizes theo-logy from this constitutional relativity – a detachment of God-talk from its dependence on the world constructs an unchanging deposit of "what we need to know" and seemingly brings the church into possession of God's revelation. Revelation here is not kenosis, relinquishment, surrender, or loss, but a treasure the church considers its task to hoard. In Francis's call for a kenotically poor church, then, there are still undercurrents of "dogmatic capitalism" – he does not apply his critique of material capitalism to the accumulation of doctrinal wealth.

A closer look, however, reveals that dogmatic capitalism follows strategies analogous to the accumulation of material goods – both are based on a politics of exclusion: Capitalism, the pope argues, relies on an unjust distribution of resources; it is an economic system in which "the powerful feed upon the powerless" (EG 53): "while the earnings of a minority are growing exponentially, so too is the gap separating the majority from the prosperity enjoyed by those happy few – it is not [their own] goods which [they] hold but [those of the poor]" (EG 56.57). "This imbalance is the result of ideologies which defend the absolute autonomy of the marketplace" (EG 56) – it is the result of an absolutization of capital (cf. EG 56): it is no longer the means to an end to which all should have access according to their needs, but has become an end in itself – it does not serve a truly human and humanizing purpose (cf. EG 55) but rules as an absolute value (cf. EG 58). The absolutization of capital from its secondary purposes has turned it into an idol (cf. EG 55) – it has led to the deification of the market whose interests have become the only rule (cf. EG 56). This results in a new quality of exclusion (cf. EG 53): When capital is absolutized, then those who are excluded from it become no longer even visible as excluded from the benefits of capital as a means to an end – "those excluded are no longer society's underside or its fringes or its disenfranchised" (EG 53). Instead, those who have no capital are simply invisible – "they are no longer even a part of [the capitalist society]. The excluded are not the 'exploited' but the outcast, the 'leftovers'" (EG 53) – they are those who do not count in the logic of the capital. A capitalist economy of exclusion makes those invisible who pay the price for the accumulation of wealth in the hands of a few.

An analogous economy of absolutization and exclusion is at work in the "accumulation of doctrinal wealth." In order to come into possession of an unchangeable "treasure of the revealed world," the church has to abort the kenotic mode of its God-talk that configures ecclesial theology as relinquishment of ownership, as loss of a possession. This dismissal of kenosis as

"The Lord, your God, is in your Midst" (EG 4)

the mode of its theology is synonymous with the concealment of the constitutive relation to its prime theological locus – for the accumulation of a safe deposit of doctrinal truths, the church has to cut itself lose from the world. The detachment of theology from its relation to the world is (literally) its absolutization – in the formation of an unchangeable dogmatic deposit, ecclesial theology becomes an end in itself rather than a means in a wider (salvific) economy. It no longer serves to relate the gospel to the world, but rules as an absolute value. Dogmatic capital thus becomes an idol, it is deified – and just like material capitalism, dogmatic capitalism relies on and reinforces an economy of exclusion: A safe deposit of absolute truth within the church is secured by the exclusion of alternative theologies whose conflicting plurality would reveal the necessarily ambivalent, plural, kenotic character of church doctrine – the kenotic mode of ecclesial theology is concealed by hiding the ambivalent plurality it produces. The absolutization of dogmatic capital erases the constitutive relation of ecclesial doctrine to the world through the exclusion of theological plurality that exposes that ecclesial theology is forged in kenosis. An unchangeable treasure of the revealed word, then, rests on those who are excluded from its consolidation; dogmatic capital is financed by those who are made invisible by its accumulation. Once it has been established, it perpetuates the exclusions in which it has been forged; the invisibility of those excluded from the economy of dogmatic capitalism serves to legitimize and reinforce their exclusion. The tradition of the Catholic Church could thus be read as a story of capitalist winners in which the appropriation of an unchangeable treasure of the revealed word facilitates the erasure of alternative theologies from this tradition. In its economy of exclusion, dogmatic capitalism keeps reinforcing its logic until there is no alternative.[23]

In other passages, Francis does display an astute awareness of the dangerous heterodoxy of such dogmatic capitalism. He harshly criticizes those within the Catholic church who rely on an established deposit of faith within the church – on "a set of ideas, … [on] a supposed soundness of doctrine" (EG 94), which they turn into "the property of a select few" (EG 95). "This is a tremendous corruption disguised as good" (EG 97). Francis criticizes the pastoral ramifications of such a nonkenotic ecclesiology – and

---

[23] The erasure of women from leadership positions in the Catholic church is a prime example of the workings of dogmatic capitalism: While records of female leadership can still be traced in New Testament and other early sources, centuries of biased transcriptions and translations of a male-dominated church have successfully concealed their prevalence. After ordained women have been made invisible from tradition, it has become impossible for the church to conceive of women as ordained.

by framing evangelization as kenosis, *Evangelii Gaudium* also offers resources to address the underlying theological problem: the dismissal of the kenotic mode of Christian theology in favor of the heretical adherence to an unchangeable treasure of the revealed word that the church supposedly has at its full disposal.

If Francis truly wants to advocate for an evangelizing church, he has to apply his harsh criticism of economic capitalism also to dogmatic capitalism – and then, the provocation that *Evangelii Gaudium* poses to the church can fully unfold. When we take Francis's call for a kenotic church to its theological conclusion, then Francis's vision for the church is to be truly dispossessed: A church that finds its mission in its relation to the world has to become poor not only in terms of its practice but also in terms of its doctrine. It cannot have any absolute dogmatic surety anymore. This is not a call for disbanding the church but a challenge to acknowledge its dependence on the world when it comes to knowing God – and it is a call to confess how throughout its history the hoarding of doctrinal wealth has impoverished, marginalized, and killed those who were excluded from the accumulation of these riches. In short, and by way of conclusion, *Evangelii Gaudium* is a call to develop a kenotic dogmatics – a theory of church doctrine that can acknowledge that God's revelation is a treasure that materializes only when the church fully lets go of it – again and again.

CHAPTER 5

"An ecclesial renewal which cannot be deferred" (EG 27–33)

Ecclesial Renewal and the Renewal of Ecclesial Structures

Sandra Mazzolini

Introduction

Evangelii Gaudium is not a simple document. The complexity of the text is underlined by the multiplicity of issues it addresses, which allows us to read this apostolic exhortation on different levels, by the acknowledgment of some ecclesiological themes, introduced by the Second Vatican Council and disregarded in postconciliar decades, such as the status of episcopal conferences and the *Ecclesia pauperum*, and by the use of some significant neologisms.[1]

Furthermore, the apostolic exhortation presents two main limitations, which have been highlighted by the Pope. The first limitation is the choice not to explore those many questions about evangelization today, "which call for further reflection and study." The second one is the fact that the Pope does not believe "that the papal magisterium should be expected to offer a definitive or complete word on every question which affects the Church and the world" (*EG* 16). Indirectly, these two limitations show how Pope Bergoglio understands the exercise of his magisterium.

We can note that the first limitation recalls the vexed question of the relationship between the ecclesiastical magisterium and theology, a question that implies the very nature of each of them. The pope has not excluded

---

[1] See Antonio Spadaro, "*Evangelii Gaudium*. Radici, struttura e significato della prima Esortazione apostolica di Papa Francesco," *Civiltà Cattolica* 4 (2013): 417–433; Daniela sala, "Parole nuove," *Il Regno-Attualità* 22 (2013): 701; Carlos María Galli, "Il forte vento del Sud," *Il Regno-Attualità* 2 (2014): 57–63.

the possibility for further reflection and study; even though implicitly, he has acknowledged the essential freedom of that reflection, which does not coincide with the pontifical teachings. The second limitation focuses instead on the pontifical magisterium from the point of view of the relationships between the Bishop of Rome and the other bishops. On one side, Pope Francis does not agree with people who think that this magisterium should be all-embracing and exhaustive. On the other, he is aware both that "[i]t is not advisable for the Pope to take the place of local Bishops in the discernment of every issue which arises in their territory," and "of the need to promote a sound 'decentralization'" (EG 16). From the ecclesiological point of view, the concept of decentralization is very relevant.[2] It refers to other notions, such as participation, joint responsibility, inculturation, and contextualization, which shape a specific ecclesiological model. Here, it is sufficient to note that this "sound decentralization" implies the notion of subsidiarity as an essential and constitutive principle of the relationships both within the Church and between the churches.[3]

The ecclesiological suggestions of *Evangelii Gaudium*, which require time for their creative implementation, are more than a mere exhortation. In fact, Pope Francis has explicitly emphasized "that what I am trying to express here has a programmatic significance and important consequences" (EG 25).[4] Therefore, he has expressed his hope "that all communities will devote the necessary effort to advancing along the path of a pastoral and missionary conversion which cannot leave things as they presently are" (EG 25).

---

[2] This concept involves issues that have been objects of heated discussions during the Second Vatican Council, as well as in the postconciliar period. Among them, we can remember the priority debate (universal or local Church?): see Patrick Granfield, "The Priority Debate: Universal or Local Church?," in *Ecclesia Tertii Millennii adventientis* (FS A. Antón), ed. Fernando Chica, sandro Panizzolo, and Harald Wagner (Casale Monferrato: Piemme, 1997), 152–161; Kilian McDonnell, "The Ratzinger/Kasper Debate: The Universal Church and Local Churches," *Theological Studies* 63(2) (2002): 227–250; Donato Valentini, "Chiesa universale e Chiesa locale. Un'armonia raggiunta?," in Idem., *Identità e storicità nella Chiesa*, ed. Aimable Musoni (Roma: Las, 2007), 93–136; Walter Kasper, "Il rapporto tra Chiesa universale e Chiesa locale. Confronto amichevole con la critica del cardinale Joseph Ratzinger," in Id. *La Chiesa di Gesù Cristo. Scritti di ecclesiologia* (Brescia: Queriniana, 2011), 453–465.

[3] Cf. "Relatio finalis Synodi episcoporum *Exeunte coetu secundo*: Ecclesia sub verbo Dei mysteria Christi celebrans pro salute mundi (7 decembris 1985)" II C8, in *Enchiridion del Sinodo dei Vescovi*, vol. 1: 1965–1988 (Bologna: EDB, 2005), 2331. See also Donato Valentini, "Valore e limiti del principio di sussidiarietà nella Chiesa quanto al ministero petrino del Papa," in Id., *Identità e storicità*, 183–198; walter Kasper, "Sul principio di sussidiarietà nella Chiesa," in Id., *La Chiesa di Gesù Cristo*, 405–414.

[4] See, also, the considerations in Chapter 6 of this volume.

"An ecclesial renewal which cannot be deferred"

My essay is in two main parts. The first one briefly deals with three themes, which summarize the main criteria of ecclesial renewal, according to the first chapter of *Evangelii Gaudium*. The transformation of the ecclesial structures (see EG 27–33), which depends on ecclesial renewal, will be analyzed in the second part of this paper.

1. Ecclesial Renewal According to the First Chapter of *Evangelii Gaudium*: Its Main Criteria and Implications

The theme of ecclesial renewal is quite complex and must be carefully assessed, without prejudice, generalization, or fear. For this reason, first, it is necessary to identify those specific criteria, on which ecclesial renewal is based, because they determine both its form and results.[5] The first chapter of *Evangelii Gaudium*, entitled *The Church's Missionary Transformation*, introduces some specific criteria, which can be summarized in three issues, that is the peculiar nature of ecclesial renewal, the identity of the Church, and the principle of pastoral conversion.

1.1. *The Nature of Ecclesial Renewal According to* Evangelii Gaudium 26

The standing point to understand the very nature of ecclesial renewal can be expressed in these terms: This renewal is not a simple reorganization or a more efficient organization of the ecclesial structures because it concerns the nature of the Church and its mystery. Referring to the invitation of Pope Paul VI to develop the call to renewal, which involves every Christian and the whole Church, Pope Francis has quoted a memorable text of the encyclical *Ecclesiam Suam*,[6] whose content can be summarized in three main points. First, the Church must develop her own awareness of her very identity. Second, this awareness leads her to compare the ideal image, namely the image of Church that Christ envisaged, wanted, and loved, and the image that the Church presents to the world today. Third, the commitment of the Church to renew herself derives from this comparison.

According to this text, there is an intrinsic correlation between the nature of the Church, ecclesial renewal, and conversion. The same correlation occurs in the paragraph, where Pope Francis has explained what ecclesial

---

[5] They also regard reasons and purposes of ecclesial renewal: see Yves Congar, *Vera e falsa riforma nella Chiesa* (Milano: Jaca Book, 1972), 55–266.

[6] See ES 9–11.

conversion is. In accordance with the Second Vatican Council, ecclesial conversion is described as the "openness to a constant self-renewal born of fidelity to Jesus Christ." Quoting UR 6, the Pope has stressed – on one side – that every renewal of the Church is essentially "an increase of fidelity to her own calling" and – on the other – that ecclesial renewal, to whom Christ calls the pilgrim Church, is continual. As the Church is a human institution here on earth, she needs continual reformation, which also concerns her structures.

The last paragraph of *Evangelii Gaudium* 26 introduces this issue in the perspective of evangelization. The pope has stressed a certain ambivalence of ecclesial structures in order to support the evangelical proclamation. Some of them "can hamper efforts at evangelization, yet even good structures are only helpful when there is a life constantly driving, sustaining and assessing them. Without new life and an authentic evangelical spirit, without the Church's 'fidelity to her own calling,' any new structure will soon prove ineffective." We can note that the pope has not emphasized if ecclesial structures are useful or not; he has rather outlined a double reason why they can support evangelization, namely "new life and an authentic evangelical spirit" and "the Church's 'fidelity to her own calling.'" In brief, we can say that, according to *Evangelii Gaudium* 26, the very nature of ecclesial renewal can only be understood with reference to the theandric nature of the Church; it also implies conversion and reformation, which contribute to shape a dynamic view of the Church and her structures.

1.2. *Ecclesial Identity: A Church That Goes Forth*

Pope Francis has described the ecclesial identity in *Evangelii Gaudium* 24: "The Church which 'goes forth' is a community of missionary disciples who take the first step, who are involved and supportive, who bear fruit and rejoice."[7] While the description of the ecclesial community as "the Church which 'goes forth'" refers to the conciliar vision of the missionary nature of the pilgrim Church (see AG 2), the expression "a community of missionary disciples" reminds us that the Church is more than its structures. The pope has emphasized who the Church is: a "community of missionary disciples" whose features are detailed by five actions (to take the first step, to be involved and supportive, to bear fruit, and to rejoice). These steps allow the pope to outline the profile of a dynamic, decentralized, welcoming,

---

[7] Again, a complementary treatment of this notion features in Chapter 6.

and inclusive Church. This profile refers specifically to the Church as sacrament, people of God, servant, and companion.

Taking the first step (*primerear* in the Spanish version) casts light on an essential theological element, namely the initiative of the Lord, who has loved us first (see 1 John 4: 10). This is the reason why the Church "can move forward, boldly take the initiative, go out to others, seek those who have fallen away, stand at the crossroads and welcome the outcast." Therefore, the possibility "to take the first step" essentially depends on the divine initiative, which also determines its content, that is the witnessing of the divine mercy, which the Church has already known.

Being involved introduces the first consequence of the ecclesial initiative of going forth, which is intended for all people, without exception. The model of the ecclesial engagement is Jesus Christ, who washed the feet of his disciples (see John 13: 1–17). The Church, involved by word and deed in people's daily lives, bridges distances, wants to abase itself if necessary, embraces human life, touches the suffering flesh of Christ in others, and takes on the "smell of the sheep." All these actions and attitudes specify the ecclesial involvement in daily human life, so that the Church is not the center of human history and divine salvation. In this perspective, serving is the key to understanding and expressing the ecclesial presence in the world.

Being supportive confirms these statements, focusing some congruous attitudes. In fact, "An evangelizing community is also supportive, standing by people at every step of the way, no matter how difficult or lengthy this may prove to be. It is familiar with patient expectation and apostolic endurance." For this reason, the community of missionary disciples of Christ is able "to bear fruit." Patience and endurance are not synonymous with passivity, namely to maintain the status quo; on the contrary, they presuppose a faithful and creative commitment, which consists in paying attention to the fruits, as well as in not being discouraged. Knowing that the Lord wants her to be fruitful, the Church that goes forth "cares for the grain and does not grow impatient at the weeds." The disciple of Christ "finds a way to let the word take flesh in a particular situation and bear fruits of new life, however imperfect or incomplete these may appear." In bearing witness to Jesus Christ, this way could also be the martyrdom, whose purpose is specified by Pope Francis: "to see God's word accepted and its capacity for liberation and renewal revealed."

Rejoicing is the last verb used to characterize the Church, which announces the Good News. Filled with joy, "an evangelizing community... knows how to rejoice always. It celebrates every small victory, every step forward in the work of evangelization." A special mention is dedicated to the "beauty of the liturgy, which is both a celebration of the task of evangelization and the source of her [of the Church] renewed self-giving." In other words, the Church evangelizes and is herself evangelized through the beauty of liturgy.

The content and implications of the previously mentioned five verbs refer to renewal, conversion, and reformation of the Church, according to the description of the Church, which goes forth as a community of missionary disciples. On one side, they allow the Church to assess what has already been accomplished and what remains to be done and, on the other, they can guide the necessary transformation.

1.3. *The Principle of Pastoral Conversion According to* Evangelii Gaudium 34–49

Pope Francis has stressed that pastoral conversion, based on a "missionary option," is the requirement of the renewal of ecclesial structures (see *EG* 27). Pastoral conversion implies three main topics: how the gospel is announced; the embodiment of the ecclesial mission within human limits; and the welcome to all, without exception.

How the gospel is announced (see *EG* 34–39). In this section of his apostolic exhortation, Pope Francis has not dealt with the means of the evangelization (e.g., announcement of the Good News, witnessing, charity, dialogue, and promotion of human rights),[8] but has rather focused on a fundamental point: to reach everyone without exception or exclusion, the evangelical message "has to concentrate on the essentials, on what is most beautiful, most grand, most appealing and at the same time most necessary" (*EG* 35).[9] It presupposes both that "[p]astoral ministry in a missionary style is not obsessed with the disjointed transmission of a multitude of doctrines to be insistently imposed," and the adoption of a "pastoral goal and a missionary style."

Although many practical consequences for the ecclesial missionary activity derive from this point, which concerns the missionary methodology and its content, Pope Francis has developed it in a more theoretical

---

[8] Some means in the practice of mission are variously developed in the following chapters of the apostolic exhortation.

[9] In *EG* 34, Pope Francis has also emphasized the necessity "to be realistic and not assume that our audience understands the full background to what we are saying, or is capable of relating what we say to the very heart of the Gospel which gives it meaning, beauty and attractiveness."

way, explaining the notion of the hierarchy of truths (see EG 36–39). After having stressed that all the revealed truths derive from the same divine source, although some of them are more important in order to express the heart of the gospel, Pope Francis has quoted *Unitatis Redintegratio* 11. Acknowledging an ancient conviction of the Church, the Second Vatican Council has stated that "in Catholic doctrine there exists an order or a 'hierarchy' of truths, since they vary in their relation to the foundation of the Christian faith." This doctrine concerns both the dogmas of faith, and the whole corpus of ecclesiastical teachings, including moral matters (see EG 36). Pastoral consequences depend on this foundational horizon (see EG 38).

The embodiment of the ecclesial mission within human limits (see EG 40–45).[10] The human limits, which Pope Francis has referred to, depend on language and circumstances. In this case, the expression "human limits" does not have a completely negative meaning, because it alludes to the evident fact that the mission of the Church is always correlated to a specific context, which is also cultural and religious. The question about how to evangelize is here evoked in the perspective of inculturation and contextualization.

The Pope's reflection is based on two premises. The first one is that the Church, as missionary disciple, needs to develop her interpretation of the divine word, as well as her understanding of truth (see EG 40). The second one is that "today's vast and rapid cultural changes demand that we constantly seek ways of expressing unchanging truths in a language which bring out their abiding newness" (EG 41). While the first premise refers to hermeneutical questions, such as the interpretation of dogmas and doctrinal development,[11] the second one focuses on the intrinsic link between evangelization and human cultures.[12]

This twofold premise has some theoretical and practical implications. Three of them are very relevant in order to approach the pope's stance about inculturation and contextualization of the evangelical announcement. First, he has not evaluated Christian doctrine as a "monolithic body

---

[10] Over the centuries, the embodiment of ecclesial mission within human limits has originated many models and paradigms of mission, see David J. Bosch, *Transforming Mission: Paradigm Shifts in Theology of Mission* (Maryknoll, NY: Orbis Books, 1991); Stephen B. Bevans and Roger P. Schroeder, *Constants in Context: A Theology of Mission for Today* (Maryknoll, NY: Orbis Books, 2004); Michael Sievernich, *Die christliche Mission. Geschichte und Gegenwart* (Darmstadt: Wissenschaftliche Buchgesellschaft, 2009).

[11] Cf. CTI, "L'interpretazione dei dogmi (1990)," in Id., *Documenti 1969–2004* (Bologna: ESD, 2006), 380–421.

[12] See *EN* 20.

of doctrine guarded by all and leaving no room for nuance" (*EG* 40). As a consequence, he has recognized that the philosophical, theological, and pastoral plurality can enable the Church to grow, if people allow the Holy Spirit to guide them, as well as that "such variety serves to bring out and develop different facets of the inexhaustible riches of the Gospel."[13]

Second, Pope Francis has introduced a theological principle in a pastoral context (see *EG* 41). The principle is the distinction between the substance of the *depositum fidei* and its expressions,[14] and the pastoral context concerns the communication of faith. The pope has stressed the necessity to transmit the unchanging meaning of the gospel message through renewed forms, because the traditional language, though orthodox, could favor a partial or wrong understanding of the evangelical truth.[15]

Third, the awareness that "the task of evangelization operates within limits of language and of circumstances" has to be put into effect. From this point of view, we can note that the pope has outlined the constant engagement "to communicate more effectively the truth of the Gospel in specific context," as well as the attitudes of a "missionary heart," which "never closes itself off, never retreats into its own security, never opts for rigidity and defensiveness. It realizes that it has to grow in its own understanding of the Gospel and in discerning the paths of the Spirit, and so it always does what good it can, even if in the process, its shoes get soiled by the mud of the street" (*EG* 45).

The welcome to all, without exception (see *EG* 46–49).[16] Two similar images express the model of the Church that goes forth: "a Church whose doors are open" (*EG* 46) and "the house of the Father, with doors always wide open" (*EG* 47). The doors are open in order to go forth and reach the fringes of humanity, as well as to welcome anyone, without exception.

---

[13] See Sandra Mazzolini, "Vissuti che trasformano le tradizioni. Una rilettura di Gaudium et spes 58," *Urbaniana University Journal* 2 (2013): 103–117.

[14] In footnote 45, Pope Francis has quoted the well-known paragraph of the speech of Pope John XXIII *Gaudet Mater Ecclesia* (October 11, 1962): "Est enim aliud ipsum depositum Fidei, seu veritates, quae veneranda doctrina nostra continentur, aliud modus, quo eadem enuntiantur."

[15] The greatest danger is to be faithful to the form, not to the substance. The Pope has quoted John Paul II, who has affirmed that "the expression of truth can take different forms. The renewal of these forms of expression becomes necessary for the sake of transmitting to the people of today the Gospel message in its unchanging meaning," *UUS* 19.

[16] This section is entitled "A Mother with an Open Heart." For the Church as mother, see Karl Delahaye, *Per un rinnovamento della pastorale. La comunità, madre dei credenti* (Bari: Ecumenica Editrice, 1974); Giampiero Ziviani, *La Chiesa madre nel Concilio Vaticano II* (Roma: Editrice Pontificia Università Gregoriana, 2001). See, also, the treatment of Francis's vision of a more inclusive church in Chapter 6 of this volume.

Pope Francis has invited Catholics not to prevent access to the house of the Father: "Frequently – he writes – we act as arbiters of grace rather than its facilitators. But the Church is not a tollhouse; it is the house of the Father, where there is a place for everyone, with all their problems" (EG 47).

From this point of view, the Church is called to avoid whatever form of exclusion[17] and to pay specific attention to the poor, who are the privileged recipients of the gospel.[18] Furthermore, "[T]he fact that it is freely preached to them is a sign of the kingdom that Jesus came to establish" (EG 48). There is, therefore, an essential bond between Christian faith and the poor; Pope Francis has not limited himself to highlighting it, but has also encouraged not weakening the clear evangelical message about the privileged role of the poor.

The nature of ecclesial renewal, ecclesial identity, and the principle of pastoral conversion give us criteria to understand properly the transformation of ecclesial structures, which must be congruent with ecclesial identity and mission in today's context.

2. The Renewal of the Ecclesial Structures According to *Evangelii Gaudium* 27–33

Evangelii Gaudium §§27–33 belong to the second section of the first chapter, a section that is entitled "Pastoral Activity and Conversion." They illustrate the theme of the renewal of ecclesial structures in the context of the missionary transformation of the Church and of pastoral conversion. The pope has proposed some guidelines more as suggestions to develop locally than as detailed rules to be put into practice everywhere in the same manner. Their evaluation, therefore, must take into account that the issue has not been developed in a systematic way.

Pope Francis has acknowledged some perspectives of the Second Vatican Council, as well as of the postconciliar magisterium of his predecessors. This acknowledgment is not a mere quote or repetition. If we compare some passages with their sources, or if we refer them to other paragraphs, chapters, and sections of *Evangelii Gaudium*, it is not so difficult to point

---

[17] The pope has not developed here the theme of policies or practices of exclusion, which are not unique to Roman Catholicism. The issue of ecclesial exclusion is quite complex; it is sufficient to remember that it affects the identity of the Christian churches. Today, the role of race, gender, immigration, social orientation, and creedal commitments challenge Christianity to rethink the question of ecclesial exclusion/inclusion. See *Ecclesiology and Exclusion: Bounderies of Being and Belonging in Postmodern Times*, ed. Dennis M. Doyle, Timothy J. Furry, and Pascal D. Bazzell (Maryknoll, NY: Orbis Books, 2012).

[18] See *LG* 8.

out what characterizes Pope Francis's understanding of the ecclesial missionary identity and its implications. The link between the mission of the Church and its structures, for example, is very significant in order to understand reasons, perspectives, and purposes of the renewal of ecclesial structures.

This link has been a constant over the centuries of Christian history. The recognition of the early centuries provides us with useful insights. In the first centuries, namely from the second to the fifth century CE, the most evident point is the spread of Christianity in a plurality of geographic and cultural areas, which were within the Roman Empire and outside its borders.[19] The increased number of Christians and Christian communities favored the reflection on the Church, as well as processes of ecclesiastical institutionalization. This evolution concerned both the structure of each Church and the relationships between the ecclesial subjects within her, and the progressive grouping of the Churches in stable forms. Though not homogenous, this institutional transformation was characterized by some common elements, such as the increase in the number and extension of dioceses; the exercise of the episcopal ministry through the mediation of the clergy and the so-called *corepiscopi*; the enhancement of coordinating centers (Rome, Antioch, Alexandria, etc.); and the search for proper means of coordination. The more complex ecclesiological model, resulting from the previously mentioned institutional transformations, also affected the ecclesial missionary activity.[20]

Over the centuries of the Church's history, the relationship between the ecclesial mission and structures has been differently outlined. Pope Francis has dealt with this issue from the point of view of the renewal of ecclesial structures, which "can only be understood in this light: as part of an effort to make them more mission-oriented, to make ordinary pastoral activity on every level more inclusive and open, to inspire in pastoral workers a constant desire to go forth and in this way to elicit a positive response from all those whom Jesus summons to friendship with himself" (EG 27).

---

[19] See *Atlante storico del cristianesimo antico*, ed. Angelo Di Berardino (Bologna: EDB, 2010).

[20] See Gustav Bardy, *La Thèologie de l'Eglise de Saint Irenée au Concile de Nicée* (Paris: Cerf, 1947); Henri Marot, "Unità della Chiesa e diversità geografica nei primi tre secoli," in *L'episcopato e la Chiesa universale*, ed. Yves M. Congar and Bernard D. Dupuy (Roma: Paoline, 1965), 699–731; Cyril Vogel, "*Unità della Chiesa e pluralità delle* forme storiche d'organizzazione ecclesiastica," ibid., 733–792; *Storia della Chiesa*, ed. Hubert Jedin, vol. 1: *Le origini*, (Milano: Jaca Book, 1976); vol. 2: *L'epoca dei concili, la formazione del dogma. Il monachesimo. Diffusione missionaria e cristianizzazione dell'impero (IV-V secolo)* (Milano: Jaca Book, 1977); Wilhelm De Vries, *Orient et Occident. Les structures ecclèsiales vues dans l'histoire des sept premiers conciles œcumeniques* (Paris: Cerf, 2011).

Evangelii Gaudium 28–32 are dedicated to the parish, other ecclesial institutions, the local Church and bishop, to the papacy, and the central structures of the universal Church. While the first four themes are illustrated from a twofold point of view, namely their nature and role as well as spaces for change, the others only refer to the change. This section of *Evangelii Gaudium* allows us both to evaluate the development of the Church in the postconciliar time,[21] and the perspectives for the future. Three concepts can summarize all the issues, namely plurality, coresponsibility, and decentralization; at the same time, they point out the direction of the renewal of the ecclesial structures according to Pope Francis's view.

2.1. Which Kind of Parish?

The Second Vatican Council did not systematically debate the theme of the parish, although the conciliar discussion on the Church, liturgy, laity, ecclesial ministry, and mission did introduce some of its elements,[22] which have not been adequately developed in the postconciliar decades. The magisterium of John Paul II is emblematic of this trend; there are in it some references about the parish, which occur in the contexts where the pope dealt with other issues, such as the catechesis, the role of the laity, and the missionary action. At the same time, he emphasized the role of the New Catholic Movements, whose dynamism contrasts with the stagnation and historical limits of the traditional parish.[23] Even the special assemblies for Africa, Asia, America, Oceania, and Europe of the Synod of Bishops paid little attention to the parish.[24] In his postsynodal apostolic exhortations, John Paul II partly acknowledged their suggestions about the nature

---

[21] Pope Francis has not limited himself to recognizing what has already been done; he has also underlined the lack of sufficient renewal of the ecclesial structures, and its necessity with reference to today's mission of the Church. He has clearly admitted the inadequacy of the efforts that have been made until now, to bring parishes "nearer to people, to make them environments of living communion and participation, and to make them completely mission-oriented" (EG 28). Pope Francis has also recognized both the small progress made in searching a new way of exercising the primacy, and the insufficient acknowledgment of conciliar desire about the episcopal conferences (see EG 32).

[22] See Giampietro Ziviani, *Una Chiesa di popolo. La parrocchia nel Vaticano II* (Bologna: EDB, 2011), 63–228.

[23] See Ziviani, *Una Chiesa di popolo*, 253–260. For an overview of the New Catholic Movements, see M. Faggioli, *Breve storia dei movimenti cattolici* (Roma: Carrocci, 2008); Id., "Inclusion and Exclusion in the Ecclesiology of the New Catholic Movements," in *Ecclesiology and Exclusion*, 199–213.

[24] See Ziviani, *Una Chiesa di popolo*, 261–267.

and role of the parish,[25] its renewal,[26] and its relationship with the New Catholic Movements.[27]

This threefold theme also occurs in *Evangelii Gaudium* 28–29. Pope Francis has confirmed that the parish is not an outdated institution; in fact, it has a great flexibility, so that it can assume different forms, which also depend "on the openness and missionary creativity of the pastor and the community" (EG 28). From this standing point, the pope has correlated the nature of the parish, its mission, and its renewal in three passages. First, he has positively described the very nature of the parish as "the Church living in the midst of the homes of her sons and daughters"; it follows that it is not "a useless structure out of touch with people or a self-absorbed group made up of a chosen few" (EG 28).[28] Second, this identity is dynamic and presupposes the capability of self-renewal and constant adaptability. Third, the articulated relationship with the people's daily life is an appropriate criterion both to understand what the parish is and acts, and to assess its renewal.

On one side, this essential link, which characterizes Pope Francis's viewpoint on the parish, determines the plurality of the parish form and favors its implementation. On the other, it therefore entails rethinking the relationships between the parish and the other ecclesial institutions, such as basic communities, small communities, and movements. Pope Francis has recognized the positive elements of these other ecclesial institutions, but at the same time has remarked that "it will prove beneficial for them not to lose contact with the rich reality of the local parish and to participate readily in the overall pastoral activity of the particular Church" (EG 29). He has also specified the purpose of this kind of integration, which is to "prevent them [the other ecclesial institutions] for concentrating only on part of the Gospel or the Church, or becoming nomads without roots." Pope Francis seems to reshape the role of these other ecclesial institutions, whose conversion and renewal depend on their contact with the rich reality of the

---

[25] See *Ecclesia in Africa*, 100 (September 14, 1995); *Ecclesia in America*, 41 (January 22, 1999); *Ecclesia in Asia*, 25 (November 6, 1999); *Ecclesia in Oceania*, 13 (November 22, 2001); *Ecclesia in Europa*, 15 (June 28, 2003).

[26] *Ecclesia in America* 41 is entirely dedicated to the renewal of the parish.

[27] This issue is more detailed in *Ecclesia in Europa* 15–16.

[28] More precisely, "The parish is the presence of the Church in a given territory, an environment for hearing God's word, for growth in the Christian life, for dialogue, proclamation, charitable outreach, worship and celebration. In all its activities the parish encourages and trains its members to be evangelizers. It is a community of communities, a sanctuary where the thirsty come to drink in the midst of their journey, and a center of constant outreach."

local parish, as well as on their involvement in the global pastoral activity of the particular Church.

Thus, which kind of parish? The pope has not detailed the features of a new kind of parish, but has introduced some main elements, such as the plurality of the parish form, its correlation with the context, its missionary and welcoming profile, and the integration of many ecclesial institutions. There is no doubt that these elements can contribute to reshape the parish form in many ways, in accordance with the missionary renewal of the particular Church, which is the primary subject of evangelization.

2.2. *The Particular Church, Primary Subject of Evangelization*

The statement that the particular Church is the primary subject of evangelization has acknowledged two relevant teachings of the Second Vatican Council. The first one concerns the essentially missionary nature of the pilgrim Church, founded in the mystery of the Triune God (see AG 2–4; see also LG 2–4). The second one refers to the nature and mission of the particular Church, according the third chapter of the decree *Ad Gentes* (see also LG 23). Regarding the Trinitarian foundation of ecclesial life and mission, the conciliar assembly has received elements of the biblical and patristic tradition, as well as changed the Catholic approach to mission.[29]

The *Missio Ecclesiae*, rooted in the *Missio Dei*, allows the Council to emphasize that the ecclesial mission is unique, although its fulfillments can be different; to go beyond the division between Christianity and missionary territories;[30] to found the missionary engagement of all ecclesial subjects in the apostolicity of the Church, as well as in a sacramental way; and to stress the role of the Holy Spirit in ecclesial life and mission.[31] These four perspectives, which have been variously developed after the Council by the ecclesiastical magisterium (see, e.g., *EN* and *RMi*) and by Christian

---

[29] See Sandra Mazzolini, *La Chiesa è essenzialmente missionaria. Il rapporto "natura della Chiesa" – "missione della Chiesa" nell'iter della costituzione de Ecclesia (1959–1964)* (Roma: Ed. Pontificia Università Gregoriana, 1999); G. Colzani, "Storia e contenuti del Decreto 'Ad Gentes.'" in Id., *Pensare la missione. Studi editi e inediti*, ed. S. Mazzolini (Città del Vaticano: Urbaniana University Press, 2012), 113–143.

[30] The question emerged before the celebration of the Council: see Henri Godin and Yves Daniel, *La France, pays de mission?* (Lyon: Les Editions de Labeille, 1943). Going beyond this distinction, the Council has also distanced itself from that missionary project, which had been intrinsically linked with a colonial project.

[31] The pneumatological references have enlarged the missionary horizons, casting light on relevant questions, such as ecclesial charismas and ministries; the salvation within and outside the Church; and the relationships between gospel and human cultures.

mission theology,[32] help us both to appreciate properly the affirmation that the particular Church is the primary subject of evangelization,[33] and to acknowledge its relevant ecclesiological consequences. Pope Francis has dealt with this theme from two points of view: the nature of the particular Church, who is called to missionary conversion (see EG 30), and the ministry of the local bishop, who has to look after the missionary communion in his diocesan Church (see EG 31).

The starting point of *Evangelii Gaudium* 30 is the description of the nature of the particular Church, which the pope has briefly outlined in positive terms, without touching some interconnected questions.[34] The particular Church is described as "a portion of Catholic Church under the leaderships of its bishop," and as "the Church incarnate in a certain place, equipped with all the means of salvation bestowed by Christ, but with local features" (EG 30).[35] In other terms, the particular Church is "the concrete manifestation of the one Church in one specific place, and in it 'the one, holy, catholic and apostolic Church of Christ is truly present and operative.'" This description emphasizes the reason why the particular Church is the primary subject of evangelization; in fact, her nature is essentially missionary, because the local Church is intrinsically correlated with the universal Church, which is essentially missionary as well (see AG 2). It follows that both the missionary engagement of each particular Church is not caused by external actors or extrinsic factors, and her missionary responsibility is not the result of some kind of devolution.

After having stressed the ecclesiological reason why the diocesan Church is the primary subject of evangelization, Pope Francis has indicated how and where each particular Church can and must express her missionary identity. In fact, the pope has emphasized that each local ecclesial community exhibits its joy in communicating Jesus Christ "both by a concern to preach him to areas in greater need and in constantly going forth to

---

[32] For an overview on the postconciliar mission theology, see *Landmark Essays in Mission and World Christianity*, ed. Robert L. Gallagher and Paul Hertling (Maryknoll, NY: Orbis Books, 2009); G. Colzani, "Verso una missione postcoloniale e postmoderna," in Id., *Pensare la missione*, 213–230; Id., "Teologia della missione," ibid., 253–295. It is also useful to consult the ecumenical document *Together Towards Life: Mission and Evangelism in Changing Landscapes. A New WCC Affirmation on Mission and Evangelism* (September 5, 2012): see http://www.oikoumene.org (accessed September 3, 2014).

[33] See *Propositio* 41, which presents the particular Church as the subject of the New Evangelization. Pope Francis has preferred not to qualify the noun "evangelization."

[34] We can remember the various questions concerning the catholicity of the local Church, its cultural identity, its relationship with the universal Church, and so on. See, e.g., Peter C. Phan, "A New Christianity, but What Kind?," in *Landmark Essays*, 201–218.

[35] See CD 11.

the outskirts of its own territory or towards new sociocultural settings."[36] Lastly, he has encouraged each particular Church "to undertake a resolute process of discernment, purification and reform," in order to make the missionary impulse "more focused, generous and fruitful."

The standing point of *Evangelii Gaudium* 31 is the pastoral ministry of the diocesan bishop, who must always favor the missionary communion of his local Church. More specifically, Pope Francis has indicated a double means in order to accomplish this task, focusing, on one side, the relationships between the diocesan bishop and his people, and, on the other, the dialogical attitude that each bishop must exercise. The pope has also added some short explanations. With regard to the first means, we can note that the relationships between the local bishop and his people shape the exercise of the episcopal ministry. Pope Francis has used a particular lexicon, which allows him to underline the dynamic profile of the episcopal ministry and some main correlated attitudes. "To go for," "to be in midst," and "to walk after" characterize the relationship of the bishop with his people; these verbal forms are referred to other expressions, which emphasize their aim, namely to point out the way and to keep the believers' hope vibrant; to maintain an unassuming and merciful presence; to help those who lag behind; and to allow "the flock to strike out on new paths." In other words, the lexicon that Pope Francis has used casts light on some main elements, which can be expressed with four relevant theological-ecclesiological notions, namely the prophecy, the being part of the people of God, the being merciful, and the discernment.

They are useful both to understand the episcopal ministry in a missionary perspective, and to introduce the second means suggested by Pope Francis, that is the dialogical attitude, which the local bishop exercises when he listens "to everyone and not simply to those who would tell him what he would like to hear."[37] From a practical point of view, this dialogical attitude requires each bishop "to encourage and develop the means of participation proposed in the Code of Canon Law, and other forms of pastoral dialogue." The thorny theme of the participatory processes in the life and mission of the Church has been variously debated in the decades after the Second Vatican Council. The pope has not dealt with its implications or consequences; he has limited himself to confirming the relevance of the participatory processes in order to foster "a dynamic, open and missionary communion," recalling the responsibility of each bishop. He has

---

[36] See AG 22; RMi 37.
[37] EG 31.

also pointed out their principal aim: "the missionary aspiration of reaching anyone," not the ecclesiastical organization.

The pope's lexicon is positive and sober, but its implications are very relevant from the ecclesiological point of view, in particular because they imply rethinking the relationships between the churches in terms of decentralization, autonomy, and subsidiarity. At the same time, they suggest that ecclesial mission is plural, namely inculturated and contextualized, and that all ecclesial subjects are involved in it. The double task of the diocesan bishop in order to favor the missionary responsibility of the particular Church certainly entails, on one side, a more participative and creative approach to the ecclesial mission; on the other, a change of mind and the will to solve some complex questions that are still open, that is, the responsibility of the laity for ecclesial life and mission, which is not yet recognized in an adequate manner.

2.3. The Conversion of the Papacy and Central Structures of the Universal Church

The dialogical attitude of each local bishop also concerns the bishop of Rome, who – as Pope Francis has underlined – is "called to put into practice what I ask of others" (EG 32). More specifically, he has introduced a reflection on the conversion of the papacy, as well as the central structures of the universal Church.[38] During the postconciliar decades, there has been a heated debate about these issues,[39] but – as the pope admits – they have not been theoretically developed or sufficiently put into practice.

With regard to the conversion of the papacy, the standing point assumed by Pope Francis is the acknowledgment of his duty, as bishop of Rome, "to

---

[38] For an historical-juridical overview, see Klaus Schatz, *Der Päpstliche Primat. Seine Geschichte von den Ursprüngen bis zur Gegenwart* (Würzburg: Echter, 1990); Yves M. Congar, *Église et Paupaté. Regards historiques* (Paris: Cerf, 1995); Niccolò Del Re, *La Curia Romana. Lineamenti storico-giuridici* (Città del Vaticano: LEV, 1998).

[39] See, e.g., Jean M. Tillard, *L'Évêque de Rome* (Paris: Cerf, 1982); Patrick Granfield, *The Limits of the Papacy: Authority and Autonomy in the Church* (New York: Crossroad, 1987); Hermann J. Pottmeyer, *Towards a Papacy in Communion: Perspectives from Vatican Councils I and II* (New York: Crossroad, 1998); John R. Quinn, *The Reform of the Papacy: The Costly Call to Christian Unity* (New York: Crossroad, 1999); *Il ministero petrino. Cattolici e ortodossi in dialogo*, ed. Walter Kasper (Roma: Città Nuova, 2004); Donato Valentini, "Il ministero petrino come servizio di unità e di comunione nella Chiesa universale," in Id., *Identità e storicità*, 139–181; Id., "Il primato petrino del Vescovo di Roma a 40 anni dal decreto conciliare 'Unitatis Redintegratio' (1964–2004). Una lettura teologica cattolica," ibid., 199–256; Walter Kasper, *Chiesa cattolica. Essenza – Realtà – Missione* (Brescia: Queriniana, 2012), 393–437.

be open to suggestions which can help make the exercise of my ministry more faithful to the meaning which Jesus Christ wished to give it and to the present needs of evangelization." This phrase introduces elements, which concerns the methodology and the content of the conversion of the papacy. The first element is a proper attitude, that is "to be open to suggestions"; the second is the purpose, which consists in making the exercise of the Petrine ministry more faithful; and the third is a double criterion, which must guide the conversion of the papacy, namely the original meaning of the Petrine ministry and the needs of evangelization today.

The perspectives of this phrase are reinforced by the quote of *Ut Unum Sint* 95, where John Paul II "asked for help in finding 'a way of exercising the primacy which, while in no way renouncing what is essential to its mission, is nonetheless open to a new situation'."[40] The request to deal with this issue within the ecumenical dialogue is in itself the most amazing innovation of the *Ut Unum Sint*, which is without precedent in the history of the Catholic ecumenism.[41] The invitation of John Paul II implies the distinction between the essence of the Petrine ministry and its forms. As many scholars have underlined, this subject is quite complex. In fact, it does not only refer to practical and pragmatic questions, but also to theological ones, which entail methodological problems[42] and specific content.[43] Pope Francis has only highlighted this distinction, recognizing at the same time the little progress made in searching for a new way of exercising the primacy. He has not tackled the reasons for this delay, limiting himself to underlining the necessity to go beyond it and to change the form of the exercise of his ministry.

The theme of the conversion of the papacy has many ecumenical implications. At the same time, it also concerns ecclesial relationships within the

---

[40] For an overview, see Sandra Mazzolini, "*Ut unum sint* 88–96. Implicazioni ecclesiologiche ed ecumeniche del ministero petrino," in *Il primato del successore di Pietro in prospettiva missionaria*, ed. Vincenzo Mosca (Città del Vaticano: Urbaniana University Press, 2013), 95–127.

[41] See Angel Antón, "El ministerio petrino y/o papado en la 'Ut unum sint' y desde la eclesiología sistemática. II," *Gr* 79/4 (1998): 650.

[42] Among them, we can recall the interpretation of dogmas, the doctrinal development, and the principle of the hierarchy of truths. See Mazzolini, *Ut unum sint*, 107–112.

[43] This distinction entails issues such as the biblical foundation of Petrine ministry and the doctrine of Vatican Councils I and II. On the interpretation of the dogmas of Vatican I, see Walter Kasper, "Introduzione al tema ed ermeneutica cattolica dei dogmi del Vaticano I," in *Il ministero petrino*, 17–27; Hermann J. Pottmeyer, "Recent Discussions on Primacy in Relation to Vatican I," ibid., 227–245. A. Antón has also emphasized the difficulty to distinguish exactly the essence of the Petrine ministry and its forms: see Antón, "El ministerio petrino y/o papado," 652–653.

Catholic tradition. From this point of view, Pope Francis has mentioned this issue again, putting it in correlation with the conversion of the central structures of the universal Church. It allows the pope to deal with the thorny question of the episcopal conferences, in particular recalling the still open problem of their statute.[44] After having quoted *Lumen Gentium* 23, Pope Francis has acknowledged that the conciliar desire of improving the episcopal conferences still "has not been fully realized, since a juridical status of episcopal conferences which would see them as subjects of specific attributions, including genuine doctrinal authority, has not yet been sufficiently elaborated."[45] In brief, the pope has focused again on the question of the statute of the episcopal conferences, which must be developed in order to promote an effective "sound decentralization." The last paragraph confirms Pope Francis's understanding of a more decentralized Church; in fact, he has underlined once more that an "[e]xcessive centralization, rather than proving helpful, complicates the Church's life and her missionary outreach."

The renewal of the ecclesial structures cannot only be understood as the static result of a unique project of reformation. *Dynamism* and *decentralization* are key words also to realize what this renewal is according to Pope Francis. On one side, he invites "everyone to be bold and creative in this task of rethinking the goals, structures, style and methods of evangelization in their respective communities" (EG 33). On the other, he "encourages everyone to apply the guidelines found in this document ... without inhibitions or fear." He concludes that the "important thing is not to walk alone, but to rely on each other as brothers and sisters, and especially under the leadership of the bishops, in a wise and realistic pastoral discernment" (EG 33).

---

[44] The Second Vatican Council has introduced this topic in *LG* 23 and *CD* 37 and 38. In the postconciliar time, the nature and the role of the episcopal conferences have been variously debated. Among others, the issue of their statute has been very relevant. Many authors have tackled this topic, which they have explained in divergent ways. Some of them have understood it in the perspective of a dynamic vision of the episcopal collegiality, which entails the ecclesiological model of the Church as *communio Ecclesiarum*, as well as the interaction between the effective collegiality and the affective collegiality. Other scholars have considered the episcopal conference as a juridical structure, whose authority derives from positive rules: see Umberto Casale, "Conferenza Episcopale," in *Dizionario di Ecclesiologia*, ed. Gianfranco Calabrese, Philip Goyret, and Orazio F. Piazza (Roma: Città Nuova, 2010), 345–354.

[45] It is interesting to note that the adjective *juridical* only appears in the English version of the text (see *EG* 32). We can wonder whether the juridical approach is sufficient to implement the role of the episcopal conferences.

CHAPTER 6

Francis's Ecclesiological Revolution

A New Way of Being Church, a New Way of Being Pope

Gerard Mannion

Evangelii Gaudium continues to represent the clearest and most detailed indication to date of Pope Francis's agenda for the church. It effectively constitutes a substantive statement of intent and mission through which Francis began to offer the church a new vision for the future. It consolidated messages we had heard from him prior to its November 2013 release in various statements and public pronouncements and also signified through many gestures and actions. And the vision contained in the document has also been subsequently and consistently confirmed in many further papal and ecclesial actions, statements, and appointments. Although the document is not a methodically structured treatise in systematic theology, it nonetheless is structured around core themes and is written to promote distinctive ends in and for the church. It is, therefore, a very ecclesiological text.

It is not just a new way of being church that we are seeing unfold before us but also a new way of being pope. This chapter considers some aspects of what is proving distinctive about both such developments. In particular, it seeks to explore in a further detail precisely what *sort* of ecclesiological vision emerges from the document.

There are many important ecclesiological themes and issues addressed in each and every one of the other contributions to this volume and, of course, especially so in those chapters preceding this one. In order to offer something here that is more complementary as opposed to repetitive of those other chapters, I will not here go into great detail on the specifics of Francis's commitment to social justice in *Evangelii Gaudium*, nor the detailed aspects concerning structural ecclesial reform or the specifics concerning the document and Francis's debt to Vatican II. Nor will I here explicate the key events, statements, gestures, and methodology behind Francis's approach to ecumenical and interfaith dialogue. These are all extremely important areas for consideration that I will touch upon (and do address in greater detail elsewhere). However, because we have several wonderful additional chapters in this volume that explore such topics, including those that explore specific themes and developments that are of much relevance to any analysis of Pope Francis's ecclesiology, this chapter will focus on the more general (or if one will, "fundamental") ecclesiological nature of his vision for the church. It will seek to identify some of the core characteristics of Francis's ecclesiological vision. I begin with an overview and work backward, like a detective story in some respects, to trace some of the most formative influences upon that vision.

In order to do so, I will offer reflections on four specific areas. First, I raise the question of *ecclesiological* continuity or discontinuity between this papacy and the previous pontificate – in general terms as well as with regard to what *Evangelii Gaudium* reveals about such a question. Second, I explore some of the key characteristics of Pope Francis's ecclesiology, particularly with regard to the most important insights into his vision and agenda for the church that the apostolic exhortation affords us. In particular, how the document displays a radical ecclesiology of openness, inclusivity, and dialogue.

Third, I briefly consider the relationship between Francis's ecclesiology and that of the Second Vatican Council before turning to consider a further especially important influence upon the ecclesiology of Pope Francis that the document appears to reveal, namely, the understanding of the church as shaped by the theology of liberation. I then turn to the refreshing ecclesiological realism seen throughout Pope Francis's exhortation and pontificate in general to date, something that owes much to both those influences earlier discussed.

In conclusion, I propose that the ecclesiological vision of *Evangelii Gaudium* is nothing short of revolutionary and, therefore, Pope Francis's agenda for the church should be judged to be equally revolutionary – as multiple developments throughout the church since March 2013 confirm.

1. Continuity, Discontinuity, and Ecclesiological "Dynamite": A New Way of Being Pope?

From the very outset of his pontificate, Pope Francis offered us many important indicators as to what sort of vision for the church and hence what type of operative ecclesiology his papacy would be shaped by. The first actual messages and signals from the new pope about what might lie ahead for the church were especially suggestive – and many of our contributors to this volume have commented upon these.

So many, around the globe, immediately sensed that this papacy would be something very different from the previous one and this, not least of all because it became clear from the outset that this first Latin American pope appeared to perceive the church from a very different perspective to his Bavarian predecessor, just as their respective ecclesial ministries and careers prior to their elections as supreme pontiff could scarcely have been more different too.

And yet, despite the highly important initial gestures and statements, this did not prevent many in the church from pushing an agenda for Pope Francis's pontificate firmly centered upon continuity with the priorities and character of the papacies of his two immediate predecessors. It even appeared at the time that some commentators were swiftly attempting to "canonize" the ethos of Pope Benedict as if a new pope could do no otherwise than slavishly imitate his predecessor. For example, George Weigel told a packed audience at a plenary session of the American Academy of Religion's Annual Meeting in Baltimore, three days before the release of *Evangelii Gaudium*, that first major teaching document from Pope Francis's own hand,[1] that there would be nothing radical in the document whatsoever. Rather, Weigel was adamant that it would be in total continuity with the ecclesial visions of Benedict and John Paul II. He has had to significantly modify his interpretation since.

Yet the clearly demonstrated reality that has come to pass is that it is beyond question that Pope Francis's agenda for the church, as set down in *Evangelii Gaudium*, is clearly revolutionary in multiple ways and yet revolutionary in a distinctive way. So, while some journalists, bishops, and spokespersons with their own agendas quickly took to mental and linguistic somersaults to paint a picture of continuity, it is difficult for anyone working in fields such as ecclesiology to reach any conclusion other than the simple fact that, on so many of the most important issues there is very little substantive continuity with the ecclesial agenda of his predecessor. In fact, the most consistent messages we are hearing from Pope Francis appear designed to try and overcome many of the most persistent stumbling blocks

---

[1] An earlier and relatively ignored encyclical, *Lumen Fidei* (June 29, 2013), http://w2.vatican.va/content/francesco/en/encyclicals/documents/papa-francesco_20130629_enciclica-lumen-fidei.html, was widely acknowledged to have been primarily the work of Benedict XVI, albeit with some additions from Francis.

that have not only been divisive, but that have also been holding the church back from fulfilling its mission in recent times.

Indeed, it would soon become clear that, in the face of the rapid ecclesial change that began to take place following the election of Francis, some in church were soon suffering from ecclesial vertigo. Not a few bishops and even cardinals began to voice their disquiet and displeasure at some of the initiatives and shifts in ecclesial direction introduced by Pope Francis. It was ironic that some of the very same people who for many years previous were ruthlessly demanding unswerving loyalty to every utterance of the pope and to the perspective of Rome were now demonstrating fully-fledged dissent in open defiance of the very same office they previously sought to protect through a veritable persecution of fellow Catholics.

In terms of that first major document, when examined in its totality, alongside the numerous other statements from Francis and his actions and agenda for the church thus far in his pontificate, it becomes clear that *Evangelii Gaudium* embodies a radically new – yet one could also say ever more authentically traditional – understanding of evangelization. What equally becomes clear is that the ecclesiologies of Francis and his predecessor are very far apart, just as their own starting contexts are so very far apart and just as many of the most vital formative influences upon their respective visions of the church differ significantly as well.

But this should be neither surprising nor controversial. For when one looks at the history of the church absolute continuity across successive papacies is rare indeed. Indeed, in general terms such is almost nonexistent for a variety of factors. Naturally there will be continuity on certain issues or in terms of organization, practice, and some personnel, but even in relation to such factors continuity is never total and all-embracing across different papacies. Why would anyone expect or even desire otherwise? Continuity in and of itself is not a virtue. Think of the election of a president or prime minister. The whole point of the election is usually the desire and/or necessity for change. Although the office of the bishop of Rome is naturally very different, we must not forget that he is elected and many of the usual trappings that surround election to other such offices surrounds that process too. Benedict XVI did not agree with John Paul II on many things (e.g., there were key differences between the two concerning interreligious and ecumenical dialogue). John Paul II had radically different priorities to Paul VI[2] (e.g., John Paul II had a much more authoritarian

---

[2] Alas John Paul I did not live long enough for us to see the outworking of his own pontifical vision, but he, Paul VI, and John Paul II were all very different in many ways.

Francis's Ecclesiological Revolution

idea of how magisterium should be practiced and further empowered the Congregation for the Doctrine of Faith [CDF] to carry out his agenda for the reach and practice of official magisterium). Paul VI was markedly different to John XXIII in so many ways, not least of all in how both wished to see the Second Vatican Council progress in terms of its core focus (For John the church's key priority, and so, also, that of the council, was opening up to and engaging with the wider world beyond the church. Paul also acknowledged this priority but believed that a more urgent priority still was addressing the internal problems and divisions within the church.). The contrasts between John XXIII and Pius XII could not be more pronounced in terms of papal style as well as pastoral focus and eccleial priorities alike, while tensions and differences between Pius XII and Pius XI are well known. Benedict XV was in many ways elected because he would pursue a very different agenda to Pius X.

And while each of these popes also shared much in common with their predecessors, none of them presided over a church or church administration that was more or less the same as that presided over by their predecessor. Every single one of them differed a great deal in ecclesiological terms from their immediate predecessor. Francis is no exception.[3]

In fact, most of the cardinals gathered in conclave who elected Francis made clear, time after time, that they *did not seek continuity* – rather they openly acknowledged that the church needed drastic, radical change and transformation. Many of them had taken wider soundings.

So in terms of those yearning for positive change in the church, the new papacy did not disappoint.

From that very moment of his emergence onto the balcony of St. Peter's, it was clear that this very first Papa Franciscus wanted to change radically how the church goes about its practice and business. He told the excited throng in St. Peter's Square upon his election that they, and indeed all the people of the church, and he were embarking upon a journey together. What an exciting and fascinating journey that would turn out to be.

Francis swiftly identified that the core priority for his papacy was to encourage the church to become a poor church *for* the poor, leading by example. Francis also rapidly began to initiate church reforms in terms of structure and eventually also canon law and doctrinal interpretation and application on a variety of issues. For example, his shift to more

---

[3] See, also, Chapter 2 by Dennis Doyle in this volume. While I argue that there is greater discontinuity between Francis and his immediate predecessors than Dennis does, I believe there are also significant points of agreement between our respective theses concerning the degree of continuity or otherwise across these papacies.

participatory governance witnessed in his creation of the C9 council of global cardinals to assist and advise him (initially a C8 until Pietro Parolin was created cardinal in his first consistory).

His emphasis upon the priority of pastoral care over doctrinal hard-line stances would be another theme that he would return to again and again, and it swiftly became clear also that he would give renewed support and energy to wide-reaching ecumenical and interfaith dialogue.

It did not take very long before this pontificate seemed to herald the dawning of an ecclesial revolution. As one of the pope's Argentine biographers, who knows him very well put it, "The revolution begins at the moment the Cardinal Archbishop of Buenos Aires, the first Jesuit to be elected to St. Peter's throne, chooses his own name.... The name is, in itself, a program of government." Saint Francis of Assisi had been called by God to repair "my house, which is in ruins." Now "Jorge Bergoglio, Pope Francis, takes up the reins of the Catholic Church, which is not in ruins but is experiencing a deep crisis."[4] She concurs that despite the efforts of Benedict XVI's supporters to strain continuity of what was rapidly identified as the opposite, "the revolution" was "already underway in his first twenty-four hours as pope. Behind the ancient walls of the Vatican, decorated with priceless frescoes, pictures and carpets, you ... [could] feel a fracture, a 'before' Francis and 'after Francis.'"[5]

Which returns us to the document *Evangelii Gaudium*. While officially an "Apostolic Exhortation on the Proclamation of the Gospel in Today's World," *Evangelii Gaudium* is a document that, in many ways, is about much more than it was supposed to be. Technically, it was supposed to be a postsynodal exhortation and response to the deliberations of the Synod of Bishops on the "New Evangelization" in 2012.[6] In fact, the references to the "new evangelization" are relatively few in total given the full title of the document (and its postsynodal status) – the term "*New* Evangelization" warrants a mention twelve times. Of course, the new evangelization (and the attendant ecclesiological framework behind it, as well as the implications of such) was a project at the very heart of the pontificate and vision for the church of Pope Benedict XVI. Yet multiple statements in *Evangelii Gaudium* and elsewhere have made it clear that Francis's and Benedict XVI's respective understandings of Christian mission and proclamation are also radically different.

---

[4] Elisabetta Piqué, *Pope Francis: Life and Revolution: A Biography of Jorge Bergoglio* (Chicago: Loyola Press, 2014), 167.
[5] Ibid., 168.
[6] See documentation at http://www.vatican.va/roman_curia/synod/.

Thus, in November 2013, Pope Francis took the opportunity to set down his own agenda for his papacy and the church of these times, as opposed to those of his predecessor. Francis also sought to try and take into account the concerns of the global bishops in a way that previous postsynodal exhortations had not always consistently done so. The times, they were a-changing indeed.

2. Unpacking Francis's Vision for the Church: A Revolution Founded on the Joy of the Gospel

Time and again throughout *Evangelii Gaudium* we encounter key principles and priorities that also appeared to shape the pastoral ministry and practice of Jorge Bergoglio as Archbishop of Buenos Aires.[7] "The challenge of Bergoglio's life and theology was a focus on mission above ecclesiology, a focus that he brought with him to the Vatican when elected the first Latin American bishop of Rome."[8] While certainly not an "anti-ecclesiology" (for there are far too many important ecclesiological insights and implications to that vision), it could be argued that the vision for the church offered by Francis is a conscious reordering of priorities – prioritizing practical, pastoral, social, and moral concerns over and against doctrinal, juridical, and fundamental theological considerations. The latter are important, of course, but only insofar as they serve the putting into practice of the gospel.

This gospel-centric vision permeates the ecclesiology of *Evangelii Gaudium* throughout. Somewhat analogous to Bill Clinton's famous election line, "It's about the economy, stupid," Pope Francis is telling all throughout the church that "Everything we do should be about the Gospel." In this document, he reminds everyone what treasures for the world lie within that gospel, which is outward looking in every respect. The document makes clear that the gospel exists to be put into practice – the faith is a gift that can and should literally change the world. The church, its structures, and ministries only exist to serve this putting into practice of the gospel and therefore to serve the world. Neither the church nor *any* particular office or officeholder within it exist for their own sake.

The pope makes clear that the document offers an agenda for the church of today and the future – at the very outset stating that its aim,

---

[7] E.g., one can see many similarities between what he tells his interviewers Ambrogetti and Rubin, in 2010, and key messages in the document, Francesca Ambrogetti and Sergio Rubin, *Pope Francis: His Life in His Own Words* (New York: G. P. Putnam's Sons, 2013; originally pub. 2010).

[8] Mario I. Aguilar, *Pope Francis: His Life and Thought* (Cambridge: Lutterworth, 2014), 179.

alongside encouraging a new chapter of evangelization characterized by joy, is to identify "new paths for the Church's journey in years to come."[9] Once again this did not suggest continuity – "business as usual" – was going to be his primary concern. The emphasis on joy in the exhortation is all consuming – and it was evident that through this document Francis was seeking to switch the mood of the church from the dark, gloomy, and foreboding tone that had become all too familiar in recent times to a more life-giving and energizing understanding, communication, and practice of the faith – he laments that "There are Christians whose lives seem like Lent without Easter."[10]

What is also clear from the outset is that, for Pope Francis, ecclesial change is urgently necessary, and he denounces as "complacent" the ecclesial standpoint that "We have always done it this way."[11] Francis maps out the exhortation's scope and limits in §16 of the document, which underlines that it is his own work, although he has taken soundings from others – itself a refreshing admission. He also seems to imply that this is not the place to settle contentious issues of doctrine,[12] indeed he even suggests that it is not the pope's place to settle every dispute in the church for were he to do so that would undermine the authority of bishops in their local churches.

With that affirmation of the local church and collegiality at one and the same time, he further surprises his readers in stating – and it is important to remember this is in the introduction of the document – that he is conscious of the need to promote a sound "decentralization"' in the church.[13] He wishes to offer "guidelines."[14] The document clearly has root and branch structural reform across the church in mind, as we shall see.[15]

The document is also somewhat unusual in how it makes no attempt to keep apart areas of concern pertaining to fundamental ecclesiology, social issues, and church-world relations. Nor are questions of dialogue treated in isolation either. It is, therefore, an example of what might be termed a both/and approach to ecclesiology, and this in a number of ways.

[9] EG, §1.
[10] §6.
[11] §33.
[12] "I have chosen not to explore these many questions which call for further reflection and study."
[13] §16.
[14] §17.
[15] §16. See Chapter 5 of the present volume by Sandra Mazzolini for a detailed discussion of certain structural ecclesial reforms advocated by Francis.

First, it seeks to bring into closer dialogue and, therefore, eventual harmony approaches to the church and its mission both from the center (or "from above") and from the periphery and the margins ("from below"). It also brings together reflections upon the church *ad intra* and those upon the church *ad extra*, allowing the two areas mutually to inform and shape one another in a more consistently successful (if less systematic) fashion than was achieved at Vatican II when one considers its texts on the whole. Finally, it is an ecclesiology that brings together theoretical and institutional questions and aspirations with practical ones – social, moral, missionary, and pastoral concerns alike. In particular, with its emphasis upon putting the gospel into practice throughout, the document turns back and forth between more traditional ecclesiological issues and questions alongside more pressing and pertinent issues for our times, just as it alternates back and forth between concerns treated somewhat separately in Vatican II's *Lumen Gentium* and *Gaudium et Spes*.[16]

In this document, as elsewhere, Francis has also made it clear that the priority for the church is to look forward not backward, that doctrinal minutiae and disputes are not more important than living the faith and putting it into practice.

And in all this there were many echoes of that other surprise appointment to the chair of Peter, Angelo Roncalli. Pope Francis has sought to follow Pope John XXIII's example in many respects. A further indication of what would come to be defining characteristics of his pontificate is offered in how this document preaches mercy, compassion, and forgiveness rather than stern admonishments and banishment. Francis states that mercy, not moralizing lie at the heart of the gospel – and he cites Thomas Aquinas in seeing mercy as the greatest virtue of all.[17]

All in all, the revolution that his biographer spoke of is clearly underlined as fact. This, again, in contrast to the perspective offered by some commentators about continuity and the oft-cited line – even from many more centrist bishops and cardinals who supported his ministry from the outset – that Francis had changed the style of the papacy but nothing of substance in the church's doctrine. *Evangelii Gaudium* does precisely that, and it is Francis's self-conscious intention in the document to do so.

---

[16] E.g., §115 even cites them one after another. While *Gaudium et Spes* does not get directly cited in the footnotes very often, it nonetheless permeates the whole document – a church going forth; a church serving the world; a sacrament of salvation; the joys, fears, sufferings, hopes, and aspirations of people are encountered in phrases throughout.

[17] §37 (citing *Summa Theologiae* II-II, q. 30, a. 4). See, also, §§3, 24, 43–44, 112, 164, 188, 194, 197–198, 252, 285 and, especially, 179, 193, and 114.

3. An Ecclesiology of Openness, Inclusivity, and Dialogue

Indeed, openness is a further defining feature of the ecclesial vision of *Evangelii Gaudium* and Pope Francis. Forms of exclusion and exclusivity are criticized in multiple parts of *Evangelii Gaudium*. An openness to and engagement with others is central to its vision (§78).[18] The title of the document not only points to this emphatic focus on the gospel but also appears to be a deliberate evocation of the spirit of Vatican II's *Gaudium et Spes*. And throughout the text Francis follows up on this. In particular, it offers a vision of a church that must "go forth." Forms of exclusion and exclusivity are criticized in multiple parts of the document. Engagement with others, outreach, and service are central to its vision (§78). The title is also evocative of another papal teaching document that left a profound impression upon the younger Jorge Bergoglio, Paul VI's own apostolic exhortation, *Evangelii Nuntiandi*.[19]

The vision for a church that "goes forth" unfolds in relation to multiple areas of ecclesial life. Whether it is the radical inclusivity that he promotes for the poor and marginalized (something broadened still further in *Laudato Si'*), to his injunction to bishops and priests to get out and become more familiar with the "smell of the sheep," to his profound commitment to the plight of migrants and refugees, to his calls for an end to racial and religious discrimination and persecution, to his radical inclusion of the homeless and poor – including initiatives introduced at the Vatican (such as showers and a hairdresser), to his preference while visiting Washington, D.C., in September 2015 to share lunch with the homeless rather than the elected power brokers of congress. It is there in his genuinely moving outreach to those with disabilities, and in his multiple statements about the need for women[20] in the church to enjoy greater involvement in the decision-making processes of the church and for their work on its behalf to be better appreciated. So, also, is this inclusivity manifest in his now famous statements of compassion to gay people ("'If someone is gay and is searching for the Lord and has good will, then who am I to judge"),[21]

---

[18] I explore Pope Francis's approach to dialogue with others – ecumenical, interreligious, and with people of no particular faith in "Pope Francis and the Wider Ecumenical Future" in *Hope in the Ecumenical Future*, ed. Mark D. Chapman and Gerard Mannion, (New York: Palgrave Macmillan, 2016).

[19] Paul VI, *Evangelii Nuntiandi* (December 8, 1975), http://w2.vatican.va/content/paul-vi/en/apost_exhortations/documents/hf_p-vi_exh_19751208_evangelii-nuntiandi.html.

[20] In *EG*, see for example, §103–104.

[21] Press Conference, Papal Flight (Sunday, July 28, 2013), http://w2.vatican.va/content/francesco/en/speeches/2013/july/documents/papa-francesco_20130728_gmg-conferenza-stampa.html.

in his calls for greater compassion toward women forced to consider and even undergo abortion, in his outreach to victims of the abuse crisis and inclusion of key survivors on a new commission to tackle the issue, and it is demonstrated clearly in the people invited to participate in the 2015 Synod, along with his inclusion of voices from around the world, including smaller and less influential countries in the College of Cardinals and departments of the Roman Curia. Francis is very serious indeed about an ecclesiology of radical openness. His marrying, at the Vatican, couples who had previously been living together and who already had children spoke further volumes about his pastoral priorities and the character of his application of the church's teaching.

Furthermore, this priority of an open and inclusive church also has doctrinal consequences too. From what Pope Francis has set down in *Evangelii Gaudium*, but equally from the very first moments of his papacy, as we have seen, as well as in his outreach to constant actions and statements in relation to others beyond the confines of the Roman Catholic family, it is clear that Pope Francis deliberately set out to banish the neo-exclusivism[22] that characterized too much of the church under his immediate predecessors and that negatively impacted ecumenical and interreligious dialogue alike.

There have been multiple changes already in canon law as well as in curial and wider ecclesial practice with regard to how people are to be treated who would previously have been shunned by the official church if they somehow did not live up to the most rigid of its doctrinal and juridical demands (e.g., Francis called for a complete reform and streamlining of how the church handles requests for a previous marriage to be annulled and these changes came to pass in the fall of 2015).

Here we see another key area in relation to which Francis has sought to follow Pope John XXIII's example in many respects. He wants a church open to and engaged with the wider world. He accentuates what people share in common rather than what divides them. The document offers a vision of *how* the church can and should be open to the world, that is outward looking and willing to engage in dialogue.

The ecclesiological vision of this the pope "from the ends of the earth," clearly has inclusivity and openness rather than the notion of a smaller, "purer" church (which often appeared to reflect the ecclesial vision of his predecessor) as core priorities. His vision is of a church that excludes nobody from its compassion, a church whose doors are always open.[23] Francis pulls no punches, "Jesus did not tell the apostles to form an

---

[22] See, e.g., §98.
[23] §46–47, 97.

exclusive and elite group."[24] And this, also, has doctrinal and sacramental – as well as pastoral – consequences, "Frequently, we act as arbiters of grace rather than its facilitators. But the Church is not a tollhouse; it is the house of the Father, where there is a place for everyone, with all their problems."[25]

The concept of "reconciled diversity" is *the* defining concept in Francis's approach not simply to ecumenical issues, but also to interfaith issues, to issues of cooperation and understanding among people of faith and those of no specific religious persuasion. Furthermore, it is the hallmark of his approach to internal divisions and differences within the Roman Catholic Church.[26] Time and again Francis affirms pluralism and diversity – indeed unity in the midst of diversity – a theme that has become the hallmark of his many statements addressed to the Catholic Church *ad intra* as much as it is of his gestures toward encouraging ecumenical and interfaith dialogue. It is a concept, borrowed from the Lutheran scholar Oscar Cullman, and one that Bergoglio was employing long before his election to the papacy.[27] This is a term has returned to on many subsequent occasions since his election.

But in *Evangelii Gaudium* it comes in a broader ranging section, on how "Unity Prevails over Conflict" (§§226–230), which addresses the necessity of facing and not ignoring conflict but also reminds us that we should keep everything in perspective. Francis argues that conflict can actually lead us to a greater realization of what we share in common, in unity with others. So, instead of ignoring the conflict or pretending it is not there, or becoming blinded by it and becoming its prisoners, so that unity is never possible, he states that "…there is also a third way, and it is the best way to deal with conflict. It is the willingness to face conflict head on, to resolve it and to make it a link in the chain of a new process. 'Blessed are the peacemakers!' (Mt 5:9)."[28] It is at this part of the document, within a larger section on "The Common Good and Peace in Society," then, rather than the specific sections on ecumenism and interreligious relations that we find his one and only use of the term *reconciled diversity* in the exhortation. Further affirming hid ecclesiology of radical openness and engagements, he tells

---

[24] He continues, "To those who feel far from God and the Church, to all those who are fearful or indifferent, I would like to say this: the Lord, with great respect and love, is also calling you to be a part of his people!," §113.

[25] §47.

[26] See, e.g., §116–117, where he speaks about cultural diversity being always part of the church throughout its history and of the great gift to the church that inculturation always has been, indeed, a gift of the Holy Spirit.

[27] See, e.g., Ambrogetti and Rubin, *Pope Francis: His Life in His Own Words*, 227–228.

[28] §227.

us that "Diversity is a beautiful thing when it can constantly enter into a process of reconciliation and seal a sort of cultural covenant resulting in a 'reconciled diversity.'"[29]

But it is beyond question that Francis has overnight given renewed energy to ecumenical and interfaith ventures in dialogue – as demonstrated in *Evangelii Gaudium*, as well as in so many of his wider actions and statements, alike. Indeed he has helped reignite the flame of dialogue on so many additional fronts, also.

This is a pastor whose own episcopal ministry in Argentina had embraced ecumenical and interfaith dialogue as nonnegotiable necessities and gifts for the church.[30] He could do no otherwise than perceive these questions and challenges in a very different way to, say Europeans or North Americans, often too imprisoned by their own cultural, social, and intellectual worldviews. This is a faith leader with whom most people who care about ecumenism, interfaith dialogue, and a better world feel they can do business.[31]

This ecclesiological openness all resonates with the dialogical significance of his actions, including his many significant and open and inclusive gestures. From washing the feet of young offenders at a correctional instate, including those of a young Muslim woman, to embracing the sick and sharing his birthday breakfast with the homeless or taking lunch with workers in the Vatican canteen. He engaged with refugees, making a special gesture toward Muslims among their number when he visited Lampedusa,[32] and made a special point of visiting Assisi, that great inspirational city of dialogue early on in his pontificate. His first visit abroad was to his home continent and World Youth Day in Brazil. Pictures of him embracing the handicapped and individuals suffering from particular afflictions to his meetings with abuse victims are further examples here. He had multiple profound statements to share with his audiences in the United States in September 2015. They included his appeal for a radical inclusivity toward the poor and migrants. He rhetorically asked both houses of Congress that surely we all want for our own children what most migrants simply want for theirs – a better future, and he further remarked on his own origins as the

---

[29] §230.
[30] For such background, see, e.g., Ambrogetti and Rubin, *Pope Francis: His Life in His Own Words* and Paul Vallely, *Pope Francis: Untying the Knots* (New York and London: Bloomsbury, 2013), *passim*.
[31] See Chapter 12 in this volume by John Borelli for further detailed considerations of Pope Francis and ecumenical and interfaith dialogue.
[32] See, also, Chapter 10 of the present volume by Maryanne Loughry.

child of migrants, just as most of the people of the Americas owe their existence to migration. Then there were his multiple statements about interreligious encounter, understanding, and harmony, especially his poignant response to the interfaith service at Ground Zero.

Without question, the style, manner, and substance of Pope Francis's ministry of unity to date have rapidly left a deep transformative impact upon intrachurch, interchurch, interfaith and faith-world dialogue alike, just as his emphasis upon a church with doors that are always open has captured the attention and affection of countless persons around the world – Catholics, "'lapsed" Catholics, other Christians, members of other faith communities, and those of no particular formal religious persuasion alike. In *Evangelii Gaudium* as elsewhere, Francis states clearly that other faiths and churches alike can bring much to Catholicism and teach it much. The superior tone of the Congregation for the Doctrine of the Faith's document from 2000, *Dominus Iesus*, is replaced by a reaffirmation throughout of universalism and a thoroughly humble and dialogical universalism at that. And the basis for Pope Francis's radically open, inclusive, and dialogical ecclesiology is nothing less than the incarnation, for, as he tells us "True faith in the incarnate Son of God is inseparable from self-giving, from membership in the community, from service, from reconciliation with others. The Son of God, by becoming flesh, summoned us to the revolution of tenderness."[33]

4. Embracing the *Ecclesiological* Legacy of Vatican II

If *Evangelii Gaudium* is indeed a substantive statement of intent and mission, one of the key inspirations behind Francis's transformative vision has been his embracing of the ecclesiological vision and priorities of Vatican II. Early in his pontificate, Pope Francis spoke of Vatican II as a "beautiful work of the Holy Spirit,"[34] and he has made council's prioritization of *aggiornamento*, reform, and dialogue equally guiding principles for his own vision for the church.[35] This is another key difference with his immediate predecessors, both of whose pontificates, as many ecclesiologists and

---

[33] *EG*, §88.
[34] In a homily preached on April 16, 2013, see http://www.news.va/en/news/pope-2nd-vatican-council-work-of-holy-spirit-but-s.
[35] Here see Chapter 3 in this volume by Massimo Faggioli and also Gerard Mannion, "Reengaging the People of God" in *Go into the Streets! The Welcoming Church of Pope Francis*, ed. Richard R. Gaillardetz and Thomas P. Rausch, S.J. (New York: Paulist, 2016). Both these essays also discuss further the parallels between Francis and John XXIII.

Francis's Ecclesiological Revolution

church historians have suggested, fostered counteractions to the vision of the majority of Vatican II fathers on several crucial issues. Instead, in both pontificates the preference was to privilege a normative "'official" ecclesiology of communion which was presented as the "real" core legacy of Vatican II. In sharp contrast to this, Pope Francis has actively rehabilitated Vatican II's understanding of the church as people of God, which was long considered to be Vatican II's core ecclesiological concept.[36]

Indeed, the notion of the church as people of God permeates the document throughout. In §114 Francis demonstrates that the concept lies at the very core of his ecclesiology "Being Church *means* being God's people, in accordance with the great plan of his fatherly love. This means that we are to be *God's leaven in the midst of humanity*."[37] The church, then, must be a people *for* others, driven by mercy.[38] Francis also rehabilitates a positive and active understanding of the *sensus fidelium*, the people of God are not to be considered "passive recipients" of some special insights from a "professional class."[39] Francis also underlines the Vatican II commitment to the vocation of the laity and again challenges a hierarchical vision of the church in §102 where he states unambiguously that "Lay people are, put simply, the vast majority of the people of God. The minority – ordained ministers – are at their service." He observes that the full responsibility of the laity is not always acknowledged in parts of the church – sometimes due to poor formation for the laity yet in others "due to an excessive clericalism which keeps them away from decision-making." And within the people of God there is diversity, so Pope Francis (here again) affirms both universalism and unity in diversity, just as the council itself affirmed such.[40]

A further key development in relation to Vatican II is how Francis has clearly sought to try and reverse the shackling of episcopal collegiality that took place in the postconciliar decades as well. For example, first of all, there is his now famed constant citing of the documents issued by different episcopal conferences from around the globe in both *Evangelii Gaudium* and *Laudato Si'* – this again in marked contrast to his immediate two predecessors who were on record as stating that episcopal conferences per se have no teaching mandate. Recall, also, Francis statement in

---

[36] Again c.f. Mannion, "Reengaging the People of God."
[37] My emphasis. Leonardo Boff has stated that Francis has placed this notion "at the center," Leonardo Boff, *Francis of Rome and Francis of Assisi* (Maryknoll, NY: Orbis, 2014), 37.
[38] Vatican II's sense of the church as transformative sacrament and as servant returning also.
[39] §120.
[40] §§111–113.

Evangelii Gaudium that it is not the pope's position to settle every question in the church *because* that would undermine local bishops. The establishment of the C9 is a further hugely important development here, as were the format of the 2014 and especially 2015 Synods of Bishops and especially Francis's call for a more truly synodal church toward the close of the 2015 gathering.[41]

And, second, while in *Evangelii Gaudium* he references John Paul II's *Apostolos Suos*, at the very same time he is, in effect, questioning the perspective and limitations upon the authority and remit of episcopal conferences contained in that document, so, in *Evangelii Gaudium* §32, we hear that,

> The Second Vatican Council stated that, like the ancient patriarchal Churches, episcopal conferences are in a position "to contribute in many and fruitful ways to the concrete realization of the collegial spirit". [LG §23] Yet this desire has not been fully realized, since a juridical status of episcopal conferences which would see them as subjects of specific attributions, including genuine doctrinal authority, has not yet been sufficiently elaborated.

At this point the document references *Apostolos Suos*.[42] And yet it immediately goes on to state that "Excessive centralization, rather than proving helpful, complicates the Church's life and her missionary outreach."[43] Yet *Apostolos Suos* was, as with the previous two papacies in general, characterized by a zealous drive toward greater centralization in the church – a drive that in many ways defined the character and agenda of the previous two papacies.

As other contributions to this volume also make clear, although this is the first pope since John XXIII called the council not to have been involved with its actual proceedings in any way, it appears that Francis will be the pope who does the most to ensure that the key intentions and legacy of Vatican II will finally come to lasting fruition in the church, albeit expanded and supplemented to take into account the very different world the church is called to serve today.

---

[41] He instructed the nuncios and episcopal conferences of the world to elicit responses about questions concerning, divorce, remarriage, and family life ahead of the 2014 Synod of Bishops, and its 2015 follow-up thereby at once helping to try and make the process more truly synodal than has been the case hitherto.
[42] John Paul II, *Apostolos Suos* (May 21, 1998): AAS 90 (1998), 641–658.
[43] EG, §32.

5. An Ecclesiology of Liberation

Francis has made justice for the poor and wider questions of social justice both his own and the church's key priority.[44] And this helps point toward one of the most important formative influences upon his ecclesiology of all, namely the vision for the church outlined in the many contributions from Latin American liberation theology. Obviously, this also suggests a further instance of discontinuity with both his immediate predecessors, especially Benedict XVI, who, when prefect of the Congregation for the Doctrine of the Faith issued the *Instruction on Certain Aspects of the Theology of Liberation* denouncing many features of this method in 1984.[45] Ratzinger was especially concerned with challenging the ecclesiological outlook of many key figures in this movement. But aside from this, it tells us so much more about Francis's own ecclesiological outlook than simply pointing toward such further differences with that of his predecessor.[46] It also points toward Francis's embracing of a polycentric understanding of the church and his affirmation of an ecclesiology from below.[47]

As with Vatican II, while it may have seemed more logical here to outline the influences upon Pope Francis's ecclesiology and his agenda for the church before outlining aspects of that agenda as outlined in *Evangelii Gaudium*, I have deliberately outlined the latter first in order that readers may all the better appreciate the formative influence of the former. This becomes especially important with regard to liberation ecclesiology.

Francis's shift toward an emphasis upon the priority of pastorally oriented practice in *Evangelii Gaudium* seems to be indistinguishable from the understanding of that vitally central concept for liberation theology in general of orthopraxis. It therefore can also be interpreted as one of many affirmations of the methods and achievements of liberation theology that we find in his statements and teachings to date.

---

[44] See, also, Chapters 8, 9, 10, respectively by Maureen O'Connell, Maryanne Loughry, and Mary Doak, in the present volume for further detailed treatments of some of the relevant themes and issues pertaining to Francis's commitment to social justice.

[45] See, e.g., the incisive account by Rosino Gibellini, *The Liberation Theology Debate* (London: SCM, 1987).

[46] A further point of relevance here is that Leonardo Boff who was reprimanded and even "silenced" under Ratzinger at the CDF and in the pontificate of John Paul II, is believed to have been an adviser to Pope Francis during the composition of *Laudato Si'*.

[47] Indeed, he employs the image of the polyhedron in *Evangelii Gaudium* – an image discussed in both Chapters 11 (Drew Christiansen) and 12 (John Borelli) of this present volume.

Indeed, I wish to suggest that Pope Francis's priorities can be summed up as being indicative of an ecclesiology driven first and foremost by liberative orthopraxis, and this helps explain each and every one of Francis's subsequent areas of focus and therefore his vision of the church in general. A church of and for the poor lies at the heart of his ecclesiology in every respect. A church that can be open to and embrace all, working for the liberation from all forms of oppression, marginalization, and exclusion of all. Everything else *serves* these priorities because the gospel has that priority.

Liberation theology, of course, has deep-rooted origins in Latin America, but one of most important epochal moments being when the groundbreaking assembly of the Latin American Roman Catholic Bishops' Conference – Conferencia Episcopal Latinoamericana (CELAM) – met at Medellín, Columbia, in 1968. This was followed up in 1979 with a further milestone meeting in Puebla, Mexico, where the bishops stated those famous words that, "We affirm the need for conversion on the part of the whole church to a preferential option for the poor, an option aimed at their integral liberation."[48] As Cardinal Bergoglio, Pope Francis was instrumental in helping CELAM reflect upon a further stage of reflection upon what this commitment means for the twenty-first century when the bishops of Latin America gathered at Aparecida in 2007 (the outcome of which we shortly turn to).

But liberation theology was to offer not just a critique of society, however, but also of the church and of the power structures and oppression within it. Indeed, that statement from Puebla is one charged with an ecclesiological vision and assertive of ecclesiological priorities. There has been much made of the idiosyncrasies of the forms of liberation theology that emerged in Argentina during the formative years of the young Jesuit Jorge Bergoglio

---

[48] CELAM III (1979), published in English as CELEM, *Puebla: Evangelization at Present and in the Future* – Official English Edition of the Third General Conference of Latin American Bishops, Puebla, Mexico (Slough, St. Paul's Publications/London, Catholic Institute for International Relations 1980), §1134. On liberation ecclesiology in general see, e.g., Gerard Mannion, "Liberation Ecclesiology," ch. 23 of *Routledge Companion to the Christian Church*, ed. Gerard Mannion and Lewis S. Mudge (London: Routledge, 2007), 425–446. Further examples of key ecclesiological writings from or about the first phase of Latin American liberation theology include Leonardo Boff, *Church, Charism and Power* (London: SCM, 1985); Leonardo Boff, *Ecclesiogenesis – The Base Communities Reinvent the Church* (London: CollinsFlame, 1996); Christopher Rowland (ed.) *The Cambridge Companion to Liberation Theology* (Cambridge: Cambridge University Press, 1993); Rosino Gibellini, *The Liberation Theology Debate*; Gustavo Gutiérrez, "The Church: Sacrament of History, A *Theology of Liberation* (London: SCM, 1974), 255–285; Gustavo Gutiérrez, "Liberating Evangelization: Church of the Poor," *Gustavo Gutiérrez: Essential Writings*, ed. with an introduction by James Nickoloff (London: SCM, 1996), 236–285.

and the battles over differing approaches that continued beyond into his episcopal ministry, as well as much being made of the fluctuating relationship between Bergoglio, liberation theology, and its different proponents in Argentina, including the notion of the "theology of the people."[49] But what seems actually clear and beyond question is that Bergoglio the priest, the bishop, and Francis the pope owe a great deal to the fundamental tenets of classical liberation theology.[50] And, perhaps above all else, the ecclesiological themes that emerged from liberation theology have left their imprint on the ecclesiology of Pope Francis, too.[51] As noted, this is most evident in that commitment to what the classical liberation theologians termed *orthopraxis* and in the approach to an ecclesiology from below.[52] This is further illustrated by then Cardinal Bergoglio's deep influence on the fifth key meeting of the CELAM bishops in 2007, the final document of which is cited frequently by Francis in *Evangelii Gaudium*. When one examines that earlier document, the links between the ecclesiological vision of the evolving liberation theology from the late 1960s and 1970s and the cardinal

[49] Space does not permit a full treatment of those debates here but see, e.g., Ivereigh, *The Great Reformer*, 110–114, 122–123, 184–186, 190–197; Vallely, *Pope Francis*, 41–61, 132–141; Aguilar, *Pope Francis*, 9–34, offers a nuanced overview of differing reactions to the emergent liberation theology across Latin America, including in Argentina.

[50] Ivereigh, somewhat contradicting some of his own arguments elsewhere in the same book, even offers evidence for this, noting Bergoglio's good relationship with former Jesuit Father General, Pedro Arrupe, including Francis own admission that Arrupe's approach to the challenges of the world for the church's mission was the correct one and that he also offered the right answers to those challenges – see his famous interview with Antonio Spadaro from September 21, 2013 (https://w2.vatican.va/content/francesco/en/speeches/2013/september/documents/papa-francesco_20130921_intervista-spadaro.html), a year in which Francis prayed fervently at Arrupe's tomb (114–116); also 184–186 (where Francis is noted for embracing the concept of inculturation as a result of Arrupe's introduction of the term to the 1974 synod on evangelization). See, also, Aguiler, *Pope Francis*, 33, "'The Jesuit response to the Medellin conference – [was] a response also embraced by Jorge Bergoglio.... Thus, the Jesuits reformed themselves while simultaneously triggering challenges and reform within the Latin American Catholic Church."

[51] In an address at Georgetown University, Washington, DC, on November 12, 2015, Fr. Juan Carlos Scannone (Pope Francis's former professor and leading figure in the Argentine interpretation of liberation theology) confirmed both that Jorge Bergoglio was heavily influenced by the ecclesiological and wider concerns of liberation theology. In private conversation following his address, he also confirmed that the ecclesiological priorities of the Argentine "'Theology of the People" and the wider liberation theology are one and the same. Scannone also confirmed that Vatican II's *Gaudium et Spes* helped give birth to the liberationist methodology that would so influence Bergoglio and come to fuller fruition in the pontificate of Francis.

[52] Both also being evident in the Aparecida document, although the latter also contains some ambivalent balancing sections more reflective of the priorities in Rome of its time. But such sit uncomfortably alongside the liberationist methods and approaches.

who became pope are clear, in particular the priority of orthopraxis. As one of Francis biographers illustrates, "Aparecida's final document was written with the help of Bergoglio's strong hand, a document that emphasises the service and mission of the Church and gives a secondary role to the expansion or self-reflection of the Church."[53] In other words, pastoral realism to be prioritized over narrow churchy evangelism and dogmatic and purely abstract ecclesiology.

We briefly consider some of the core themes in liberation ecclesiology in order to help appreciate these parallels and its influence upon Pope Francis's vision for the church further still. In doing so, I suggest we find echoes in *Evangelii Gaudium* and in the vision and agenda of Pope Francis in general at each and every turn.

> Because the Church has inherited its structures and its life style from the past, it finds itself today somewhat out of step with the history which confronts it. But what is called for is not simply a renewal and adaption of pastoral methods. It is rather a question of a new ecclesial consciousness and a redefinition of the task of the Church in a world in which it is not only *present*, but of which it *forms a part* more than it suspected in the past. In this new consciousness and redefinition, intraecclesial problems take a second place.[54]

So spoke the person widely acknowledged as the "father" of Latin American liberation theology, Gustavo Gutiérrez. But those words would not at all have looked out of place had they appeared in *Evangelii Gaudium* or featured in one of the many public addresses that Pope Francis has made to date. Gutiérrez went on to state that "[t]he unqualified affirmation of the universal will of salvation has radically changed the way of conceiving the mission of the Church in the world," a shift from a preoccupation with "guaranteeing heaven" to instead seeing "[t]he work of salvation" as "a reality which occurs in history" and that "gives to the historical becoming" of humanity "its profound unity and its deepest meaning."[55] Again, what we read in *Evangelii Gaudium* is but the logical outcome of a pastor who

---

[53] Aguilar, *Pope Francis*, 34. See, also, 130, "A day after his appointment as president of the writing commission for Aparecida, Bergoglio presided at the Eucharist with all the bishops and spoke quietly about his own interpretation of the general theme of the meeting: a Church that would not focus on herself and her self-sufficiency, but a Church that would reach out to every periphery, accepting an invitation to mission. This theme became central in the final document." Further parallels between Aparecida and the substance of *Evangelii Gaudium* are discernible at 130–131.
[54] Gutiérrez, *A Theology of Liberation*, 255.
[55] Ibid.

Francis's Ecclesiological Revolution

wholeheartedly agrees with such a perspective and who has spent many decades seeking to live out such an ecclesiology in practice.

Writing in 1977, T. Howland Sanks and Brian Smith summarized the key components of the liberationist approach to ecclesiology as follows,

> [T]he main characteristics of the ecclesiology of liberation theology are (1) the affirmation of the universal salvific will, (2) the consequent "uncentering" of the Church in the work of salvation-liberation, (3) understanding the Church as the reflectively conscious part of humanity, whose function is to be a sign to the rest of humanity, (4) the specification of this function always in terms of the concrete historical realities in which the Church finds itself, and hence (5) the necessity for an analysis of the society's socio-political-economic situation.[56]

It is an approach to understanding and empowering the church that does not focus on hierarchical categories or older symbols that accentuate the power and authority of the institutional church and its key leaders. Elsewhere, I have suggested that "[l]iberation theology realises that, sufficiently transformed from the sinful ways present throughout its own structures and ways, the church can be one of the most powerful agents *for* human liberation and *for* building the kingdom. In essence, liberation ecclesiology seeks an understanding and structure of church that is *non-hierarchical*, viewing all leadership purely in terms of and as *service* to the community."[57] In *Evangelii Gaudium* we see such dimensions of a liberative ecclesiological vision also embraced from Rome – arguably for the first time in living memory if not in history. Latin American liberation theologians developed an ecclesiology that might better serve the needs of the people of this huge yet impoverished and oppressed continent. Pope Francis builds on such an understanding of the church and its mission in order to expand the relevance of such a commitment to integral human and ecological liberation to the entire world.

These key themes and components of the liberationist approach to ecclesiology are also underlined by the Mexican ecclesiologist Alvaro Quiroz Magaña, who has emphasized how the challenges of ever-changing historical and sociopolitical realities cry out for a new way both of understanding and of being church. In Magaña's analysis, the primary foci of liberation ecclesiology entail a church understood as the people of God and as the sacrament of historical liberation – at one and the same time both a sign

---

[56] T. Howland Sanks and Brian H. Smith, "'Liberation Ecclesiology: Praxis, Theory, Praxis," *Theological Studies* 38(1) (March 1977): 3–38 at 15.
[57] Mannion, "Liberation Ecclesiology," 426.

and servant of the Reign of God. This demands an acknowledgment and commitment to overcoming of the divisions within the church. In turn, such will entail new structures, ministries, and modes of service within the church. The church's mission is to proclaim the gospel in solidarity with all who are exploited and oppressed – the church is charged with making the reign of God a reality in the midst of human history.

Magaña particularly highlights how liberation ecclesiology interlinks the concepts of "church," "Reign of God," and "world" in its efforts to aid the church's mission of accompanying the poor along the road to genuine social and historical transformation. For Magaña, liberation ecclesiology is a task that is never complete, constantly demanding responses to the ever-changing situation of the people of God. Theologians and church leaders are actually evangelized *by* the poor, who constitute "the most important agent of ... evangelizing liberation."[58] A further parallel here is with Pope Francis's affirmation of popular piety and of the poor and their experience as a locus of theology in *Evangelii Gaudium*.[59]

In liberation ecclesiology we, of course, see the profound influence of many of the core ecclesiological themes that came to prominence at Vatican II, and applied in particular to the Latin American context. But today we can also see in outline the fundamental themes that would eventually come to be put into practice in the vision for the church of Pope Francis, and we see parallels with the core themes of liberation ecclesiology that come to the fore in *Evangelii Gaudium* in particular.

Sanks and Smith help further unpack the character of liberation ecclesiology in highlighting its contention that human beings are not created to join the church, rather the church came into being to serve humanity ergo (drawing on the ecclesiology of Juan Luis Segundo) "'the Church is part of humanity, not some entity over against humanity."[60] Furthermore, "the Christian must be open to and engage in analysis of the political, economic, and cultural situation in which the Church is to function as a sign. The Church has something to learn from the world as well as something to contribute."[61] Indeed, the incarnation impresses upon the church an obligation to fashion a radically transformative and salvific ethics, and

---

[58] Alvaro Quiroz Magaña, "Ecclesiology in the Theology of Liberation" in *Systematic Theology – Perspectives from Liberation Theology*, ed. Jon Sobrino and Ignacio Ellacuria (London: SCM, 1996).

[59] E.g., §126.

[60] Sanks and Smith, "Liberation Ecclesiology," 8. They are drawing, in particular, upon Juan Luis Segundo, *The Community Called Church*, trans. John Drury (Maryknoll, NY: Orbis, 1974).

[61] Ibid., 10; see Segundo, *Community Called Church*, 99.

so, citing Segundo in part, "the Church is called upon to 'adopt a deeper moral attitude,' a morality that is creative, progressive, and social, directed toward building the human community, rather than a moral attitude preoccupied with 'wanting to know how we (individually) will be judged.' All our actions and attitudes should be concerned with the other person's salvation, not our own."[62]

It is thus that doctrine serves the pastoral mission of the church and not the other way around. Doctrine must never stand in the way of the dialogue and cooperation between the wider world and the church, "The Church's doctrines should not be an obstacle to this dialogue, because they are open-ended and by their very structure admit of being questioned."[63] Sanks and Smith further analyze the ecclesiology of Gutiérrez,[64] in which the prominent themes of focus include the emphasis upon the fact that the church does not stand over and above the world but rather exists in its midst and in the midst of historical and political reality to serve humanity and bring about liberative salvation through the building of the kingdom, "This integral relationship between liberation from sin and political, social, and economic liberation has obvious consequences for the self-understanding of the Church and its mission."[65]

These are self-evident ecclesiological truths that seem to have been embraced clearly by Jorge Bergoglio, and regardless at what stage of his own ministry such an embrace took place, it nonetheless took place. Now as Pope Francis, they are also clearly ecclesiological truths and guiding principles that have left a deep imprint on *Evangelii Gaudium* and *Laudato Si'* alike.

A further parallel is the acceptance and encouragement of de facto ecclesiological pluralism that liberation theology helped encourage. This draws together several components of Pope Francis's agenda for the church. As Sanks and Smith concluded, "Pluralism in ecclesiology is no more unthinkable than pluralism in theology in general. A plurality of ecclesiologies may be mutually illuminating. It may be the function of liberation theology to nudge us in this direction."[66] In fact, as Francis's fellow

---

[62] Sanks and Smith, "Liberation Ecclesiology,"; Segundo, *Community Called Church*, 110–111.
[63] Sanks and Smith, "Liberation Ecclesiology," 11; Segundo, *Community Called Church*, 126.
[64] They cite the US edition, Gustavo Gutiérrez, S.J., *A Theology of Liberation: History, Politics, Salvation*, trans. and ed. Sister Caridad Inda and John Eagleson (Maryknoll, NY: Orbis, 1973).
[65] Sanks and Smith, "Liberation Ecclesiologies," 14.
[66] T. Howland Sanks and Brian H. Smith, "Liberation Ecclesiology: Praxis, Theory, Praxis," *Theological Studies* 38(1) (March 1977): 3–38 at 38.

Jesuit, Marcello De C. Azevedo once suggested, perhaps liberation ecclesiology (he was specifically thinking of the Base Ecclesial Communities movement), could serve as a meeting point for ecclesiologies in general.[67] Pope Francis appears, in effect, to be widening this suggestion to liberation ecclesiology in general – which may yet come to serve as unifying energy that resolves decades and more of divisive battles between competing ecclesiological visions within Catholicism. But, and here is the twist, that unity must, for Francis, be a unity in diversity, one that embraces "healthy decentralization."[68] When one examines the detailed proposals concerning church reform of, for example, Leonardo Boff in the 1980s,[69] one cannot but conclude that such a vision is one shared by Pope Francis in so many ways, especially with regard to the need for such a decentralization.[70] Francis's reported recent praise of and consultations with the likes of Gutiérrez, Boff, and Jon Sobrino underlines all this further.

Furthermore, as Gutiérrez noted back in that epoch-defining study, in coming to realize commonality in fighting against injustice and the need to collaborate to bring about human liberation, to defeat "misery and injustice," Christians from differing churches find a much stronger commitment around which ecumenism may prosper – one that "unites them more strongly than intraecclesial considerations" and that presents a pathway for Christian unity very different to those traditional ecumenical ideals long favored in Europe (and, one must say, also in Northern America). Gutiérrez believes this will lead toward a "'new kind of ecumenism,'" and one that will involve traversing pathways that lead "'through unecclesiastical places.'"[71] Pope Francis also clearly acknowledges this potential, indeed this priority, too, and has widened it further still beyond the Christian ecumenical collaborative scope to that among people of many faiths and of no particular formal religious persuasion – as *Evangelii Gaudium* also demonstrates.

In his thoroughgoing realism about the plurality of the world, Pope Francis, clearly building on the legacy of liberation theology, is doing so much more than nudging us in the direction of simply acknowledging

---

[67] Marcello De C. Azevedo, "Basic Ecclesial Communities: A Meeting Point of Ecclesiologies," *Theological Studies* 46 (1985): 601–620.

[68] *EG*, §16 – *healthy* is a far better translation of the Spanish ("saludable 'descentralización'") than the official English term used (*sound*), which has authoritarian connotations that might work against Pope Francis's clear intentions in making this statement.

[69] E.g., in *Church, Charism and Power*, especially and also *Ecclesiologenesis*.

[70] Such a need is viewed very differently from Latin America than it might be from the heart of Europe, of course – or at least it was in the 1980s. Today the reality is quite something else.

[71] Gutiérrez, *Theology of Liberation*, 278.

ecclesiological pluralism. Francis encourages the harmony of multiple voices[72] and endorses pluralism in cultural but crucially also religious and theological forms. Ergo he also endorses it in terms of ecclesiology and here, again, is a further lesson from liberation theology and also from Vatican II. We now turn to consider such realism in further detail.

6. Embracing Ecclesiological Realism

A final key characteristic of the ecclesiological vision of Pope Francis is something that I believe is also heavily shaped by Vatican II and liberation ecclesiology. This is its refreshing realism. Francis does not hold an idealist vision of a pure church free of blemishes. Far from it. He is astonishingly refreshing in acknowledging just how much of a mess the church is in – including, especially, its central offices and leadership. There is no pretense that somehow the church and the messy fallible humans who constitute its people can somehow be separated. He knows drastic structural and existential change is necessary. And he has set about implementing such (this again is something he has brought with him from the lessons learned during his episcopal ministry in Argentina). In §49, one of the most evocative passages from *Evangelii Gaudium* that was quickly cited around the globe and captured the attention of so many, soon after the exhortation's release, we see a passage that is among the most suggestive of his ecclesiological vision and priorities of all and in which he makes priorities as clear as possible,

> Here I repeat for the entire Church what I have often said to the priests and laity of Buenos Aires: I prefer a Church which is bruised, hurting and dirty because it has been out on the streets, rather than a Church which is unhealthy from being confined and from clinging to its own security. I do not want a Church concerned with being at the centre and which then ends by being caught up in a web of obsessions and procedures. If something should rightly disturb us and trouble our consciences, it is the fact that so many of our brothers and sisters are living without the strength, light and consolation born of friendship with Jesus Christ, without a community of faith to support them, without meaning and a goal in life. More than by fear of going astray, my hope is that we will be moved by the fear of remaining shut up within structures which give us a false sense of security, within rules which make us harsh judges, within habits which make us feel safe, while at our door people are starving and Jesus does not tire of saying to us: "Give them something to eat" (Mark 6:37).

---

[72] See, e.g., EG, §117 – *harmony* is a word that occurs frequently throughout the document.

These words, too, encapsulate the ecclesiological revolution that Francis wished to commence in multiple ways.

On a vital number of long-divisive ecclesiological issues *Evangelii Gaudium* is clear and unambiguous. Addressing multiple aspects of the crises the church has faced in recent times, in *Evangelii Gaudium*, he calls for a church that realizes it must not become obsessed with doctrinal disputes and alienating lines in the sand. Rather the gospel is about responding to the love of God in like kind.

The change that Francis knows is necessary in the church entails a radical overhaul of magisterium in theory and practice.[73] This, again brings together the influences of Vatican II and liberation ecclesiology upon his own thinking. As José Comblin has encapsulated liberation ecclesiology's appropriation of Vatican II's great insights on the *sensus fidelium* entailing that the entire people of God participate in the exercise of ecclesial magisterium (LG §12),[74] and this is something Francis has consciously affirmed time and again – not least of all in the 2015 Synod of Bishops when he directly cited the very same section from *Lumen Gentium*.[75] Francis envisions a church that teaches with authority only for the sake of putting the gospel into practice in an open and dialogical fashion. If people are leaving the church, that suggests a fault on the part of the church and therefore on the part of its shepherds and leaders.[76] As Comblin puts it, in a manner which I think Francis would wholeheartedly agree, "The point is not to pit the people against the hierarchy, but to situate the hierarchy where it belongs, within the people."[77] The people, as Comblin (almost) puts it, "have [magisterial] agency."[78] Francis, it would appear, has set about

---

[73] I have explored matters with regard to such reform in more detail in "Reengaging the People of God" and in the inaugural Irish Theological Quarterly Lecture, "Pope Francis and the Art of Magisterium" (St. Patrick's College, Maynooth University, Kildare, Ireland, October 7, 2015).

[74] José Comblin, *People of God* (Maryknoll, NY: Orbis, 2004), 191–194.

[75] Address of His Holiness Pope Francis Ceremony Commemorating the 50th Anniversary of the Institution of the Synod of Bishops, Paul VI Audience Hall (Saturday, October 17, 2015), http://w2.vatican.va/content/francesco/en/speeches/2015/october/documents/papa-francesco_20151017_50-anniversario-sinodo.html.

[76] E.g., §63, "We must recognize that if part of our baptized people lack a sense of belonging to the Church, this is also due to certain structures and the occasionally unwelcoming atmosphere of some of our parishes and communities, or to a bureaucratic way of dealing with problems, be they simple or complex, in the lives of our people. In many places an administrative approach prevails over a pastoral approach, as does a concentration on administering the sacraments apart from other forms of evangelization."

[77] Comblin, *People of God*, 194.

[78] Ibid.

Francis's Ecclesiological Revolution

helping to remind the church of this and helping to make it once again the empowering reality throughout the church it once was long before anyone had ever heard of that dusty Latin concept of magisterium that really only became fashionable in the nineteenth century.

This again highlights what would become a further common theme in Francis's papal discourse and actions: church doctrines, structures, organization, ministries, and offices exist to serve the gospel and the world, not the other way around. In *Evangelii Gaudium* Francis even states boldly that "[t]he papacy and the central structures of the universal Church also need to hear the call to pastoral conversion."[79] "Healthy decentralization" coming to the fore, once again, just as it did in October 2015 when Francis called for a more truly synodal church at each and every level.[80]

The root and branch structural reform[81] that Francis has made clear is needed across the church has not only been witnessed in action through his rapid reforms to the curia (including planned restructuring of the different departments and discasteries within) but also in relation to several inspired episcopal appointments and the fundamental transformation in how he as pope and the official church in Rome simply goes about its business. Francis also, as mentioned, drastically transformed the procedures and *modus operandi* of the synod of bishops, returning it to something much closer to the representative body and more active forum originally envisaged at Vatican II. So, also, did he revise the style and size of the pallium and its ceremony – something that had been elaborately enlarged by his predecessor. This, also, is an affirmation of collegiality and a further statement about collegiality and decentralization.[82]

In *Evangelii Gaudium*, Francis warns against "'a nostalgia for structures and customs which are no longer life-giving in today's world.'"[83] Everything must be understood not in the framework of rigid doctrine and canon law but rather in terms of a "missionary key."[84] Again like John XXIII, he has said that in the church, above all else, charity must prevail in all things. He

---

[79] EG, §32.
[80] Address of His Holiness Pope Francis Ceremony Commemorating the 50th Anniversary of the Institution of the Synod of Bishops, http://w2.vatican.va/content/francesco/en/speeches/2015/october/documents/papa-francesco_20151017_50-anniversario-sinodo.html.
[81] Again, see §16.
[82] See, e.g., http://en.radiovaticana.va/news/2015/01/29/pope_modifies_and_enriches_pallium_investiture_ceremony_/1120538, http://www.news.va/en/news/list-of-archbishops-who-will-receive-the-pallium-a, http://ncronline.org/news/vatican/francis-changes-pallium-ceremony-nod-decentralization.
[83] Ibid., §108.
[84] §§33–34.

has condemned ecclesial vendettas and witch hunts, as well as enmity and unchristian behavior toward others in the church,

> It always pains me greatly to discover how some Christian communities, and even consecrated persons, can tolerate different forms of enmity, division, calumny, defamation, vendetta, jealousy and the desire to impose certain ideas at all costs, even to persecutions which appear as veritable witch hunts. Whom are we going to evangelize if this is the way we act?[85]

Again, this stands in marked contrast to the atmosphere in the church that prevailed under Francis's predecessor when certain groups and individuals were allowed to engage in such witch hunts and in the castigation of fellow Catholics with impunity. Even church leaders would engage in this "policing" of the faith and the atmosphere of a rigid supposed orthodoxy being held up over and against others as a weapon with which to judge and exclude them.

It is therefore evident that Francis today rejects ecclesiological idealism – there is no pretense that the reality of the church today is anything other than what it is with all its messiness and failings. And *Evangelii Gaudium* makes clear that this will be his default stance throughout his pontificate.

So Francis prefers an ecclesiological realism, acknowledging the reality of the messiness of the church (alongside its gifts and charisms as well). This leads to him embracing the need for a thoroughgoing ecclesial repentance. When he apologizes for mistakes the church has made, he apologizes for the church and does not attempt some neoscholastic mental gymnastics to try and protect some imagined pure and pristine institution that can never be at fault, as was the case when then Cardinal Ratzinger urged John Paul II not to make a millennium apology on behalf of the church, but rather to make the distinction of apologizing for failings on the part of individuals within the church rather than the church. Francis has apologized for an enormous range of failings on the church's part, from its handling of the abuse crisis to its exploitation of indigenous peoples[86] to its treatment of women and exclusion of them from the highest decision-making arenas of the church; from its involvement in the persecution of Waldensians, to that of Pentecostals in 1930s Italy, to members of others churches and faiths for the Roman Catholic Church's failings toward them also. He has outlined

---

[85] §100–101.
[86] See, e.g., http://www.independent.co.uk/news/world/americas/pope-francis-apologises-for-catholic-crimes-against-indigenous-peoples-during-the-colonisation-of-the-americas-10380319.html, http://www.cruxnow.com/church/2015/07/09/pope-francis-apologizes-for-exploitation-of-native-peoples-calls-for-economic-justice/.

how his church must share its part of the blame for why ecumenism has not made greater progress.

And if we consider the roots of Pope Francis's ecclesiological realism, we are drawn back to the enduring value of that theological approach that some critics had long dismissed as passé. For it is in the theology of liberation that we also find the roots of Francis's ecclesiological realism. For, as we have sought to here emphasize, in liberation ecclesiology we find the most thoroughgoing down to earth approach of an ecclesiology from below.

7. Conclusions

As we strive to emerge from a period of dark and divisive times for the church, a dispositional framework that accentuates the openness of the church, its welcoming, compassionate, and loving character by default has now come to the fore in the ecclesiological vision of Pope Francis. A marked shift away from the punitive and legalistic centralization of recent decades has clearly begun and gathers pace. Many will not like that but it was inevitable and desperately necessary.

Logically speaking, if this papacy has made charity, joy, mercy, and tenderness core ecclesial virtues and so guiding ecclesiological principles, the simultaneous message is an admission that the church of recent decades must somehow have been too characterized by the opposite of such virtues – that charity was too often lacking, that joy was absent, that stern authoritarianism and harsh and unchristian treatment was too often allowed to prevail in the church. In the previous two pontificates there was an ecclesiological shift from the open church of Vatican II to increased centralization and neo-exclusivism. Francis's agenda is reversing this and moving the church from a vicious to a virtuous ecclesiological circle in a short space of time. He has demonstrated that not only is it possible, desirable and even necessary, for Catholicism to embrace a new way of being church, but that it is also possible, desirable, and indeed necessary for him to follow a very different way of being pope.

Shaped by Vatican II and liberation ecclesiology, with a thoroughgoing ecclesiological realism guiding all he does, the ecclesiological revolution of Francis (whose very name evokes the tenderness that he appends to the incarnation-inspired revolution he speaks of in *Evangelii Gaudium*) is now firmly ecclesial reality.

Yes, the real challenge and test will be what further substantial changes are forthcoming in the ecclesial culture and structures long term. It will not be enough to talk about love, mercy, and compassion and yet leave in place the conditions for the possibility of a return to a church of cold individualistic piety that makes little difference in the real world. The church has been suffering from a great deal of social sin in recent decades. This is another concept of central importance to liberation theology. It must take steps to atone for that social sin in its own midst and with regard to its attitude to those beyond the Catholic family.

Finally, it is significant that Pope Francis has not simply gone about following *his own* agenda – he is following the mandate laid down for him by the many discussions of the College of Cardinals prior to the conclave that elected him. As noted, many of those cardinals had taken soundings from those in their differing contexts around the wider world. There was a consensus that today's church and world needed a pope with a very different outlook and that the church required change and reform.[87] In effect, the cardinals decided the church needed a thoroughgoing dose of ecclesiological realism. Pope Francis's agenda is also reflecting the collective CELAM agenda of Aparecida, something further reflected in his approach to synods and his October 2015 call for a truly synodal church, where he further underlined his agenda for a dialogical, participatory, and decentralized model of magisterium, of a listening church.[88] That this pope is embracing a wider more collaborative and participatory understanding of the church and forms of authority is itself a further break with his immediate predecessors and, once again, the signs are that such is a step deliberately taken. The ecclesiological revolution has indeed begun.

---

[87] This was explicitly confirmed, e.g., by the Irish former Archbishop of Westminster, Cardinal Cormac Murphy O'Connor in conversation with (amongst others) Paul Vallely, see the latter's, *Pope Francis*, 157.
[88] Address of His Holiness Pope Francis Ceremony Commemorating the 50th Anniversary of the Institution of the Synod of Bishops, http://w2.vatican.va/content/francesco/en/speeches/2015/october/documents/papa-francesco_20151017_50-anniversario-sinodo.html.

PART II

A Church of and for the Poor: The Social Vision of *Evangelii Gaudium*

CHAPTER 7

The Social Vision of *The Joy of the Gospel*

Four Questions

William Werpehowski

Pope Francis cautions that *The Joy of the Gospel* is "not a social document," by which he means a statement of the sort we find in the Roman Catholic social encyclicals from 1891's *Rerum Novarum* forward.[1] Nevertheless, he does consider at least four closely related, even overlapping questions in chapter Four and elsewhere that bear on Christian theological and social ethics. There are more than that, of course; but in order to order my reflections, I will pose the four along with the exhortation's answers, as I understand them, and accompany those answers with commentary that reaches to consideration of what in fact *is* "a social document," the Pope's May 2015 contribution to Catholic social teaching, *Laudato Si'*.

1. In the Light of Christian Faith, What Is Economic Justice?

Francis composes the answer in trinitarian terms. To believe in a father who loves human beings infinitely means that the Father confers upon each of them an infinite dignity. To believe that we are redeemed and ennobled by the Incarnation of the son means that "the social relations existing" between human beings are redeemed also, that is, liberated from a bondage ensnaring us in self-absorption, defensiveness, isolation, and self-understandings dependent upon one or another form of exclusion.

---

[1] Pope Francis, *Evangelii Gaudium* (2013), at http://w2.vatican.va/content/francesco/en/apost_exhortations/documents/papa-francesco_esortazione-ap_20131124_evangelii-gaudium.html, no. 184. Hereafter references to numbered paragraphs in this document will appear in the body of the essay.

To believe that the Holy Spirit is at work is to realize that the spirit seeks "to penetrate every human situation and all social bonds" for the sake of "genuine fraternal love" before God (178–179). The "social dimension of evangelization" involves responding to God's love in a way that desires and promotes the good of others in and by the power of, if you will, that very spirit. From the standpoint of economic justice, the good of others that is sought to forge and deepen fraternal bonds must be understood in terms of persons' fundamental equality, their equal claim to integral development, or authentic human flourishing *with oneself and with others*.

"As long as the problems of the poor are not radically resolved by rejecting the absolute autonomy of markets and financial speculation and by attacking the structural causes of inequality, no solution will be found for the world's problems or, for that matter, to any problems. Inequality is the root of social ills" (202; cf. 53–60). The pope imagines out loud that we may find these words "irksome" (203), and we might, if for no other reason than for their seeming hyperbole. Yet were we Roman Catholics, we would need to reckon with the idea that since the Second Vatican Council, Catholic social teaching has more or less consistently moved "in an egalitarian direction," identifying economic justice with "solidaristic equality," and the "common good" with the "inclusive sharing in a common quality of life" that is mutually fulfilling."[2] Vast differences in economic prospects and wherewithal undermine that kind of sharing.

In an essay written thirty years prior to *The Joy of the Gospel*, Drew Christiansen, S.J., presented this general case accurately and effectively. Relative equality, "the idea that wealth and resources ought to be regularly redistributed to redress the differences between groups, sectors, and even nations," has its precedent in Pope John XXIII's claim in *Mater et Magistra* that the common good requires making "accessible the goods and services for a better life to as many persons as possible," and "to eliminate or hold within bounds the inequalities that exist between different sectors of the economy."[3] This theme is variously affirmed and developed in subsequent magisterial documents, including *Pacem in Terris* (1963), *Gaudium et Spes* (1965), *Populorum Progressio* (1967), and *Octagesima Adveniens* (1971). Its theological core, simply enough, is the conviction that we are one human family created and redeemed by God in Jesus Christ; thus social

---

[2] Drew Christiansen, S.J., "On Relative Equality: Catholic Egalitarianism after Vatican II," *Theological Studies* 45 (1984): 674.
[3] Ibid., 652. The quotation from John XXIII is from his 1961 encyclical *Mater et Magistra*, par. 79.

and economic inequalities ought to be held within moral limits set *"by the cardinal norm of communitarian equality with its aim of sustaining and enhancing the bonds uniting people to one another."*[4] We are brothers and sisters to one another and should treat one another in tune with that fact, being ever vigilant about conditions that manifest isolation or exclusion. So "the common good, reconceived in theological terms ... is the image of familial sharing in the banquet of life: Lazarus and the rich man sitting down together at the Lord's table."[5]

Not long after the publication of Christiansen's study, Catholic social teaching further advanced the moral considerations he highlights. In *Economic Justice for All* (1986), the US Catholic Bishops defended a moral norm of justice as participation to govern economic life, relations, and institutions.

> *Basic justice demands the establishment of minimal levels of participation in the life of the human community for all persons.* The ultimate injustice is for a person or group to be treated actively or abandoned passively as if they were nonmembers of the human race.... This can take many forms, all of which can be described as varieties of marginalization, or exclusion from social life.... The poor, the disabled, and the unemployed too often are simply left behind.[6]

A year later, in *Solicitudo Rei Socialis*, Pope John Paul II reflected at length on the virtue of solidarity, which (1) may emerge upon the recognition that our human interdependence is not only a "fact" and a "system" but also a *"moral category"*; (2) is a persevering commitment to the common good – "that is to say to the good of all and of each individual, because we are *all* really responsible for *all*"; (3) categorically excludes the "exploitation, oppression and annihilation of others"; (4) would see the "other," that is, the *neighbor,* "as a sharer, on a par with ourselves, in the banquet of life to which are all equally invited by God."[7] Christian believers in the common fatherhood of God, the brotherhood of Christ, and the life-giving work of the Holy Spirit inspires discernment of "a new *model* of the *unity* of the human race, which must ultimately inspire our *solidarity.*"[8]

---

[4] Ibid., 653–654, italics in text.
[5] Ibid., 675.
[6] US Bishops, *Economic Justice for All* (Washington, DC: National Conference of Catholic Bishops, 1986), par. 77.
[7] *Solicitudo Rei Socialis*, in *Catholic Social Thought: The Documentary Heritage*, ed. David O'Brien and Thomas A. Shannon (Maryknoll, NY: Orbis Books, 2006), 421–423 (par. 38–39), italics in text.
[8] Ibid., 423 (par. 40), italics in text.

The subsequent history of John Paul II's pontificate and that of his successor Benedict XVI continues the appeal to equality, solidarity, and "inclusive sharing in a common quality of life;" in the latter case, we need note only Benedict's 2013 World Day of Peace Message, "Blessed are the Peacemakers." "It is alarming," he writes, "to see hotbeds of tension and conflict caused by growing instances of inequality between rich and poor, by the prevalence of a selfish and individualistic mindset which also finds expression in an unqualified financial capitalism."[9] Recognizing "above all ... that we are, in God, one human family," humanity may seek its peace "principally [in] the attainment of the common good in society at its different levels."[10] The pope emphasizes here not only the defense and promotion of human life, but also the need for economic models of development built on "the principle of gratuitousness as an expression of fraternity and the logic of gift."[11] His proposal for a "pedagogy of peace" includes a "pedagogy of pardon" along with "activity, compassion, solidarity, courage, and perseverance."[12]

It is as important as it is obvious to insist at this point that Francis's social analysis, critique, and moral vision announce no fundamental change in Catholic teaching.[13] He has continued to communicate that teaching in his 2015 encyclical on the environment and "care for our common home," *Laudato Si'*. Citing the Bolivian Bishops in 2012, he stresses that the gravest effects of deterioration of the environment are suffered by the poor; "a true ecological approach *always* becomes a social approach; it must integrate questions of justice in debates on the environment, so as to hear "*both the cry of the earth and the cry of the poor.*"[14] Francis also recurs to the idea of a universal and interdependent family inclusive of all creation, human and nonhuman, while decrying "the enormous inequalities in midst,"

> whereby we continue to tolerate some considering themselves more worthy than others. We fail to see that some are mired in desperate and degrading poverty, with no way out, while others have not the faintest idea of what to do with their possessions, vainly showing off their supposed superiority and leaving behind so much waste which, if it were the case everywhere, would destroy the planet.[15]

---

[9] Benedict XVI, "Blessed are the Peacemakers," at http://w2.vatican.va/content/benedict-xvi/en/messages/peace/documents/hf_ben-xvi_mes_20121208_xlvi-world-day-peace.html, par. 1.
[10] Ibid., par. 3.
[11] Ibid., par. 5.
[12] Ibid., par. 5.
[13] For an alternative perspective, see Chapter 6 of the present volume.
[14] Pope Francis, *Laudato Si'*, at http://w2.vatican.va/content/francesco/en/encyclicals/documents/papa-francesco_20150524_enciclica-laudato-si.html, par. 48–49.
[15] Ibid., par. 90.

Where "growing numbers of people are deprived of human rights and considered expendable, the principle of the common good immediately becomes, logically and inevitably, a summons to solidarity and a preferential option for the poorest of our brothers and sisters."[16] Crucially, he interprets the long-standing Catholic account of the subordination of the right to private property to common destination of the goods of creation, that is, "that the earth is essentially a shared inheritance, whose fruits are meant to benefit everyone," to be "a golden rule of social conduct and 'the first principle of the whole ethical and social order.'"[17] This interpretation echoes what we find earlier in *The Joy of the Gospel*, though with particular reference to the virtue or "mind-set" of solidarity, which is described as "a spontaneous reaction by those who recognize that the social function of property and the universal destination of goods are realities which come before private property" (188, 189).

Thus far I have described the *general* case for "solidaristic equality" as we find it in Christiansen's work and its later expressions. Specific prudential applications, recommended policy proposals, and personal and institutional priorities are matters in which differences and disagreements can and will exist. For example, Christiansen understands his norm of relative equality to lead to a "least difference" criterion, that is, that any decrease in the absolute between lesser and greater entitlements is ipso facto "more equal."[18] One might contrast this with *Economic Justice for All*'s idea that justice demands basic "minimum levels of participation" in communal life. As for what Francis may or may not say on this score, we turn to the second question.

2. Given This Vision of Economic Justice, What Are the Religious and Moral Priorities for Christians "going forth from ourselves towards our brothers and sisters" (179) to Seek Justice and "make the Kingdom of God present in our world" (176)?

Before delivering "the answer," let me say a word about the terms of the question. First, it asks about religious and moral "priorities," and just so is intended to return us to a signature feature of *Economic Justice for All*. In a section entitled "Moral Priorities for the Nation," the letter declares that *"the poor have the single most urgent economic claim on the conscience*

---

[16] Ibid., par. 158.
[17] Ibid., par. 93. Here Francis quotes directly from John Paul II, *Laborem Exercens* (1983), par. 19. See Christiansen, "On Relative Equality," 658–652, for a good discussion of the patristic and more contemporary legacy of this rule.
[18] Christiansen, "On Relative Equality," 667.

of the nation," and that "*the fulfillment of the basic needs of the poor is of the highest priority.*"[19] "Increasing active participation in economic life" by those "excluded" or "vulnerable" takes on a "high social priority."[20] Following that, there is a sharp criticism of social and economic investment producing "luxury consumer goods" and "military technology," rather than directing "wealth, talent, and human energy" to benefit poor or economically insecure fellow citizens.[21] As we shall see, Pope Francis's account of "priorities" in *The Joy of the Gospel* is related to but surely distinct from *Economic Justice for All*'s moral guides to public policy.

Second, the question relies on the sense and image of "going forth." "The word of God," Francis writes, "consistently shows us how God challenges those who believe in him 'to go forth.'" Witness the calls to Abraham, Moses, and Jeremiah, let alone Jesus's own command to "go and make disciples." Christians today are also "to take part in this new missionary 'going forth,' to obey his call to go forth from our own comfort zone in order to reach all the 'peripheries' in need of the light of the Gospel" (20). Ecclesially, Francis wishes for a "missionary impulse" that channels everything that the Church is and does "for the evangelization of today's world rather than for her self-preservation" (27). He encourages each particular Church "to undertake a resolute process of discernment, purification and reform" so that that impulse to proceed "to the outskirts of its own territory or towards new sociocultural settings" may become "ever more, focused, generous, and fruitful" (30). In the case of social ethics or, more precisely, "the social dimension of evangelization" as it makes the Kingdom present by doing justice, Francis similarly envisions going forth "from ourselves," from our constricted need for self-preservation and our cherished "comfort zones" "towards our brothers and sisters" in self-giving love.

3. What Does This Mean?

I think that this very form of a "missionary impulse" *is* for Pope Francis, as he says, "the absolute priority"; it should "ground every moral norm" and be "the clearest sign for discerning spiritual growth in response to God's free gift" (EG 179). From the standpoint of moral and spiritual practice, he mentions two subsidiary "priorities" in the service of this "absolute."

---

[19] *Economic Justice for All*, par. 86, 90, italics in text.
[20] Ibid., par. 90.
[21] Ibid., par. 92.

The Social Vision of *The Joy of the Gospel*

Constructively, Francis first urges that Christians "be docile and attentive to the cry of the poor and to come to their aid.... The old question returns: 'How does God's love abide in anyone who has the world's goods, and sees a brother or sister in need and yet refuses help?' (1 Jn 3:17)." There is a great deal at stake here, as *hearing* the plea of the poor in their need is itself named a "*need* ... born of the liberating action of grace within each of us" in virtue of our life and faith in Jesus Christ, "who became poor, and was always close to the poor and the outcast" (EG 186–188, my italics).

Critically, and second, Christians are exhorted simply to wake up from a faithless, "new self-centered paganism." "Sometimes we prove hard of heart and mind; we are forgetful, distracted and carried away by the limitless possibilities for consumption and distraction offered by contemporary society" (195–196). Correlatively, waking up *from* "ourselves" in our indolence is also awakening *to* the clear, unqualified, and stringent and at the same time healing word "that our mercy to others will vindicate us on the day of God's judgment." We cut off our iniquities by showing mercy to the oppressed, and almsgiving atones for sin as water extinguishes fire (193). "This message is so clear and direct, so simple and eloquent, that no ecclesial interpretation has the right to relativize it.... We should not be concerned simply about falling into doctrinal error, but about remaining faithful to this light-filled path of life and wisdom" taught us in the words and actions of Christ (195).

In short, the message of the gospel is to show "brotherly love" and offer "humble and generous service" in "justice and mercy" toward the poor, the lost, "those whom society discards" (194–195). In union with the God who hears the cry of the poor, Christians do, too. The practical program that Francis lays out includes structural reform, promoting the integral development of the poor, and performing "small daily acts of solidarity in meeting the real needs which we encounter" (188); but that program is rooted in the aforementioned absolute and supporting religious and moral priorities.

Laudato Si' works from and builds upon them. The centrality of the "absolute" comes clear in paragraph 208.

> We are always capable of going out of ourselves towards the other. Unless we do this, other creatures will not be recognized for their true worth; we are unconcerned about caring for things for the sake of others; we fail to set limits on ourselves in order to avoid the suffering of others or the deterioration of our surroundings. Disinterested concerns for others, and the rejection of every form of self-centeredness and self-absorption, are essential if we truly wish to care for our brothers and sisters and for the natural environment. These attitudes also attune us to the moral imperative

of assessing the impact of our every action and personal decision on the world around us.[22]

The ecological crisis that Francis describes in chapter 1 of the encyclical is "a summons to profound interior conversion"; "a more passionate commitment for the protection of our world ... cannot be sustained by doctrine alone," without an "ecological spirituality," an "'interior impulse which encourages, motivates, nourishes and gives meaning to our individual and communal activity."[23] Note Francis's direct quotation of words from paragraph 261 of *The Joy of the Gospel*, which clearly hearkens back to the governing commendation of the "missionary impulse" considered in the preceding text.

The encyclical also returns us to the priorities of "hearing" and "awakening." I have already noted its injunction to heed both the cry of the earth and the cry of the poor. One ground for the conjunction is stressed again and again – that "everything is connected."[24] "The violence present in our hearts ... is also reflected in the symptoms of sickness evident in the soil, in the water, in the air and in all forms of life. This is why the earth herself, burdened and laid waste, is among the most abandoned and maltreated of our poor."[25] Creaturely interdependence extends deeply and thoroughly to include the universe as a whole.[26] "We are faced not with two separate crises, one environmental and the other social, but rather with one complex crisis that is both social and environmental. Strategies for a solution demand an integrated approach to combating poverty, restoring dignity to the excluded, and at the same time protecting nature."[27] And the goal of *understanding* the realities of pollution, climate change, water poverty, the loss of biodiversity, and the like is "to become painfully aware, to dare to turn what is happening in the world into our own personal suffering and thus to discover what each of us can do about it."[28]

As for "awakening" to the social and environmental crisis and its challenges, the encyclical also repeatedly points out "lack of interest," "obstructionist attitudes," "denial," "indifference," "nonchalant resignation," "blind confidence in technical solutions," lack of awareness, the "mental pollution" brought on by digitally induced "overload and confusion," the

---

[22] *Laudato Si'*, par. 208.
[23] Ibid., par. 216–217.
[24] Ibid., par. 91. See also par. 70, 86, 92, and 139.
[25] Ibid., par. 2,
[26] Ibid., par. 86.
[27] Ibid., par. 139.
[28] Ibid., par. 19.

"numbing of conscience," and general strategies of evasiveness, or self-imposed blindness by which sinful human beings "contrive to feed their self-destructive vices." A globally destructive "technocratic paradigm" bent on possession, control, and mastery of "formless" and "external" objects in nature leads human agents to ignore or forget the *realities and accompanying limits* they confront in nature, and the same paradigm in corporate capitalist economy promotes "a whirlwind of buying and selling" that "leads people to believe that they are free as long as they have the supposed freedom to consume."[29] These are the forces and associated dispositions we need to recognize, shake off, and finally awaken from.

In his biography of Pope Francis, Austin Ivereigh reflects on one of a number of similarities he sees between his Jesuit subject and Ignatius of Loyola:

> They share ... a constant attention to spiritual discernment – where is God calling us? What are the temptations and the distractions from this call? – in hours of dawn prayer as well as in reflecting on the most mundane of activities.... For both Ignatius and Francis, radical reform is ultimately about the courage to strip away the accrued layers of distraction to recover what has been lost. It is a going back in order to go forward.[30]

My treatment of the second question has centered on the priorities of "going forth," hearing the cry of the poor and the earth as a direction for where God is calling us today, and awakening from layers of somnolent "distraction." If that account is on the right track, then it may well be that which might first strike one as an improbable or impertinent comparison contains, after all, quite a great deal of truth.

4. As Christians Live in and Live Out a "Missionary Impulse" toward the Poor (and the Earth), What Spiritual Energies, Dispositions, and Forms of Discernment Characterize Their Service for Justice?

The most basic message of the apostolic exhortation is that the Gospel is good news in the deepest possible sense. It is the love of God in Jesus Christ for our liberation to new and authentic life. Hence their *being* in Christ is nothing other than the central source of joy in Christians' lives. But joy as an expression of one's own most being has an infectious quality. "Christians

---

[29] Ibid., par. 14, 30, 47, 49, 59, 106, 109, 203.
[30] Austin Ivereigh, *The Great Reformer: Francis and the Making of a Radical Pope* (New York: Henry Holt, 2014), 55.

have the duty to proclaim the Gospel without excluding anyone. Instead of seeming to impose new obligations, they should appear as people who wish to share their joy, who point to a horizon of beauty and who invite others to a delicious banquet. It is not by proselytizing that the Church grows but 'by attraction'" (EG 15).

The gospel that Christians are called forth bodily to proclaim is, in its true and manifest appearance, beautiful. Francis gives his fullest explication of this idea in a discussion of catechesis.

> Every form of catechesis would do well to attend to the "way of beauty" (*via pulchritudinis*). Proclaiming Christ means showing that to believe in and to follow him is not only something right and true, but also something beautiful, capable of filling life with new splendor and profound joy, even in the midst of difficulties. Every expression of true beauty can thus be acknowledged as a path leading to an encounter with the Lord Jesus. This has nothing to do with fostering an aesthetic relativism which would downplay the inseparable bond between truth, goodness and beauty, but rather a renewed esteem for beauty as a means of touching the human heart and enabling the truth and goodness of the Risen Christ to radiate within it. If, as St. Augustine says, we love only that which is beautiful, the incarnate Son, as the revelation of infinite beauty, is supremely lovable and draws us to himself with bonds of love. (*EG* 167)

Elsewhere in the exhortation the pope makes a similar claim about communicating the gospel in its consummate attractiveness. Evangelization with joy "becomes beauty in the liturgy, as part of our daily concern to spread goodness" (24). In the gospel's "basic core" and "heart," "what shines forth is the beauty of the saving love of God made manifest in Jesus Christ who died and rose from the dead" (36). The homily, then, "far from dealing with abstract truths or cold syllogisms," must communicate "the beauty of the images used by the Lord to encourage the practice of good" (142).

In all these texts Francis seems to presuppose (1) that beauty "is in some sense specific to the modalities of sense, particularly to sight and hearing, or ... to the modalities of sensible appearance of those things said to be beautiful"; (2) that "appearance," and of course the appearance of the gospel we would communicate, is not merely "cosmetic" or external to truth and goodness, but is "the shining forth of the thing's nature"; and (3) that (and here recall his appeal to a Augustine in a neoplatonic moment) the good to be loved (erotically) is integrally involved with what we are attracted to.[31]

---

[31] I draw here from a marvelous study by Aryeh Kosman, "Beauty and the Good: Situating the *Kalon*," *Classical Philology* 105 (2010): 354–356.

The upshot is a straightforward rejection of "aesthetic relativism" and, more importantly, the strong (and characteristically but not exclusively Catholic) suggestion that the beautiful, "as the intentional object of proper desire ... governs our moral life."[32]

In summary, our going forth from ourselves to others in joy may not only prompt eager human interest; the beauty of the gospel may yet elicit the love of it. Christian "missionary zeal" is for the sake of "rhetoric" in the best sense, that is, getting the point across, communicating the beauty of the gospel, the beauty of life in Christ, joyfully."[33]

But we do not and cannot do that if we are self-absorbed, indifferent, "deadened" to the cry of the poor by our "culture of prosperity," and the like (54).

In the case at hand, we may embody new life, as we have already noted in the preceding text, by acknowledging the extent to which we share and sustain a lifestyle that excludes others, and by refusing to cloud over – in the many ways we so cunningly can – something "so simple and eloquent" as the claim that it is by the works of justice and mercy that we will be judged. "We may not always be able to reflect adequately the beauty of the Gospel, but there is one sign which we should never lack: the option for those who are least" (EG 194–195). Third, beyond programs and specific practices of promotion and assistance, Christians need to nurture what Francis describes as an "attentiveness which considers the other in a certain sense at one with ourselves," and with that an appreciation of the poor in their goodness, experience, culture, and faith. True love has a "contemplative" character that permits us to serve another "not out of necessity or vanity, but rather because he or she is beautiful above and beyond mere appearances" (199).

The distinction between apprehending the authentic beauty of the poor and moving past "mere appearances" works to confirm my analysis in the preceding text. Aside from that, I believe that Francis's brief but rich reflection on beauty, attentiveness, communion, and love is especially significant because it points to a spiritual stance he deems constitutive of service, one of *encounter, dialogue,* and, within both, *"being in the heart of the people."*[34]

---

[32] Ibid., 356.
[33] Note Kosman's situating a certain sense of the beautiful, captured in the Platonic and Aristotelian category of the *kalon*, within a "rhetoric of being," "the realm of being's presentation to our subjective awareness." Ibid., 354.
[34] EG, 273. The following explication of this spiritual stance is informed by Ivereigh's discussion of related themes. See *The Great Reformer*, 110–117, 141–143, 183–184, 213–216.

A posture and, socially considered, a culture of *encounter* (220) rules out exclusion in its many forms, including discarding and ignoring others in their vulnerability and need. Positively, encounter means engaging the neighbor in his or her lives and struggles. The gospel "tells us constantly to run the risk of face-to-face encounter with others, with their physical presence which challenges us, with their pain and their pleas, with their joy which infects us in our close and continuous interaction" (88). We "accept and esteem them as companions along the way"; "better yet," we are "learning to find Jesus in the faces of others, in their voices, in their pleas" (91). Encounter in this eminently concrete sense, rooted in personal encounter with Jesus Christ (e.g., 264) and prompting discovery of the neighbor's beauty, "is what makes the authentic option for the poor differ from any other ideology, from any attempt to exploit the poor for one's own personal or political interest. Only on the basis of this real and sincere closeness can we properly accompany the poor on their path of liberation" (199).

Commitment to and involvement in *dialogue* "as a form of encounter" (239; cf. 238ff.). Pope Francis/Jorge Mario Bergoglio's theology of the "*pueblo fiel*," the "holy people of God," can be said to feature this spiritual moment. Austin Ivereigh explains, while sketching the development of this vision in Argentina in the 1970s with special reference to its "pioneer," theologian Lucio Gera, and to Bergoglio's own "mission" as Jesuit Provincial:

> Who is *el pueblo*? ... Gera defined it in terms of the despised and marginalized majority, from which whom comes the desire for justice and peace. For Gera, *el pueblo* is an active agent in history, not, as liberals and Marxists view it, a passive mass needing to be made aware. "The people have a rationality." Wrote Gera. "They have their project; we don't give it to them." The role of theologian was not to impose categories, he argued, but to interpret the people's project in light of its salvation history....
>
> ... In the idea of "God's holy faithful people" Bergoglio had what theologians call a hermeneutic – an interpretive key, or yardstick – that would allow him to reform and unite the province, beyond ideology, by focusing very directly on the poor ... he did not believe that the clergy, or the bishops, or Rome were in possession of the truth that they distributed downwards, but that the Holy Spirit was revealed through a dialogue between the *pueblo fiel* and the universal Church.[35]

In *The Joy of the Gospel*, Francis stresses two conditions for this dialogue (122). One is taking seriously the *historical agency* of the poor. "In their

---

[35] Ibid., 112–113. Ivereigh cites the source in Gera to be "Cultura y dependencia, a la luz de la reflexion teologica," *Stromata*, Ano XXX (January–June 1974), no. 1/2.

daily lives people must often struggle for survival and this struggle contains within it a profound understanding of life which often includes a deep religious sense. We must examine this more closely in order to enter into a dialogue like that of the Lord and the Samaritan woman at the well where she sought to quench her thirst" (72). Indeed, "in their difficulties" the poor know "the suffering Christ" (198). The other condition is welcoming the *culture* and *popular piety* of the marginalized, their "ways of living the faith" (199). The pope praises Paul VI for giving a "decisive impulse in this area" when he writes in *Evangelii Nuntiandi* that popular piety "manifests a thirst for God which only the poor and simple can know"[36] (123). Francis adds that "[u]nderlying popular piety, as a fruit of the inculturated Gospel, is an active evangelizing power which we must not underestimate" (125–126). It follows that "we" who may and must have a dialogue with the poor "need to let ourselves be evangelized by them. The new evangelization is an invitation to acknowledge the saving power at work in their lives and to put them at the center of Church's pilgrim way" (198).[37]

Encounter and dialogue both require and develop a lively recognition "that we are a people," which generates a spiritual "savour" or "taste for being close to people's lives.... Mission is at once a passion for Jesus and a passion for his people.... He takes us from the midst of his people and sends us to his people; without this sense of belonging we cannot understand our deepest identity" (268). Our *"being in the heart of the people"* follows and is moved by Jesus's example; we want "to enter into the reality of other people's lives and know the power of tenderness" (270). One does not so much have this mission; one *is* this mission, this *"being."* "But once we separate our work from our private lives, everything turns grey and we will always be seeking recognition or asserting our needs. We stop being a people" (273).

In *Laudato Si'*, the option for the poor, as shown in the preceding text, continues to be prominent. Ideas of beauty, encounter, dialogue, and the "spiritual savour of being a people" may be said to play a background,

---

[36] Paul VI, *Evangelii Nuntiandi* (1975), at http://w2.vatican.va/content/paul-vi/en/apost_exhortations/documents/hf_p-vi_exh_19751208_evangelii-nuntiandi.html, par. 48.
[37] *The Joy of the Gospel* also discusses the theme dialogue in contexts other than what is treated here. See, e.g., 132–134, 137–138, 140–144, 238–258. Francis also asks God "to give us more politicians capable of sincere and effective dialogue aimed at healing the deepest ... of the evils in our world!" (205). One can reasonably argue that the pope's strong words against "trickle down" economics (54) and "the invisible hand of the market" (204) are first of all aimed at *ideology* that all too confidently and no doubt evasively resist the sort of dialogue he commends. On this point, consider Ivereigh, 213–214, and John L. Allen, Jr, *The Francis Miracle* (New York: Time Books, 2015), 146–148.

regulative role. Surely nothing in the encyclical is at odds with them. In addition, the letter does make a few telling appeals with ecological resonance. For example, the pope writes:

> By learning to see and appreciate beauty, we learn to reject self-interested pragmatism. If someone has not learned to stop and admire something beautiful, we should not be surprised if he or she treats everything as an object to be used and abused without scruple.[38]

The "mental pollution" that Francis decries is explicitly cited as impeding the acquisition of "true wisdom, as the fruit of self-examination, dialogue, and generous encounter between persons."[39] Also, Francis takes the lack of awareness and "numbing of conscience" about how environmental degradation damages the "excluded" to be "due partly to the fact that many professionals, opinion makers, communications media and centers of power ... are far removed from the poor, with little direct contact with their problems," that is, to the "lack of physical contact and encounter."[40] It is important not to overlook, moreover, that the entirety of *Laudato Si'* is framed in terms of the author's urgent appeal "for a new dialogue to protect our common home," "a conversation that which includes everyone, since the environmental challenge we are undergoing, and its human roots, concern and affect us all.... We require a new and universal solidarity."[41] Finally, the spirit and the logic of "being in the heart of the people," a logic, that is, of entering into and truly sharing the reality of others and hence knowing the power of tenderness, is extended to include all of creation. "Ecological conversion ... entails a loving awareness that we are not disconnected from the rest of creatures, but joined in a splendid universal communion. As believers, we do not look at the world from without but from within, conscious of the bonds with which the Father has linked us to all beings."[42] To illustrate this "sublime communion," Francis is pleased to repeat a passage from *The Joy of the Gospel*: "God has joined us so closely to the world around us that we can feel desertification of the soil almost as a physical ailment, and the extinction of a species as a painful disfigurement" (215).[43]

---

[38] *Laudato Si'*, par. 215.
[39] Ibid.,
[40] Ibid., par. 49.
[41] Ibid., par. 14. See also par. 163–201.
[42] Ibid., par. 220.
[43] Ibid., par. 89. For more on "ecological conversion," cf. par. 220–232.

5. Given the Differences, Disagreements, and Conflicts That Would Separate or Divide Human Persons, How Do We Move Forward in Building a People Seeking Together a Common Good in Peace, Justice, and Fraternity?

Moving forward depends on four "principles" that are derived from the "pillars of the Church's social doctrine." They are "related to constant tensions present in every social reality" (*EG* 221).

Recall that recognition that we *are* a "people" emerges through encounter and dialogue. Thus Francis argues that to *become* a people devoted to its common good requires an ongoing, intergenerational "process" driven by a "desire for integration" and the will "to achieve this through the growth of a peaceful and multifaceted culture of encounter" (220). One must accept "the tension between fullness and limitation," between "complete possession" of the final cause or ideal that "draws us to itself" and the limited moment in which the good is sought (222). Francis associates "fullness" with "time," the circumscribed moment with "space," and writes that the first principle is that *"time is greater than space."* Giving priority to time is to stay the course to a shared life patiently and purposively "without being obsessed with immediate results ... which yield easy, quick short-term political gains, but do not enhance human fullness." When space is decisive, processes directed toward authentic human existence are "crystallized" through the attempt "to possess all the spaces of power and self-assertion" (*EG* 222–224). Implicit in this principle is a critique of bureaucratic and other narrowly political practices that subordinate encounter, inclusion, and development for the common good to gaining advantages within an ever-contested and normatively unmoored balance of power. Francis invokes this principle explicitly in *Laudato Si'*:

> A politics concerned with immediate results, supported by consumerist sectors of the population, is driven to pursue short-term growth. In response to electoral interests, governments are reluctant to upset the public with measures which could affect the level of consumption or create risks for foreign investment. The myopia of power politics delays the inclusion of a far-sighted environmental agenda within the overall agenda of governments. Thus we forget that "time is greater than space," that we are always more effective when we generate processes rather than holding on to positions of power.[44]

---

[44] *Laudato Si'*, par. 178.

Francis hardly denies, however, that building a community constitutively involves reckoning with contestation, conflict, and power. "Conflict cannot be ignored or concealed," but if we stay trapped in it, our moral and spiritual horizons "shrink" (226). Facing conflict over how to live together "head on," persons may be able to build "communion amid disagreement" so long as they are "are willing to go beyond the surface of the conflict and see others in their deepest dignity" (227–228). Yet *that* clear-sightedness requires acknowledging a second principle: *"unity is greater than conflict."* The promise of peace in unity given in Jesus Christ offers the possibility of persons' achieving a "reconciled diversity" that is neither the absorption of difference nor a "negotiated settlement"; it is rather "a resolution that takes place on a higher plane and preserves what is valid and useful on both sides" (EG 228–230). Again, we find this principle employed in the encyclical letter.

> Politics and the economy tend to blame each other when it comes to poverty and environmental degradation. It is to be hoped that they can acknowledge their own mistakes and find forms of interaction directed to the common good. While some are concerned only with financial gain, and others with holding to or increasing their power, what we are left with are conflicts or spurious agreements where the last thing either party is concerned about is caring for the environment and protecting those who are most vulnerable. Here, too, we see how true it is that "unity is greater than conflict."[45]

Returning to *Evangelii Gaudium*, a third tension is "between ideas and realities." A "continuous dialogue" between the two is necessary, "lest ideas become detached from realities"; for – *"realities are more important than ideas."* Concepts and conceptions must always be "at the service of communication, understanding, and praxis" (EG 232). The pope warns against a "mere rhetoric" of "pure ideas" estranged from being. He rejects "the various means of masking reality," including "angelic forms of purity, dictatorships of relativism, objectives more ideal than real, empty rhetoric, brands of ahistorical fundamentalism, ethical systems bereft of kindness, intellectual discourse bereft of wisdom." The principle of reality is that of "a word already made flesh and constantly striving to make flesh anew" (EG 231–233). While urging "an open and respectful dialogue ... between the various ecological movements" in *Laudato Si'*, Pope Francis allows that among such movements "ideological conflicts are not infrequently encountered. The gravity of the ecological crisis demands that we look

[45] Ibid., par. 198.

The Social Vision of *The Joy of the Gospel*

to the common good, embarking on a path of dialogue which demands patience, self-discipline and generosity, always keeping in mind that 'realities are greater than ideas.'"[46]

Finally, social life consists of a fourth tension between "globalization and localization." Looking beyond the confines of our particular neighborhoods, persons are tempted to an abstract, consumerist combination of aestheticism and conformity. We fall "into step behind everyone else, admiring the glitter of other people's worlds, gaping and applauding at all the right times." Staying too close to home, we risk contentment with "a museum of local folklore, a world apart" without novelty and immune to "the beauty which God bestows beyond [our] borders." Living within the tension may prevent us from falling within one or the other extreme, as we "sink our roots deeper" into our native place, but do so with a broader view "to the greater good which benefits us all." To do that well, we recognize – principle four – that *"the whole is greater than the part"* but also "greater than the sum of its parts." "The global need not stifle, nor the particular prove barren" in a lived history of building a "convergence of peoples who, within the universal order, maintain their own individuality" (EG 234–236). The pope does not refer us to this guideline in the letter on the environment. Something like it, however, appears to be in play when he warns that a "consumerist vision of human beings, encouraged by the mechanisms of today's globalized economy, has a leveling effect on cultures" and insists that, in contrast, care for our common home "demands the constant and active involvement of local people *from within their proper culture.*"[47]

Generally speaking, how are we to understand the four principles? Ivereigh argues persuasively that for Francis they are "a kind of sapiential wisdom captured in a series of criteria for discernment" that work together to resist one-sided ideologies and the domination of a "people" by "elites" of any stripe.[48] Let me conclude this section, and this essay, with a brief ecumenical comment and analysis that follows Ivereigh's lead in a complementary way.

In a classic chapter from his classic 1932 study of *Moral Man and Immoral Society*, Reinhold Niebuhr addressed the topic of "The Preservation of Moral Values in Politics."[49] He argued for a "Christian realism" that denied

---

[46] Ibid., par. 201, citing EG, 231.
[47] Ibid., par. 144
[48] Ivereigh, *The Great Reformer*, 142. Note also the very brief but informative account of the history and sources of the four norms, 142–143
[49] Reinhold Niebuhr, *Moral Man and Immoral Society* (New York: Charles Scribner's Sons, 1932), 231–256.

that political and social life is a morally blind power struggle, and that commended an equal justice practically favoring those who are vulnerable and disempowered. For this great Protestant theologian, conflict was constitutive of collective life; but he insisted also that the law of life normatively is the law of love. Accordingly, human beings in Christian vision are created for and ordered to unity. Niebuhr also criticized naïve and sentimental sorts of Christian idealism that projected, we can say in light of the foregoing, "angelic forms of purity," and "objectives more ideal than real" upon political existence.

Niebuhr does not consider the tension between "globalization" and "localization" as such. But that does not matter for our purposes. His consideration of the tensive relation between moral fulfillment and power, fellowship and conflict, and reality and idea invites the suggestion that Francis's four principles represent a parallel and distinctively Roman Catholic account of the conditions for preserving moral, and just so authentically human, values in public life. They work out of characteristic Catholic frameworks of teleology, an ethic and spirituality of the virtues, humanity as a universal family, incarnational realism, and the common good. In keeping with its missionary call to forging, through encounter, dialogue, and a nonnegotiable option for the poor, a people in solidaristic equality, *The Joy of the* Gospel thus resists the reduction of a people's being, becoming, and flourishing to collective self-assertion and a "fetishism of immediate, visible results";[50] of hope for unity to a divisive cynicism; of the reality of praxis under God to abstract evasion and illusion; and of genuine community to either life unrooted or a life buried in silos underground.

---

[50] Thomas Merton, *Passion for Peace* (New York: Crossroad Publishing Company, 2006), 98.

CHAPTER 8

Taking on the "Smell of the Sheep"

Racial Justice in the Missionary Key of *Evangelii Gaudium*

Maureen O'Connell

Evangelli Gaudium might be the best document that we have to date in Catholic Social Teaching for animating racial justice work.[1] It is particularly helpful for those of us living in the United States where racial difference irrefutably fuels the economic disparity with which Pope Francis is so concerned and where the lingering legacy of white supremacy sustains the "globalization of indifference"[2] he compels us to interrupt. I root my optimism in a tactile, sensorial image of evangelization that Francis invokes early in the document: "An evangelizing community gets involved by word and deed in people's daily lives; it bridges distances, it is willing to abase itself if necessary, and it embraces human life, touching the suffering flesh of Christ in others," explains the pope. "Evangelizers thus take on the 'smell of the sheep' and the sheep are willing to hear their voice. An evangelizing community is also supportive, standing by people at every step of the way, no matter how difficult or lengthy this may prove to be."[3]

In what follows I will offer three points to unpack the potential of this significant image of "taking on the smell of the sheep" for understanding racial justice work as constitutive of evangelization. First, Francis's embodied identity as the first Euro-American pope offers a much-needed site for raising historical consciousness about the role of religion in the racing of the peoples of the Americas, as well as an opportunity to name

---

[1] For comprehensive overview of Catholic Social Teaching on racism, particularly in the American context, see Bryan Massingale, *Racial Justice and the Catholic Church* (Maryknoll, NY: Orbis, 2010).
[2] Pope Francis, *EG*, §54.
[3] *EG*, §24.

the enduring and embodied legacy of whiteness as a theological problem. Second, his description of the global economy as reflective of a culture of exclusion squarely places racially driven economic inequality in the United States at the forefront of responding to the gospel message of love and lifts up culturally particular responses to it as viable alternatives. Third, his emphasis on mercy as the proper response to individual and collective sinfulness provides a viable affective form of resistance to the "acedia" of white supremacy. I conclude by raising a concern about the biblical text shaping the pope's missionary vision for evangelization in an increasingly racialized global community, all of which might spark further engagement of his text for folks taking up the work of racial justice in the United States.

1. Francis Is "White Like Me"

First, Pope Francis's physical body and cultural heritage cannot be separated from the words he writes and speaks, and even more importantly those he acts. While the significance of his South American roots and choice to live and work among the poor in one of that continent's biggest and poorest cities has been much celebrated, Francis is the first *Euro-American* pope. In other words, he is "white like me," to use a phrase that Christian critical race theorist Tim Wise invokes when attempting to raise race consciousness among fellow whites who often enjoy the privilege of moving through social spaces impervious to privileges and advantages afforded us by virtue of our white skins.[4] As such, Francis cannot transcend a complicated and ugly history of colonial imperialism – economic, political, cultural, ecclesial – that systematically disadvantaged people with dark skin, whether in the genocide and forced labor of Amerindians or the enslavement of Africans brought to the Americas at very outset of our current global economy. This violently unjust history has been justified by a "racial frame"[5] of Christian white supremacy, which racially categorized the indigenous and enslaved peoples of Francis's home continent as well as our own, and

---

[4] Tim Wise, *White Like Me: Reflections on Race from a Privileged Son* (Brooklyn, NY: Soft Skull Press, 2005).

[5] Joe Feagin understands whiteness as a way of "framing," or "unifying perceptions that help with cognition and understanding" with varying levels of intentionality. He roots white supremacy in the dominance of the centuries-old "white racial frame," which draws on the twin pillars of negative ideas, emotions, and images of African Americans, and positive ideas, emotions, and images about whites and white institutions. See, *The White Racial Frame: Centuries of Racial Framing and Counter-Framing* (New York: Routledge, 2009), 93. The frame is aggressively proposed and defended by whites, and internalized by many other racial groups.

which continues to inform social perceptions of racial difference and organize society according to racial preferences.

By a frame of "Christian" supremacy, I mean the dispositions and practices, both individual and collective, that position Christianity over and against other religions, initially Judaism and later the religions of the Americas, Africa, and Asia, and in turn posit Christians, most notably white or European Christians, as intellectually, morally, and culturally superior persons.[6] By a frame of "white supremacy" I mean the dispositions and behaviors that reflect and defend the normativity and superiority of white experience[7]; justify continued racial inequality by assessing people of color as culturally or morally deficient[8]; motivate weak commitments to racial justice through inflated notions of white innocence and moral goodness[9]; and shape encounters with racially different others with the twin responses of fear and guilt.[10] Several critical race theorists contend that the former, Christian supremacy, provided the historical platform for the latter, white supremacy.[11] As such Karen Teel notes "'whiteness is a properly and peculiarly white Christian theological problem that demands a white theological response.'"[12]

If people of European decent in the Western Hemisphere pay attention to the way that Francis is "white like us," then it becomes more difficult to dismiss the problem of whiteness, contained in the very history of Pope Francis's native Argentina, a history that continues to drive the

---

[6] See J. Kameron Carter, *Race: A Theological Account* (New York: Oxford University Press, 2008); Willie Jennings, *The Christian Imagination: Theology and the Origins of Race* (New Haven, CT: Yale University Press, 2011); and James Perkinson, *White Theology: Outing Supremacy in Modernity* (New York: Palgrave Macmillan, 2004).

[7] See Peggy McIntosh's now classic "White Privilege: Unpacking the Invisible Knapsack," http://www.amptoons.com/blog/files/mcintosh.html. See also Wise, *White Like Me*.

[8] Assumptions of the intellectual, moral, and cultural inferiority of people and communities of color is a central component of what Joe R. Feagin calls the "white racial frame," which he unpacks in *The White Racial Frame: Centuries of Racial Framing and Counter-Framing* (New York: Routledge, 2009).

[9] See Barbara Applebaum, *Being White Being Good: White Complicity, Moral Responsibility, and Social Justice Pedagogy* (Lexington, KY: Lexington Books, 2011).

[10] George Yancy, *Black Bodies, White Gazes: The Continuing Significance of Race* (Lanham, MD: Rowman and Littlefield Publishers, 2008).

[11] I am grateful to work of Jeannine Hill Fletcher in bringing her work on feminist approaches to interreligious dialogue to bear on the racial dimensions of kyriarchy in our engagement with the religious "other" in "Warrants for Reconstruction: Christian Hegemony, White Supremacy." Working paper, Department of Theology, Fordham University, New York, 2014. See also Carter, *Race: A Theological Account*; and Joseph Barndt, *Becoming an Anti-Racist Church: Journeying toward Wholeness* (Minneapolis, MN: Augsburg Fortress, 2011).

[12] Karen Teel, "What Jesus Wouldn't Do," in *Christology and Whiteness: What Would Jesus Do*, ed. George Yancy (New York: Routledge, 2012), 19–35 at 20.

economic disparity that limits possibilities for flourishing of people of color of the Americas. Consider, for example, that Francis hails from a region of Argentina that was the first port of entry for tens of thousands of African slaves as early as the sixteenth century[13] and a city whose population was at least one-third African by the early 1800s. In fact, black slaves built and maintained the largest Jesuit mission property in the Americas during the seventeenth century, and represented 65 percent of troops in the army that fought for independence from Spain between 1810 and 1818. And yet in a 2010 census, Afro-Argentines represented less than half of 1 percent of the population.[14] In short, our first Euro-American pope hails from what many to consider the most "European" or white of the countries in Latin and South America, a reality that belies the vibrant indigenous culture of nineteen different peoples that flourished prior to the arrival of the Spanish in 1536 and the contributions of a "forcibly indigenized"[15] Afro-Argentinian population from the sixteenth through nineteenth centuries, as well as the experiences of more recent arrivals, either from the African continent or from other countries that comprise the African Diaspora in South America.[16]

Attention to the "whiteness" of the new pope's identity might allow similarities between Francis's Argentina and Euro-American Catholics' United States to come into better focus when considering the construction and ongoing maintenance of racial hierarchies in the Americas. For example, both countries were colonized at the burgeoning of our global economy

---

[13] David Eltis et al., *Atlas of the Transatlantic Slave Trade* (New Haven, CT: Yale University Press, 2010).

[14] See Rachel DeCoste, "Why Are There So Few Black Men on the Argentina Football Team?," *Huffington Post*, July 9, 2014, http://www.huffingtonpost.ca/rachel-decoste/argentina-world-cup-_b_5571761.html?view=print&comm_ref=false; and Josh Ghosh, "Blackout: How Argentian 'Eliminated' Africans from Its Historical and Consciousness," *International Business Times*, June 4, 2013, http://www.ibtimes.com/blackout-how-argentina-eliminated-africans-its-history-conscience-1289381.

[15] I encountered this term through Jeannine Hill Fletcher's work with Stephen Ray's "Contending for the Cross: Black Theology and the Ghosts of Modernity," *Black Theology: An International Journal* 8(1) (2010): 53–68.

[16] Scholars currently debate the reasons for the absence of African decedents in the contemporary landscape along genocidal, whitening, and invisibility trajectories, all of which surface evidence of a European rejection the dignity of persons of African descent in Argentina and a preference for lighter-skinned Europeans. See Patricia D. Fox, *Being and Blackness in Latin America: Uprootedness and Improvisation* (Gainesville: University of Florida Press, 2006); George Reid Andrews, *The Afro-Argentines of Buenos Aires: 1800–1900* (Madison: University of Wisconsin Press, 1980); Martin A. Lewis, *Afro-Argentine Discourse: Another Dimension of the Black Diaspora* (Columbia: University of Missouri Press, 1995); Donald S. Castro, *The Afro-Argentine in Argentine Culture: El Negro Del Acordeon* (Lewiston, NY: Edwin Mellen Press, 2001).

that bound nations, colonies, and peoples around the Atlantic in the trade of 12.5 million Africans, and during the Enlightenment age that privileged Anglo-Saxon ways of knowing and being, and law and government.[17] The accumulation of wealth in both countries depended upon violent acquisition of resources of indigenous peoples and the slave labor of indigenous and forcibly indigenous populations, and was consolidated in the white hands of owners of land, people, and industry. Both countries embraced what Charles Mills calls a "racial contract," a political and moral social arrangement created by whites, which justified race-based discrimination in the name of "securing the privileges and advantages of the full white citizens and maintaining the subordination of nonwhites," and which continues to require "a certain schedule of structured blindness and opacities in order to establish and maintain white polity."[18] The Christianity that flourished in both countries initially participated in all of this – we have, for example, historical records of Jesuit slave owning in both countries[19] – and for the most part failed to take up these contradictions and social inequalities that result from them. Bloodlines in both countries historically privileged whiteness, shaped perceptions of social status, and determined access to social goods: the "one drop rule" in the United States rendered whites with African lineage as black, whereas in Argentina European bloodlines render Afro-Argentines as white even today. A "melting pot" national identity and ideology, which privileges the nineteenth- and twentieth-century European immigrant experience in both countries, assumes there is nothing of cultural import from indigenous or forcibly indigenized peoples, or simply ignores their contributions.[20]

While it might be too much for us to expect the pope to speak directly to this history and its unfolding effects, philosopher George Yancy reminds us that we carry these histories in our bodies because racism is always mediated in and through bodies and experienced in the "quotidian, everyday level of social transaction."[21] For people of color, racism often means experiencing one's body as a "battleground" where one constantly mediates the projections of whites, which are necessary in order for whites to sustain our frames of superiority and are dependent on historically constructed

---

[17] Kelly Brown Douglas, *Stand Your Ground: Black Bodies and the Justice of God* (Maryknoll, NY: Orbis Books, 2015), 3–47.
[18] Charles Mills, *The Racial Contract* (Ithaca, NY: Cornell University Press, 1997), 14 and 19.
[19] Thomas Murphy, *Jesuit Slave Owning in Maryland: 1717–1838* (New York: Routledge, 2001).
[20] Fox, *Being and Blackness in Latin America*, 3. C.f., also the revelations concerning the complicity of Georgetown University in the slave trade as detailed in The Report of the Working Group on Slavery, Memory, and Reconciliation, Washington, D.C., 2016 available at http://slavery.georgetown.edu/report.
[21] George Yancy, *Black Bodies White Gazes: The Continuing Significance of Race* (Lanham, MD: Rowman and Littlefield Publishers, 2008).

understandings of black bodies as unlawful, unintelligent, and hypersexualized. "I am that premarked Black *thing*," notes Yancy, "Within the context of white North America, before I am born, my body's meaning has been defined by those historically embedded racist practices, discourses, and institutional forces that often remain invisible."[22]

For white people like myself and the pope, the somatic experiences of racism in everyday social exchanges mean to experience our racial identity as an invisible or inconsequential facet of our self of sense or our ways of making meaning. It is to be impervious as to the ways in which our bodies participate in an ongoing performative narrative that denies the full humanity of people who do not look like us (clutching purses, crossing streets, or locking car doors as men of color approach; politely tolerating racialized jokes; policing our interactions for political correctness; harboring thoughts of superiority; denying that we "see color") and to be beneficiaries of systems (employment, education, judicial, health care, housing, etc.) that perceive us and our bodies as normative or that against which all other bodies must be measured or that through which other experiences must be filtered. As Teel puts it, "to be white to is have unbelievable power, power that is unearned and undeserved and unjust, and, typically, to be virtually unaware of it."[23]

If attention to Francis's white body exposes the problem of whiteness, then it also reveals possible ways of taking up this problem, particularly in and through evangelization as he understands it. While *Evangelii Gaudium* does not speak directly to racism, his attention to cultural distinctiveness and the inculturation of the gospel provides important insights for resisting the dominance of whiteness in the Americas. For example, he explicitly rejects the normativity of European experience when he notes, "We cannot demand that peoples of every continent, in expressing their Christian faith, imitate modes of expression which European nations developed at a particular moment of their history, because the faith cannot be constricted to the limits of understanding and expression of any one culture."[24] By naming popular piety or the people's mysticism as "a *locus theologicus* which demands our attention,"[25] Francis reminds theologians: "We would not do justice to the logic of the incarnation if we thought of Christianity as monocultural and monotonous." He goes on to say that the variety of cultures within the church "reflect the beauty of her varied face."[26] Perhaps

[22] Ibid., 26.
[23] Teel, "What Jesus Wouldn't Do," 21.
[24] *EG*, §117.
[25] *EG*, §126.
[26] *EG*, §116–117.

Taking on the "Smell of the Sheep"

a reflection of his Ignatian sensibilities, which trusts in finding God in all things or is animated by a missionary zeal to go to the periphery, this pope does not seem to be fearful of difference.

Through his confidence in inculturation, Francis explicitly resists a monolithic European Christianity, and implicitly rejects the historical white washing of history and flattening out of cultural distinctiveness that comes with a narrow Euro-American[27] racial frame. Critical race theorists continue to identify the wisdom, dispositions, and practices of distinct cultures, as well as the kind of bonding social capital generated by multicultural communities, as antidotes to white supremacy.[28] In this way, Francis's call to evangelization in and through culture can be easily translated into an invitation to perceive and resist a monolithic and empty culture of whiteness. For example, African American theologian William Jennings calls Christians to take up the "imaginative capacity to redefine the social, to claim, to embrace, to join, to desire" – practices generally rejected in white culture but embraced in more multicultural ways of knowing and being.[29] Furthermore, cultural distinctiveness has long provided bodies of color – individual and collective, physical and symbolic – an antibody for the dehumanizing pathologies of white supremacy. We might use Francis's celebration of cultural distinctiveness to recover a variety of ethnic mysticisms lost to the North American indigenous and immigrant church in the process of assimilation to white culture. Francis's attention to the inculturation of the gospel might help Catholics who share his European lineage to reject the arbitrary binaries of whiteness or blackness and illuminate instead a far more multivalent and adaptable context and character of multiculturalism. He notes that it is in the beauty of the varied face of the inculturation of the gospel that its message becomes most alluring and most attractive.

Moreover, that *Evangelii Gaudium* reflects a "broad" understanding of evangelization as white theologian Avery Dulles explains it, with a more subtle focus on unbelievers or nonbelievers than that of his immediate predecessors, might also temper the explicit superiority of Catholicism that has historically worked in tandem with the superiority of whiteness to justify oppression of the racial and religious other in our contemporary

---

[27] Reference is frequently made to "Euro-North American" mind-sets and cultural biases. Here I speak of Euro-American to include those other parts of the Americas where such prejudices exert influence, too, specifically in terms of issues of racism and inclusion.

[28] See practical examples in J. Love Calderon and Marcella Runell Hall, *Love, Race and Liberation: Til the White Day Is Done* (New York: Love-N-Liberation Press, 2010).

[29] Jennings, *The Christian Imagination*, 6.

reality.[30] In Francis's estimation, for example, it is not unbelievers that present the greatest threat to the vitality of the faith, but rather a lack of zeal within the Christian community. Moreover, he understands dialogue as a kind of encounter, and one that must be inclusive and oriented toward peace: "It is time to devise a means for building consensus and agreement while seeking the goal of a just, responsive and inclusive society," he notes. "The principal author, the historic subject of this process, is the people as a whole and their culture, and not a single class, minority, group or elite. We do not need plans drawn up by a few for the few, or an enlightened or outspoken minority which claims to speak for everyone. It is about agreeing to live together, a social and cultural pact."[31]

In short, if we agree with the pope's claim that local cultures provide an undeniable locus for theological reflection, then his physical Euro-Argentine embodiment provides the possibility for reflecting on a history of the social construction of race, the Church's involvement with this, and its contemporary implications for global economies, which disproportionately exclude people of color.[32] Again, while none of this is immediately operative in the document, the first apostolic exhortation by the first Euro-American pope provides an important opportunity to consider his words in the context of his socially constructed embodiment and, in so doing, brings new levels of meaning to them. In other words, becoming aware of his embodiment might enable those who are white like him to ask ourselves: What it might mean to "take on the smell of the sheep"[33] when that odor is infused with the social suffering caused by the superiority awarded him and other Euro-Americans because our lighter-colored and thereby more desirable wool?

2. Color-blind Racism as Sustaining Economic Exclusion in the United States

According to Francis, "Inequality is the root of social ills."[34] Just as his physical body provides a site for taking up the problem of whiteness, Francis's simple assertion that economic inequality fuels the vast majority of our

[30] Avery Dulles, "Vatican II and Evangelization," in *The New Evangelization: Overcoming the Obstacles*, ed. Steven Boguslawski, OP, and Ralph Martin (New York: Paulist Press, 2008), 1–12.
[31] EG, §239.
[32] Sentiments further underlined by the implications of Francis's statements about the exploitation of Africa during his in-flight press conference following his 2015 trip to Africa.
[33] Ibid., §24.
[34] Ibid., §202.

social problems creates an irrefutable causal link between poverty and racism in the United States, particularly in light of the new dimension he brings to the Catholic social tradition's ongoing conversion about poverty: exclusion. "Exclusion ultimately has to do with what it means to be a part of the society in which we live; those excluded are no longer society's underside or its fringes or its disenfranchised – they are no longer even a part of it. The excluded are not the 'exploited' but the outcast, the 'leftovers.'"[35] That he describes poverty in terms of "exclusion" aptly captures the reality of racial inequality in the United States because racial difference fuels economic inequality. Francis's focus on the economically excluded, as well as the dynamics with fuel their exclusion, requires that American Catholics turn and face the harsh reality that the #BlackLivesMatter movement began to lift up in August 2015 after the shooting dead of African American Michael Brown by white police officer Darren Wilson in Ferguson, Missouri: that people of color in the United States disproportionately experience the exclusion that comes with various forms of poverty now affecting more than one in five of all Americans.

In anticipation of the fiftieth anniversary of the passage of the Civil Rights Act in on July 2, 1964, the *Huffington Post* ran a series of charts pointing to markers of race-based economic disparity in the United States today.[36] *The New York Times* ran a similar piece in late August 2–14, in order place the shooting death of Michael Brown in Ferguson and the protests that followed into a larger social context.[37] The data captured from a variety of sources – 2010 Census, The Federal Reserve, The Urban Institute, US Department of Education for Civil Rights to name a few – highlights the connection between race and poverty. For example, white Americans constitute 64 percent of the population but hold 88 percent of the nation's wealth and the income gap between whites and people of color has tripled since 1984. When it comes to housing, affluent people of color live in poorer neighborhoods than working-class whites, and people of color were more likely than whites to be targeted by subprime lenders and less likely to receive conventional mortgages. Educational markers are also dismal when we consider that 74 percent of African American and 80 percent of

---

[35] Ibid., §53.
[36] Braden Goyette and Alissa Sheller, "15 Charts That Prove We Are Far from Post-Racial," *The Huffington Post*, June 2, 2014, http://www.huffingtonpost.com/2014/07/02/civil-rights-act-anniversary-racism-charts_n_5521104.html.
[37] Neil Irwin, Claire Cain Miller, and Margot Sanger-Katz, "America's Racial Divide, Charted," *The New York Times*, August 19, 2014, http://mobile.nytimes.com/2014/08/20/upshot/americas-racial-divide-charted.html?_r=1.

Hispanic children attend segregated schools and African American preschoolers are more likely to be disciplined through suspension than white preschool children. Whites use drugs with greater frequency, but blacks are three times as likely to be arrested for drug use and the duration of sentencing for the latter is nearly twenty times that of the former. One in three black men will be incarcerated at some point in their lives. This last point is unique to our economic context in the United States, where corporations make $50 billion a year in the very process of turning people into "leftovers" in our economy through the prison industrial complex, which some say is returning us to our colonial roots where wealth was generated through the enslavement and disenfranchisement of a particular racial group.[38]

Francis's assessment of an economy of exclusion, when coupled with this evidence of race-based social inequality, makes the persistent problem of racism much more difficult to sidestep with the distinctively Euro-North American appeal to "color-blind" ways of perceiving economic inequality in the United States that prevail in our post–civil rights public discourse. Hispanic sociologist Eduardo Bonilla-Silva suggests that "color-blind racism" is anchored by four operative frames that shape white logic around racial encounters or analysis of racial data like that listed in the preceding text, all of which function to deny the reality of racism: abstract liberalism with its appeals to equal opportunity and free choice; naturalization or the sense that "like naturally stick with like"; cultural racism or stereotyping; and the minimalization of racism.[39] Because it refuses to acknowledge that racism exists on every level of human relationship (with self and others, in social structures and cultures), colorblindness is increasingly the way in which white dominance is maintained, and as such, a way by which economies continue to exclude disproportionately people of color. Consider the way in which the "#AllLivesMatter" response to the movement spawned by police shootings of unarmed African Americans obfuscates the race-based disparities in policing and the criminal justice system, not to mention the internalized dispositions of white superiority that created and maintain them.[40]

---

[38] See Michele Alexander's *The New Jim Crow: Mass Incarceration in an Age of Colorblindness* (New York: The New Press, 2012). For Catholic responses to the prison industrial complex, see Alex Mikulich, Laurie Cassidy, and Margie Pfeil, *The Scandal of White Complicity in US Hyper-incarceration: A Nonviolent Spirituality of White Resistance* (New York: Palgrave MacMillan, 2013).
[39] Eduardo Bonilla-Silva, *Racism without Racists: Colorblind Racism and Racial Inequality in Contemporary America* (Lanham, MD: Rowman and Littlefield, 2015), 25–52.
[40] See Douglas's explanation of the black body as a guilty body in *Stand Your Ground*, 48–89.

Fortunately, Francis implicitly offers an alternative to color-blind racism when he names economic exclusion as the manifestation of kind of culture, a " 'throw away' culture"[41] or a "culture of prosperity"[42] or a "culture where each person wants to be bearer of his or her own subjective truth,"[43] all of which undermine commitments to the common good. While not necessarily new given John Paul II's frequent invocation of the "culture of death" or Benedict XVI's notion of "culture of moral relativism," Francis's repeated analysis of culture, a word that appears nearly sixty times in *Evangelii Gaudium*, underscores an important middle way for examining and responding to the complicated interplay between interpersonal and systemic relationships of racial domination and oppression in our current economy. It is in the notion of culture that we might find alternatives to Euro-American colorblindness.

Francis notes, "[Culture] has to do with the lifestyle of a given society, the specific way in which its members relate to one another, to other creatures and to God. Understood in this way, culture embraces the totality of a people's life."[44] African American Catholic ethicist Bryan Massingale has been arguing for a similar cultural shift when it comes to our understanding of racism. Racism is not simply individual acts of prejudice or hate or even limited only to structures that exclude. Rather, racism is a way of making meaning about ourselves and others that is learned and practiced, that informs and forms us individually and collectively, and as such makes exclusionary practices and structures largely invisible to those already included.[45] Focus on an economy that excludes presents an opportunity for an even more challenging focus on the "whitely" dimensions of our economic culture of exclusion. In other words, by calling attention to a culture of exclusion, Francis allows us to move beyond thinking about racial inequality in terms of interactions between individual persons, whether white or of color, or even beyond a focus on how racism disadvantages some, and toward facets of white *culture* that exclude based on socially constructed and institutionally sustained assumptions of racial superiority. "Today," notes Massingale, "the continuing resistance to racial equality, despite undeniable progress, can be largely explained by a fundamental ambivalence on the part of the majority of white Americans: their desire to denounce blatant racial injustices, and yet preserve a situation of white

[41] EG, §53.
[42] Ibid., §54.
[43] Ibid., §62.
[44] Ibid., §115.
[45] Massingale, *Racial Justice and the Catholic Church*, 13–33.

social dominance and privilege. To say it plainly, most Americans are committed to both interpersonal and systemic inequality."[46]

Individual and collective commitments to systemic inequality or social exclusion come in many forms and are too numerous to mention here but generally include antipathy to difference, a sense of entitlement to social advantages, denial of the reality of racism or shock when confronted with overt expressions of racism, or guilt about racial injustice. Psychologist Derald Wing Sue calls the exclusionary practices of the dominant white culture "micro-aggressions" through which superiority is individually and collectively performed and cultures of exclusion are sustained.[47] Social justice educator Barbara Applebaum associates the common denominators of whiteness with the "belief in one's authority and in one's own experience as truth" along with "an unwillingness to be challenged that is protected by perceived white moral goodness or white benevolence."[48] Both make communities of faith, particularly those seeking the security of their own goodness and innocence, susceptible to the exclusionary culture of whiteness.

Francis implicitly resists the exclusion that comes with colorblindness with his insistence that evangelization must go hand in hand with inculturation. What does inculturation have to do with racial justice? First, inculturation bolsters the agency of those who receive the message of the gospel, while ensuring the freshness and newness of its message about the radical inclusivity of God's love. Communities far from the center of ecclesial, political, or economic power have long incarnated the gospel in their particular cultural practices and as such have prevented the tradition from turning a blind eye to the varied gifts and needs of the universal Church. Recall, again, his words in *Evangelii Gaudium*: "We would not do justice to the logic of the incarnation if we thought of Christianity as monocultural and monotonous".[49] That he invokes the wisdom of more than ten bishops' conferences around the world throughout *Evangelii Gaudium*, reflects a

---

[46] Ibid., 41.
[47] Psychologist Derald Wing Su describes these habits in terms of "microaggressions" or regular insults, assaults, or invalidations unknowingly communicated verbally, nonverbally, or symbolically by good intentioned whites that convey messages of our own superiority or normativity and another's inferiority or difference. These might include inabilities to properly pronounce or remember names of persons of color, inquiring as to their country of origin or qualifications for a job or degree, or invalidating their experience by simply not asking about it. See *Microaggressions in Everyday Life: Race, Gender and Sexual Orientation* (New York: Wiley, 2010).
[48] Applebaum, *Being White, Being Good*, 16 quoting Marilyn Frye's "White Woman Feminist," in her *Willful Virgin: Essays in Feminism 1976–1992* (Freedom, CA: Crossing Press), 151.
[49] EG, §117.

commitment to celebrate cultural difference in the midst of ecclesial unity. Perhaps more importantly, he links the agency of inculturation with an agency denied to those excluded in our economy in such a way that cultural expressions of gospel values might become an antidote to a culture that excludes in the name of colorblindness. "We can see that the different peoples among whom the Gospel has been inculturated are active collective subjects or agents of evangelization. This is because each people is the creator of their own culture and the protagonist of their own history."[50] He identifies expressions of popular piety or "the people's mysticism" as sources of theological insight, sources that contemporary theologians of color have long lifted up as alternatives to strictly white ways of knowing, believing, and acting, as well as more accurate ways of understanding the urgency of social inequality.[51]

Finally, his repeated use of the term *encounter* suggests that Francis sees embodied connection among people who would otherwise remain distant from each other as the antithesis to exclusion. White historian Joseph McCartin notes *encounter* occurs thirty-one times throughout *Evangelii Gaudium*.[52] In order to resist the "defensive attitudes with today's world imposes on us," Francis notes "the Gospel tells us constantly to run the risk of a face-to-face encounter with others, with their physical presence which challenges us, with their pain and their pleas, with their joy which infects us in our close and continuous interaction."[53] Such encounters invite us to dwell near each other, the very definition of what it means to be neighborly in Yancy's estimation. It is in proximity with those otherwise excluded, that those who fuel economic disparity with our colorblindness and false sense of superiority – intellectual, moral, cultural – can, in Yancy's words, become vulnerable or undone or unsutured from the tight bindings of white culture.[54] Only when we dwell near to each other can we take on the smell of each other, and perhaps replace the odor of the dominant white culture with a multicultural scent that reflects the diverse communities that comprise our North American landscape. White pastor and theologian

---

[50] Ibid., §122.
[51] Ibid., §124. For other examples scholars who argue for turn to beauty and the imagination in order to respond more effectively to the signs of the times, see, respectively, the works of scholars such as Roberto Goizueta on liberation aesthetics; see Pineda Madrid on Juarez; see O'Connell on murals in Philadelphia.
[52] In his contribution to the Georgetown University symposium in March 2014, out of which this volume originated.
[53] *EG*, §83.
[54] George Yancy, "Being Black, Being a 'Problem,'" La Salle Lecture on Religion and Culture, April 14, 2014, Philadelphia, PA.

Joseph Barndt suggests that such a stance makes it possible for predominantly white churches to "birth" what he calls an "anti-racist multicultural church," or communities of individuals committed to developing an analysis of structural racism in their church, devising strategies for dismantling, and creating a new institutional identity that seeks relationships with other churches, particularly those of color.[55]

3. Mercy as Antidote to White Acedia

Ideas about encounter lead to my third and final point regarding Francis's potential contribution to racial justice work and critical race theory, a discourse with which Catholic theologians have only recently begun to engage.[56] Francis identifies several symptoms of a Church that has lost its zeal and fallen instead into a state of "paralysis and acedia"[57] – fear, despair, disillusionment, indifference, fatigue, and insecurity.[58] Critical race theorists would recognize many of these affective realities as pathologies of whiteness or white culture or white supremacy.[59] Among the ranks of pastoral workers in the Church to whom Francis speaks, these symptoms arise as a result of a diminishing commitment and fervor in the face of the evils of the world and within the Church. Might we also recognize these symptoms among those who benefit from an economy of exclusion in the United States? Are they not akin to what Joe Feagin and Herman Vera identify the "social alexithymia" of whiteness or the sense that "white racism involves a massive breakdown of empathy, the human capacity to experience the feelings of members of an out group viewed as different"?[60] Jennings names this lack of empathy as evidence of a "distorted relational imagination" among white Christians who have failed to come to terms with the historical contradiction of colonialism and continued rejection of the Christian call to intimacy for the sake of "ways of being in the world that resist the realities of submission, desire, and transformation."[61]

---

[55] Barndt, *Becoming and Anti-Racist Church*, 145–184.
[56] Most notable is Alex Mikulich, Laurie Cassidy, and Margie Pfeil, *Interrupting White Privilege: Catholic Theologians Break the Silence* (Maryknoll, NY: Orbis Books, 2007). See also Bryan Massingale's review of this discourse in Catholic moral theology and social ethics in "Has the Silence Been Broken? Catholic Theological Ethics and Racial Justice," *Theological Studies* 75(1) (2013): 133–155.
[57] EG, §81.
[58] Ibid., §78–86.
[59] Mary Elizabeth Hobgood, *Dismantling Privilege: An Ethics of Accountability* (Cleveland, OH: The Pilgrim Press, 2000), 56–59.
[60] Joe Feagin and Herman Vera, *White Racism: The Basics* (New York: Routledge, 1995): 16.
[61] Jennings, *The Christian Imagination*, 8 and 4.

Taking on the "Smell of the Sheep"

If Euro-North Americans liken themselves to zealless pastoral ministers in the Church, then the pope's exhortation invites us to consider the causes of our paralysis and acedia. In some cases our symptoms may stem from dealing – or perhaps not dealing – with the painful contradictions with which most Euro-American Catholics in the United States must contend: contradictions in our founding civil documents where all persons are recognized as equals, except some; contradictions in our immigrant history and present reality where we stand in solidarity with some immigrants, but not all; and contradictions in our current commitments to evangelization when the Jesus of the last judgment is among those from whom we voluntarily segregate ourselves from in our churches, neighborhoods, and schools. Perhaps most profound is the challenge white supremacy presents to the very kerygma of the gospel that Francis identifies as central to evangelization – the call to recognize that we are loved by God and to love in return – when we consider white ethicist Mary Elizabeth Hobgood's claim that white supremacy stems from an inability of whites for self-love because to maintain racial hierarchies whites need constantly to deny fundamental things about our own humanity in order to justify dehumanizing others: "Because white status depends on denying the deepest parts of the relational self, our humanity is impoverished, and our capacity to be moral – in right relationship with others – is diminished."[62]

It is in identifying this acedia that Francis makes the most significant contribution to those wading into waters troubled by the ongoing legacy of these contradictions. The antidote to fear, despair, indifference, and insecurity is mercy, which for Francis involves an ongoing and heartfelt acknowledgment that one is both sinner and loved. In ways that may be influenced by his own personal experience of failing to stand up to the contradictions in the political and ecclesial contexts of Argentina, Francis identifies mercy as arising from the three-part kerygma that animates his understanding of evangelization: Jesus loves us, Jesus dies for us, and he is with us every day loving us.[63] Moreover, he marshals extensive exegetic support in identifying God's mercy as the primary message of the gospel, and therefore of evangelizers, and as such "demands on the part of the evangelizer certain attitudes which foster openness to the message: approachability, readiness for dialogue, patience, a warmth and welcome which is non-judgmental."[64]

[62] Ibid., 48.
[63] EG, §164.
[64] Ibid., §165.

Mercy compels us to acknowledge simultaneously our finitude when it comes to our complicity in sin, whether personal or structural, *and* our beloved status in the eyes of our God. As such for Francis mercy is an emotional experience, not a rational or logical or intellectual one, that frees us to love our flawed selves so as to love our neighbor, frees us from the binds of exclusivity to be evangelizers of a message of radically inclusive love, frees us to take on the smell of the sheep tainted by a history of suffering at the hands of white supremacy.

How might Francis's notion of mercy function in the context of racial justice work? First, a disposition toward acknowledging our complicity in the ongoing dynamics of racism potentially moves Euro-Americans beyond our color-blind default positions that simply reject the severity of racial injustice in post–civil rights America, deny our complicity in a culture of racism, and lack historical consciousness where the construction and maintenance of racial hierarchies is concerned. In other words, mercy frees Euro-Americans to take on the smell of our white supremacy, which has tinged all wools, regardless of racial identity, and in so doing liberate ourselves and others from it.[65]

Moreover, acknowledging our sinfulness when it comes to racism, rather than sidestepping it, can undo the paralyzing bindings of rejection, denial, or voluntary ignorance that keep Euro-Americans wound up in defensive postures around our brothers and sisters of color. Much in the way that mercy can transform a church that is "healthy from being confined and from clinging to its own security" into one that is "bruised, hurting and dirty,"[66] mercy might allow Euro-Americans to become, in the words of Yancy, vulnerable or "unsutured" or undone with ugliness of our white supremacy.[67] A disposition toward acknowledging that we are profoundly loved for who we are – and not for the cultural trappings awarded us by the color of skin *and* despite our complicity in cultures of exclusion – can counter the lack of self-love that Hobgood identifies as the catalyst for white supremacy.

Moral theologian James Keenan suggests that mercy is the virtue that enables us to enter into the chaos of other people's lives and ought to

---

[65] Alexander Mikulich, Laurie Cassidy, and Margaret Pfeil describe what such a stance looks like in the context of mass incarceration in *The Scandal of White Complicity in US Hyper-Incarceration: A Nonviolent Spirituality of White Resistance* (New York: Palgrave Macmillan, 2013).

[66] *EG*, §49

[67] George Yancy, *Look, A White! Philosophical Essays on Whiteness* (Philadelphia: Temple University Press, 2012).

animate Christian life because it best captures the work of God in salvation history.[68] Francis reminds that we are most effective in doing so when we acknowledge that we are both sinners and loved, and then commit ourselves to live in the freedom God's mercy awards us. As such mercy becomes the ability for white Christians in the United States to enter into the chaos that sustaining white supremacy has created in our individual lives and white communities, before attempting to address the damage it continues to cause in our wider communities. Turning a critical and yet loving eye inward – onto the white self or onto the white parish or onto the white neighborhood – may assist white Christians in moving beyond paralyzing guilt or defensive anger about racism toward an affective desire for encounter – with the merciful God of the gospel, as well as with neighbors excluded by a culture of white supremacy.

4. Conclusion: Process and Periphery

To be sure, the scriptural model of evangelization in the document, taken from Matthew 28: 19–28 (*Go, and make disciples of the nations*), can dangerously reinforce many kinds of superiority that whites like myself perpetuate in our work for social justice, even the necessary work of racial justice. Systematic theologian Jeannine Hill Fletcher has recently applied a feminist hermeneutic of suspicion to the history and practices of religious pluralism in order to identify white supremacy at the heart of Christians' engagement with the religious other throughout American history, noting ways in which biblical passages like this one were invoked to justify the discrimination of people of color who refused to give way to Western expansion or assimilate to the norms of Christian citizenship. Moreover, Applebaum's observations of white educators' and students' persistent claims to the superiority of their intellect, goodness, and innocence even in the context of social justice pedagogy ought to raise concerns about ways in which social engagement stemming from mission or vision statements invoking gospel language may dangerously reinscribe the very racial hierarchies we intend to dismantle through this work.[69] Finally, Francis's biblical image of evangelization rooted in missionary disciples might reinforce the assumption that racism is something that Euro-American Christians need to engage

---

[68] See James F. Keenan, *Jesus and Virtue Ethics: Building Bridges Between New Testament Studies and Moral Theology* (New York: Sheed and Ward, 2005), 67–73; "Virtue and Identity," *Concilium* (2000/2): 69–77; and *The Works of Mercy: The Heart of Catholicism* (Lanham, MD: Rowman and Littlefield Publishers, 2007).
[69] Applebaum, *Being White Being Good*, 27–51 and 91–118.

by going to the familiar front lines of injustice, rather than seeing that racism is perpetuated within the familiar boundaries of our white worlds – neighborhoods, classrooms, churches, police departments – through the assumptions and practices of white superiority.

That said, Francis offers, perhaps inadvertently, two important conditions for the missionary discipleship that attend to these concerns and as such can shape Euro-American Catholics in our work for racial justice. First he insists that time must take priority over space in evangelizers' work for peace and justice. "One of the faults which we occasionally observe in sociopolitical activity is that spaces and power are preferred to time and processes," he notes:

> Giving priority to space means madly attempting to keep everything together in the present, trying to possess all the spaces of power and of self-assertion; it is to crystallize processes and presume to hold them back. Giving priority to time means being concerned about initiating processes rather than possessing spaces.... What we need, then, is to give priority to actions which generate new processes in society and engage other persons and groups who can develop them to the point where they bear fruit in significant historical events. Without anxiety, but with clear convictions and tenacity."[70]

This preference for time over space echoes the "antiracist racist" stance that many critical race theorists recommend for white Americans when it comes to the necessary work of racial justice[71] because such an individual and collective self-understanding accepts rather than denies the reality of racial injustice, embraces responsibility that comes with complicity, and acknowledges that deconstructing racism is a continual process with an arch at least as long as the one that continues to construct it. Yancy notes that whites cannot claim to be antiracist racists by pointing to a particular set of strategies or goals that will create spaces free of racial conditioning, but rather must continually aspire to *become* persons liberated from such conditioning by working alongside those oppressed by them. Working for a pragmatic fix places too much emphasis on a point of "arrival,"[72] a space in Francis's sense of the word, and in the process of trying to arrive at that space can easily replicate the habits of whiteness we have explored here.

---

[70] EG, §223.

[71] Barndt, *Becoming and Anti-Racist Church*, 145–200; and Alex Mikulich, Laurie Cassidy, and Margaret Pfeil, *The Scandal of White Complicity in US Hyper-Incarceration: A Nonviolent Spirituality of White Resistance* (New York: Palgrave Macmillan, 2013), 167–185.

[72] Yancy, "Exploring Race in a Predominantly White Classroom," Pedagogy Workshop hosted by the Philosophy Graduate Student Association at Villanova University (20th September, 2013).

The notion of time or process, by contrast, offers the promise of personal and social liberation through a gradually transformative conversion that is never fully complete, where humble recommitments replace guilt, where ongoing critical self-examination replaces voluntary ignorance, where a willingness to remain engaged in the messy work of undoing racism replaces a triumphant sense of being one of the "good" white people who is somehow above the fray or beyond reproach.

Second, Francis notes "all of us are asked to obey his call to go forth from our respective comfort zones in order to reach all the *'peripheries'* in need of the light of the Gospel."[73] When it comes to racial justice work, the periphery for Euro-American Catholics is our own psyches and subconscious selves where many of us are haunted by those painful contradictions at the heart of our self-understandings as white American Catholics and where the ongoing work of deconstructing socially conditioned racist dispositions and practices needs to happen. As evangelizers called to take on the smell of the sheep, Francis compels white Catholics to go to the uncomfortable periphery of our otherwise comfortable relationships with friends, family members, or colleagues by naming manifestations of our participation in a culture that excludes in the context of our friendships, our families, and our places of work and ministry.

For this kind of evangelizing work, for the courage to take on the smell of the sheep, we must pray for mercy.

---

[73] EG, §20, emphasis mine.

CHAPTER 9

A Church of and for the Poor

The Social Vision of *Evangelii Gaudium* through the Eyes of a Scholar-Practitioner

Maryanne Loughry, AM, RSM

The Apostolic Exhortation of Pope Francis, *Evangelii Gaudium*[1] given in Rome on November 24, 2013, the solemnity of Christ the King, marked the end of the 2012–2013 Year of Faith and as such can be seen as the concluding "book end" to that Year of Faith alongside Pope Benedict XVI's Apostolic Exhortation *Porta Fidei*,[2] the opening "book end." This chapter is concerned with the significant events that took place between these two "book ends" that foreshadowed the text and teaching of *Evangelii Gaudium*. Of special significance for *Evangelii Gaudium* and this Year of Faith is that not only, over a period of five months, were there two different papal authors for these two "book end" exhortations, but also two living popes, monumental Church events and all within a year of tumultuous world events.

This twenty-first century Year of Faith was invoked with several foci. It marked the fiftieth anniversary of the opening of the Second Ecumenical Vatican Council. It was also a celebration of the twentieth anniversary of the *Catechism of the Catholic Church* and the witness of charity. Furthermore, as Pope Benedict XVI wrote in *Porta Fidei (The Door of Faith)*, the Year of Faith was a "summons to an authentic and renewed conversion to the Lord, the one Savior of the world,"[3] all of this was an invitation for Catholics to

---

[1] Pope Francis, *EG*, http://www.vatican.va/evangelii-gaudium/en/.
[2] Pope Benedict XVI, Apostolic Exhortation, *Porta Fidei*, http://www.vatican.va/holy_father/benedict_xvi/motu_proprio/documents/hf_ben-xvi_motu-proprio_20111011_porta-fidei_en.html.
[3] Ibid.

A Church of and for the Poor

experience conversion through turning back to Jesus and entering into a deeper relationship with him. *Porta Fidei*, also called for the Year of Faith to be specifically dedicated to the profession of the true faith and its correct interpretation through the reading of, or better still, the pious meditation upon, the documents of the council fifty years on and the articles of the *Catechism of the Catholic Church*. Plenary indulgences were to be earned for these activities.[4] As an apostolic letter, *Porta Fidei* exemplified the dense theological treatises that had come to characterize Pope Benedict's communication with the faithful. What no one was to know was how profound Pope Benedict's invitation to conversion was going to become in the light of the momentous events that unfolded in the first months of this Year of Faith.

The next part of this unfolding story is already recent history but, as already indicated, the momentous events of 2013 came to shape the Year of Faith in ways not envisioned *in Porta Fidei* on October 11, 2011.

Monumentally, on the February 11, 2012, four months into the Year of Faith, the Vatican announced that Pope Benedict XVI would be resigning due to old age and poor health. This announcement took all by surprise because in the modern era all popes had held the position from their election till their death and the last resignation of a pope had been that of Pope Gregory XII in 1415 (which was involuntary). As we now know, following Pope Benedict's resignation, the Conclave of Cardinals was convened and Cardinal Jorge Mario Bergoglio, then Archbishop of Buenos Aires, Argentina was elected pope. Bergoglio was the first non-European pope in nearly thirteen hundred years, the first from the Southern Hemisphere and the first Jesuit. Significantly he chose Francis as his papal name after St. Francis Assisi. The first months of Pope Francis's papacy heralded what was to be the cornerstone message of *Evangelii Gaudium*, a passionate call to the Church to go out and not be indifferent to the poor and suffering in the world today.

From the beginning Pope Francis's papacy was punctuated with signs and exhortations that signaled a new energy for the papacy and the Church. Energy charged with a renewed enthusiasm for the poor. Significantly Pope Francis also communicated in a more direct and plain language than his predecessor making his messages a great deal more accessible. These key elements of Francis's early months of papacy came to be transmitted and amplified in Pope Francis's first Apostolic Exhortation *Evangelii Gaudium*, which spelled out Pope Francis's agenda for the Church.

[4] Retrieved from http://www.annusfidei.va/content/novaevangelizatio/en/annus-fidei/indulgentia.html.

This chapter will concentrate on three papal actions, or rather three particular events that occurred early in Francis's papacy and that arguably are markers of Pope Francis's social agenda. These events foreshadowed and exemplified in action the text and emphasis of *Evangelii Gaudium*. They are: the immediate events surrounding Pope Francis's election, his celebration of Holy Thursday in Rome, and his first trip out of Rome to Lampedusa. All three of these events came to shape what some have now called the "Francis Effect" and acted as markers of Pope Francis's unfolding social agenda.

1. Pope Francis's Election

1.1. *His Preconclave intervention*

Pope Francis's election was clearly the first time that we received a first sense of not only who the cardinals thought was the right person to address the needs of the Church at this time but also what particular agenda many hoped the next pope would bring to address these needs. Preconclave general congregation meetings of all cardinals who could be present commenced on March 4, 2013 and in the midst of the many issues discussed at these "closed" meetings opinions were canvassed on the problems facing the church at the moment and what characteristics would ideally be embodied in the next pope. It has been reported in the media that, at the usually "secretive" second to last preconclave general congregation meetings of the cardinals, Cardinal Bergoglio addressed his brother cardinals on these topics commencing with an opening quote from Paul VI on the sweet and comforting joy of evangelizing, our first signal of the emphasis to come of his future apostolic exhortation and a possible reference to the eventual title of *Evangelii Gaudium*.

Cardinal Bergoglio spoke of the future pope as needing to be "a man who, from the contemplation and adoration of Jesus Christ, helps the Church to go out to the existential peripheries, that helps her to be the fruitful mother, and who gains life from evangelizing."[5] In the same address Cardinal Bergoglio spoke of the Church needing to "come out of herself" both geographically and to where there is the greatest need.

---

[5] Informal quote of Cardinal Bergoglio, Vatican Radio Report, http://en.radiovaticana.va/storico/2013/03/27/bergoglios_intervention_a_diagnosis_of_the_problems_in_the_church/en1-677269.

A Church of and for the Poor

> Evangelizing pre-supposes a desire in the Church to come out of herself. The Church is called to come out of herself and to go to the peripheries, not only geographically, but also the existential peripheries: the mystery of sin, of pain, of injustice, of ignorance and indifference to religion, of intellectual currents, and of all misery.[6]

Cardinal Bergoglio went on to talk of the present Church being in need of healing from within, a Church preoccupied with self:

> When the Church does not come out of herself to evangelize, she becomes self-referential and then gets sick (cf. the deformed woman of the Gospel). The evils that, over time, happen in ecclesial institutions have their root in self-referentiality and a kind of theological narcissism. In *Revelation*, Jesus says that he is at the door and knocks. Obviously, the text refers to his knocking from the outside in order to enter but I think about the times in which Jesus knocks from within so that we will let him come out. The self-referential Church keeps Jesus Christ within herself and does not let him out.[7]

And again of direct relevance to the future Apostolic Exhortation *Evangelii Gaudium*, Cardinal Bergoglio extolled his wish for the Church to come out of itself and evangelize:

> When the Church is self-referential, inadvertently, she believes she has her own light; she ceases to be the mysterium lunae and gives way to that very serious evil, spiritual worldliness (which according to De Lubac, is the worst evil that can befall the Church). It lives to give glory only to one another. Put simply, there are two images of the Church: Church which evangelizes and comes out of herself, the *Dei Verbum religiose audiens et fidente proclamans*; and the worldly Church, living within herself, of herself, for herself. This should shed light on the possible changes and reforms which must be done for the salvation of souls.[8]

He finally described the attributes of the future pope as being out going and enlivened by the joy of evangelizing.

> Thinking of the next Pope: He must be a man who, from the contemplation and adoration of Jesus Christ, helps the Church to go out to the existential peripheries that helps her to be the fruitful mother, who gains life from 'the sweet and comforting joy of evangelizing.'"[9]

---

[6] Ibid.
[7] Ibid.
[8] Ibid.
[9] Ibid.

Further media reports describe Bergoglio's intervention at this preconclave meeting as so significant and relevant to the challenges for the Church identified by members of the conclave that the intention to elect Bergoglio gathered significant momentum after this intervention even though his name had not been widely discussed in the weeks leading up to the Conclave.[10]

1.2. The Papal Name

Cardinal Bergoglio was elected pope on March 13, 2013 after five ballots, and it is reported that, unlike many if not most earlier conclaves of relatively recent memory, this election was strongly influenced by the robust preconclave meetings.[11] Cardinal Ortega of Havana had been so moved by the earlier intervention of Cardinal Bergoglio that he had asked him for a copy of the written text. When Bergoglio was elected, Cardinal Ortega asked for permission to share the text more widely. As mentioned, this text was our first indication of the agenda for the Church of the man who was to become Pope Francis. What followed next was the choice by Bergoglio of the papal name of Francis after St. Francis Assisi. The choice of this name provided the next clue of the profound social agenda for the Church that Pope Francis had in mind from the outset. It was the first time any pope had chosen the name Francis and from the first words uttered by the newly elected pope it was evident that he had chosen the name Francis out of recognition of St. Francis of Assisi's love of 'Lady Poverty.'"[12]

1.3. Pope Francis's First Address

On the evening of his election Pope Francis deviated from former protocol and appeared on the balcony of St. Peters in a white cassock rather than a red ermine trimmed mozzetta (shoulder cape) with his pectoral cross from Argentina. More astonishingly Pope Francis then asked the thousands gathered in St. Peter's Square to pray over him silently before he gave his first "Urbi et Orbi" blessing to the church and the world.[13] It was as if a breath

---

[10] See the report at http://chiesa.espresso.repubblica.it/articolo/1350484?eng=y.
[11] Christopher Lamb, "Five Ballot Wonder," *Tablet* (March 23, 2013), 4.
[12] A little less than two months before the publication of *Evangelii Gaudium*, Pope Francis visited Assisi on the feast day of St. Francis and in his homily spoke of St. Francis's love for the poor and his imitation of Christ in his poverty being inseparably united like the two sides of a coin. See the official report at http://www.news.va/en/news/popes-homily-for-solemn-mass-in-assisi.
[13] Robert Mickens, "Francesco di Roma," *Tablet* (March 23, 2013), 6.

of fresh air had blown through the church. In the days that followed Pope Francis was pictured catching the bus with his fellow cardinals and paying his own hotel bill after the conclave. He did not move into the official papal residence at St. Peters but rather chose to stay at the Vatican guest house, Casa Santa Marta. These were further early signs of Pope Francis's agenda for the Church and the world alike.

1.4. Holy Thursday 2013

A little over two weeks after his election all eyes were on Pope Francis with many wondering how he would participate in his first Easter ceremonies as pontiff. At the Mass of the Chrism, on the morning of March 28, 2013, a Mass traditionally celebrated with the clergy of the diocese, Pope Francis again spoke of the need to go out to the edges:

> We need to "go out", then, in order to experience our own anointing, its power and its redemptive efficacy: to the "outskirts" where there is suffering, bloodshed, blindness that longs for sight, and prisoners in thrall to many evil masters. It is not in soul-searching or constant introspection that we encounter the Lord: self-help courses can be useful in life, but to live our priestly life going from one course to another, from one method to another, leads us to become pelagians and to minimize the power of grace, which comes alive and flourishes to the extent that we, in faith, go out and give ourselves and the Gospel to others, giving what little ointment we have to those who have nothing, nothing at all.[14]

In this homily Pope Francis is clearly addressing the clergy and imploring them to not only go to serve the poor but also to move from being internally focused so as to find the Lord in outreach and ministry, particularly to those who are suffering and poor.

Later that day, Pope Francis put actions to the words of his homily and celebrated the Holy Thursday ceremony in Casa del Marmo, a juvenile detention center on the outskirts of Rome. At Casa del Marmo he deviated significantly from tradition by washing the feet of twelve young detainees, two of whom were women and at least one a Muslim. Previous popes have celebrated Holy Thursday mass in basilicas in Rome and only washed the feet of males. This, however, was reportedly not a new practice for Pope Francis who had previously celebrated Holy Thursday mass in hospitals

---

[14] Pope Francis, Homily for the Mass of Chrism 2013, http://w2.vatican.va/content/francesco/en/homilies/2013/documents/papa-francesco_20130328_messa-crismale.html.

and prisons in Argentina.[15] These words and actions of Pope Francis so soon after his election amplified and put flesh to the words of his preconclave intervention: *"The Church is called to come out of herself and to go to the peripheries."*[16]

2. Pope Francis's First Trip Outside Rome

Four months into his papacy, and after significant appointments in Rome including the establishment of a permanent advisory council of eight (later nine) cardinals tasked with assisting him to reform the Vatican bureaucracy, Pope Francis made his first trip out of Rome (on July 8, 2013). Where he went was the most telling indication yet of his desire for the Church to go beyond its normal boundaries. Pope Francis went to the island of Lampedusa. This island, located in the Mediterranean off the coast of Sicily, is the point of arrival for many thousands of asylum seekers by boat. In 2013 almost 45,000[17] asylum seekers arrived in Lampedusa from African countries including Mali, Senegal, and Eritrea, 11,300 of the arrivals were from Syria.[18] These asylum seekers have fled their countries for many reasons: "Countries are spitting out their people for different reasons: war, revolution, bad governance, dead-end economies, climate change, poverty, persecution."[19]

Most had crossed by land to Libya and then taken an unsafe or rickety boat in the hope of being granted asylum in the European Union. The morning the pope arrived on Lampedusa a boat containing 165 from Mali pulled into shore and the Sunday before 120 were rescued off Lampedusa when their boat capsized. Amongst those rescued were pregnant women. These unauthorized boat arrivals and sea rescues had taxed the local inhabitants of Lampedusa as well as the Italian and European Union authorities for several years. The question of how to address this issue of the asylum seekers arriving by boat was a vexed issue and also evoked much larger

---

[15] C. Glatz, "Pope Washes the Feet of 12 Young Detainees to 'Serve Them from the Heart.'" National Catholic Reporter, March 28, 2013. Retrieved from http://ncronline.org/news/vatican/pope-washes-feet-12-young-detainees-serve-them-heart.

[16] See the report Vatican Radio at http://en.radiovaticana.va/storico/2013/03/27/bergoglios_intervention_a_diagnosis_of_the_problems_in_the_church/en1-677269.

[17] 160,000 asylum seekers have arrived in Lampedusa in the first nine months of 2014. See http://www.theguardian.com/world/2014/oct/20/-sp-migrants-tales-asylum-sea-mediterranean.

[18] See http://www.unhcr.org/5347d8fa9.html.

[19] M. Rice-Oxley and M. Mahmood, "Migrants' Tales: I feel for those that were with me. They got asylum in the sea," *Guardian* (October 21, 2014), see http://www.theguardian.com/world/2014/oct/20/-sp-migrants-tales-asylum-sea-mediterranean.

A Church of and for the Poor

issues, including the responses to conflict in the Middle East; the issue of conflict and wealth distribution in Africa; and the questions of protection and visa options for asylum seekers and refugees in general. Thousands have died attempting this crossing.

Pope Francis going to Lampedusa could be likened to his going to Guantanamo Bay in the United States or Christmas Island in Australia for his first visit. All of these places are lightning rods for debate on global/regional policy in relation to those who are poor and conflict impacted.

In Lampedusa Pope Francis celebrated mass on an altar shaped as a boat. In his homily he spoke of "a painful thorn" in his heart when he thought of the many immigrants that die at sea when their "vehicles of hope become vehicles of death."[20] Drawing on a reference from the book of Genesis, Pope Francis asks the congregation "Where is your brother?" referring to the asylum seekers as brothers and sisters of ours who are escaping difficulty in the hope of finding peace and serenity for their families. In a reference to the faithful having lost their bearing or orientation, a theme consistent with Pope Francis's concern for the Church being too focused on its own internal matters, he talked of "'the other' no longer being considered a brother or sister but rather simply as one who disturbs us, interrupts our lives. He then spoke about globalized indifference, how the world has become indifferent to the suffering of others; a theme that returns powerfully in *Evangelii Gaudium*.

> The culture of comfort, which makes us think only of ourselves, makes us insensitive to the cries of other people, makes us live in soap bubbles which, however lovely, are insubstantial; they offer a fleeting and empty illusion which results in indifference to others; indeed, it even leads to the globalization of indifference. In this globalized world, we have fallen into globalized indifference. We have become used to the suffering of others: it doesn't affect me; it doesn't concern me; it's none of my business![21]

Referring again to those lost at sea while seeking asylum Pope Francis asks

> "Has any one of us wept because of this situation and others like it?" Has any one of us grieved for the death of these brothers and sisters? Has any one of us wept for these persons who were on the boat? For the young mothers carrying their babies? For these men who were looking for a means of supporting their families? We are a society which has forgotten

---

[20] Pope Francis, Homily at Lampedusa (July 8, 2013), http://w2.vatican.va/content/francesco/en/homilies/2013/documents/papa-francesco_20130708_omelia-lampedusa.html.
[21] Ibid.

how to weep, how to experience compassion – "suffering with" others: the globalization of indifference has taken from us the ability to weep![22]

At Lampedusa, in this significant visit, Pope Francis's call to attend to the suffering of those displaced resonated with Catholic Church teaching on refugees and migrants and heralded for the Church and world his agenda for the poor and his request that their plight not be ignored.

3. *Evangelii Gaudium*

At the end of the Year of Faith, on the Feast of Christ the King, November 24, 2013, Pope Francis produced his apostolic exhortation on the proclamation of the gospel in today's world: *Evangelii Gaudium*. It actually contained few surprises. Much of the 206-page exhortation resonated with the message that Pope Francis had been proclaiming since his election as well as in his earlier life. *Evangelii Gaudium* is a teaching document that is long, passionate, and full of citations from around the world, as well as being largely in a simple straightforward language – in stark contrast to Benedict XVI's *Porta Fidei*. *Evangelii Gaudium* is written in very warm and pastoral style reflecting Pope Francis's preference for addressing the entire family of the Church, something that is a further reflection of the humble manner in which Pope Francis has embraced his papacy.

3.1. *Poor Church for the Poor*

It is not only this refreshing style but also Pope Francis's passionate explication of earlier communications with the Church that has come to characterize this encyclical as Pope Francis's agenda for his papacy.[23] With regard to Pope Francis's social agenda, Julian Filochowski, formerly director of the nongovernmental organization, CAFOD (the official Catholic aid agency for England and Wales) and now at Jesuit Mission UK, described *Evangelii Gaudium* as a charter for a Vatican Spring, an indirect reference to the "Arab Spring" that had been changing the face of the Middle East in the years preceding 2013.[24] Filochowski, an international development scholar welcomed the "freshness and fragrance of springtime" on every page of the encyclical. He also described *Evangelii Gaudium* as having

---

[22] Ibid.
[23] John Allen (March 16, 2013); see http://ncronline.org/blogs/francis-chronicles/pope-francis-i-would-love-church-poor.
[24] http://www.indcatholicnews.com/news.php?viewStory=24305.

A Church of and for the Poor

two fundamental foci: "first, transforming the way we live as Church and reenergizing us to become a genuinely 'missionary Church'; and second, putting the poor back where they belong at the very center of the Church's mission."[25]

Bernd Nilles, Secretary General of CIDSE (Coopération Internationale pour le Développement et la Solidarité – i.e., International Cooperation for Development and Solidarity), an International Alliance of Catholic Development agencies, and another Church international development specialist described *Evangelii Gaudium* as an exhortation that put the poor and vulnerable at the heart of the document and offering help and guidance on the path toward global justice.[26]

Obviously Pope Francis has a vision and an agenda for the Church and the world. To come to fully understand this agenda, particularly Pope Francis's social agenda, *Evangelii Gaudium* needs to be read alongside of Pope Francis's earlier homilies and his actions. Each of these interventions is also given greater clarity when considered within the context of daily global events such as the conflicts in the Middle East and the global financial crisis.

Filochowski suggested that the opening paragraphs of *Evangelii Gaudium* serve as a summary of the two key foci of Pope Francis. There Francis stated that,

> The greatest danger in today's world, pervaded by consumerism, is the desolation and anguish born of a complacent yet covetous heart, the feverish pursuit of frivolous pleasures, and a blunted conscience. Whenever our interior life becomes caught up in its own interests and concerns, there is no room for others, no place for the poor.[27]

This also a clear echo of the agenda outlined by Pope Francis's immediately prior to his election calling for the Church and its faithful to look outward so as to be able to embrace the poor. Furthermore, at the outset of the exhortation, the Christian faithful are encouraged to see this as a "new chapter of evangelization, one marked by joy," a reference to the title of the exhortation.

3.2. The Poor

With regard to Pope Francis's social or global agenda, obviously the poor are central,

---

[25] Julian Filochowski, "Reflection on *Evangelii Gaudium* – The Joy of the Gospel" (March 9, 2014), http://www.indcatholicnews.com/news.php?viewStory=24305.

[26] See the report at http://en.radiovaticana.va/news/2013/12/03/evangelii_gaudium:_offering_help_and_guidance_on_the_path_towards/en1-752225.

[27] EG, §2.

> The Pope loves everyone, rich and poor alike, but he is obliged in the name of Christ to remind all that the rich must help, respect and promote the poor. I exhort you to generous solidarity and a return of economics and finance to an ethical approach with favors human beings.[28]

Here Pope Francis not only implores all to promote the poor, but he also includes a light touch referring to his own obligations and emotional investment; a refreshing message of encouragement prefaced by Pope Francis's own emotional investment.

Pope Francis reminds us that the poor are central to the gospel: "God's heart has a special place for the poor, so much so that he himself 'became poor' (2 Cor. 8:9)."[29] The encyclical goes on to remind us that: "For the Church, the option for the poor is primarily a theological category rather than a cultural, sociological, political or philosophical one. God shows the poor 'his first mercy'.... Inspired by this, the Church has made an option for the poor which is understood as 'a special form of primacy in the exercise of Christian charity, to which the whole tradition of the Church bears witness.'" Quoting Benedict XVI Pope Francis goes on to explain that this option is "implicit in our Christian faith in a God who became poor for us, so as to enrich us with his poverty."[30]

Pope Francis then reminds the faithful that the poor are central in his agenda for the Church and the world:

> This is why I want a Church which is poor and for the poor. They have much to teach us. Not only do they share in the *sensus fidei*, but in their difficulties they know the suffering Christ. We need to let ourselves be evangelized by them. The new evangelization is an invitation to acknowledge the saving power at work in their lives and to put them at the center of the Church's pilgrim way. We are called to find Christ in them, to lend our voice to their causes, but also to be their friends, to listen to them, to speak for them and to embrace the mysterious wisdom which God wishes to share with us through them.[31]

Here making clear that any proclamation of the gospel, any act of evangelization needs to be centered in engagements with the poor, another reference to the Church needing to be outward in focus. And, when specifically referring to the poor Pope Francis also embraces "new forms of poverty and vulnerability." Here he specifically mentions "the homeless, the addicted,

---

[28] Ibid., §58.
[29] Ibid., §197.
[30] Ibid., §198.
[31] Ibid.

A Church of and for the Poor

refugees, indigenous people, the elderly who are increasingly isolated and abandoned, and many others."[32]

Further into *Evangelii Gaudium* Pope Francis addresses the challenging issue of Interreligious Dialogue. When Pope Benedict XVI invoked the Year of Faith the world was in the grips of that aforementioned "Arab Spring," a series of antigovernment protests that were spreading across the Middle East, even overturning governments in some lands. By the time Pope Francis was elected conflict had erupted in a significant number of Arab nations. Recall that on his first Holy Thursday as Pope, Francis washed the feet of at least one young Muslim detainee. This was not inconsequential but rather a symbol of Pope Francis's agenda. In *Evangelii Gaudium* he refers to the relationship between evangelization and interreligious dialogue, describing how both "mutually support and nourish one another."[33] In reference to Islam he says: "Our relationship with the followers of Islam has taken on great importance, since they are now significantly present in many traditionally Christian countries";[34] he then speaks of Muslim immigrants, "we Christians should embrace with affection and respect Muslim immigrants to our countries in the same way that we hope and ask to be received and respected in countries of Islamic tradition,"[35] here directly referring to the ongoing conflicts in the Middle East and the persecution of Christians.

Significantly, and possibly shedding further light on Pope Francis's choice of Lampedusa for his first visit out of Rome Pope Francis then refers to migrants. "Migrants present a particular challenge for me, since I am the pastor of a Church without frontiers, a Church which considers herself mother to all."[36] He next elaborates on victims of human trafficking[37] and "doubly poor those women who endure situations of exclusion, maltreatment and violence,"[38] one of the references to women in Pope Francis's agenda that would become more frequent in later pronouncements, addresses, and actions.

When addressing challenges of today's world Pope Francis refers to global advances in areas such as health care and education but follows up quickly that globally the majority are not enjoying these advances

---

[32] Ibid., §210.
[33] Ibid., §251.
[34] Ibid., §252. See, also, Chapter 12 of the present volume on interreligious dialogue and EG.
[35] Ibid., §253.
[36] Ibid., §210.
[37] Ibid., §211.
[38] Ibid., §212.

preoccupied with subsistence living. He then powerfully speaks of an "economy of exclusion."

> Just as the commandment "Thou shalt not kill" sets a clear limit in order to safeguard the value of human life, today we also have to say "thou shalt not" to an economy of exclusion and inequality. Such an economy kills.[39]

Pope Francis then clearly targets modern economic policy for strong criticism:

> In this context, some people continue to defend trickle-down theories which assume the economic growth, encouraged by a free market, will inevitably succeed in bringing about greater justice and inclusivity in the world. This opinion, which has never been confirmed by the facts, expresses a crude and naïve trust in the goodness of those wielding economic power and in the sacralized workings of the prevailing economic system.[40]

Pope Francis returns to further criticize the global financial systems when addressing "the economy and the distribution of income." Building on an earlier pronouncement by Pope Benedict XVI, Pope Francis strongly asserts that inequality and the structures that keep people unequal must be addressed with urgency:

> The need to resolve the structural causes of poverty cannot be delayed, not only for the pragmatic reason of its urgency for the good order of society, but because society needs to be cured of a sickness which is weakening and frustrating it, and which can only lead to new crises.... As long as the problem of the poor are not radically resolved by rejecting the absolute autonomy of markets and financial speculation and by attacking the structural causes of inequality, no solutions will be found for the world's problems or, for that matter to any problems. Inequality is the root of social ills.[41]

Pope Francis continues, calling for an active interventionist role:

> We can no longer trust in the unseen forces and the invisible hand of the market. Growth in justice requires more than economic growth, while presupposing such growth: it requires decisions, programmes, mechanisms and processes specifically geared to a better distribution of income,

---

[39] Ibid., §53. See, also, esp. Chapter 10 of the present volume.
[40] Ibid., §54.
[41] Ibid., §202.

the creation of sources of employment and an integral promotion of the poor which goes beyond a simple welfare mentality.[42]

He returns to the faithful and admonishes those who are only looking after themselves and not concerned with what is happening to the poor, repeating the powerful phrase from his homily at Lampedusa – a *globalization of indifference*. More like a lamentation, Pope Francis elaborates this phrase:

> Almost without being aware of it, we end up being incapable of feeling compassion at the outcry of the poor, weeping for other people's pain, and feeling a need to help them, as though all this were someone else's responsibility and not our own.[43]

Yet Pope Francis's words have not sat comfortably with some of the faithful. In a media interview, soon afterward, Cardinal Dolan attempted to explain that Pope Francis's words were not directed at all billionaires, especially not US billionaires.[44]

Returning to Pope Francis's visit to Lampedusa and his homily, the action of going to Lampedusa powerfully spelt out who was of concern to him. His concern for refugees and migrants arriving in Lampedusa was not new to the Church as it has always been that the Church has always adopted a wider definition of who is a refugee than the United Nations 1951 definition.[45] What was significant was his highlighting the people who were crossing borders, without visas to flee poverty and poor governance. He was "updating" and putting flesh on those who earlier Church teachings have expressed concern about. Pope Francis in *Evangelii Gaudium* is reprioritizing and making the Church's social agenda more contemporary. It is a little like he is pressing a soft "reset" button for the Church, encouraging a refocusing. Earlier learning and memory is retained but there is a new emphasis and orientation made more explicit by actions.

Pope Francis's words and actions are counter the prevailing culture but consistent with the message of the gospel, the life of Jesus, and earlier Church teaching. In many senses Pope Francis's actions speak louder than words, but for those who missed the actions the words are in *Evangelii Gaudium*. His actions are more a further enunciation of these words.

---

[42] Ibid., §204.
[43] Ibid., §54.
[44] See http://news.genius.com/Ken-langone-the-pope-hates-us-billionaires-annotated.
[45] In the 1992 Vatican document: *Refugees: A Challenge to Solidarity*, the Pontifical Council "Cor Unum" and the Pontifical Council for the Pastoral Care of Migrants and Refugees used the term *refugee* in a broader sense and refers to the need to be inclusive of victims of armed conflict, erroneous economic policy, or natural disasters.

Indeed, this chapter was initially going to be called "'Actions Speak Louder Than Words." The social justice agenda of *Evangelii Gaudium* can better be understood when *Evangelii Gaudium* is read alongside the signs of our times as well as Pope Francis's ongoing actions and words in his many addresses.

From his early preconclave intervention where, as Cardinal Bergoglio, he powerfully and inspirationally outlined his hopes for the Church and the characteristics that he hoped would be present in the next pope through to *Evangelii Gaudium*, Pope Francis has very firmly called on the Church to turn from being rich and internally focused. He has put on the Church's agenda the means for doing this in active engagement, on the margins, with the poor. Pope Francis sees this as essential for the Church and a constitutive element of proclaiming the gospel in today's world.

What he has then gone on to reiterate is that this will not only assist the Church to get back on track, but it will be the saving of the Church. Pope Francis has put flesh on the words that were being generated in *Evangelii Gaudium*, and he has done so in a very passionate, bold, and vigorous manner. This is truly the "Francis Effect" that has captured the Church, the faithful, and the disillusioned:

> I exhort all countries to a generous openness which, rather than fearing the loss of local identity, will prove capable of creating new forms of cultural synthesis. How beautiful are those cities which overcome paralysing mistrust, integrate those who are different and make this very integration a new factor of development![46]

Furthermore, as Julian Filochowski celebrated, *Evangelii Gaudium* "is telling us quite bluntly that the option for the poor is no matter for esoteric deconstruction. It's simple and it's an imperative. The option for the poor means that the poor come first-first in our priorities, first in our pastoral plans, first in the use of our time, first in the call on our financial and human resources. It will be hard to swallow for the rich Church in the rich world."[47]

Other events in 2013 also shed light on Pope Francis's social agenda. This chapter has concentrated on the first few. At a Vatican conference to commemorate the fiftieth anniversary of *Pacem in Terris* (held on October 3, 2013, although the document was actually officially released on April 11,

---

[46] Ibid., 210.
[47] Filochowski, "Reflection on *Evangelii Gaudium*."

A Church of and for the Poor

1963) when one can only imagine that the finishing touches were being put on *Evangelii Gaudium*, Pope Francis referred again to events at Lampedusa because of yet another boat drowning. He spoke of how *Pacem in Terris*, fifty years ago, focused on: "a basic consequence: the value of the person, the dignity of every human being, to be promoted, respected and safeguarded always."[48] He further affirmed that every person must also be effectively offered access to the basic means of sustenance, food, water, housing, medical care, education, and the possibility to form and support a family. In terms of social agenda, he powerfully stated that: "these are the goals which must be given absolute priority in national and international action and indicate their goodness." Pope Francis then asked "[D]o they exist in practice?" Returning in this address to the daily tragedies occurring on route to Lampedusa and the causes behind people taking these risky journeys Pope Francis further elaborated upon the plight of those he was talking about:

> Speaking of peace, speaking of the inhuman global economic crisis that is a grave symptom of the lack of respect for man, I cannot but recall with great distress the victims of the umpteenth tragic shipwreck which occurred off the shore of Lampedusa today. The word "disgrace" comes to mind! It is a disgrace! Let us pray together to God for those who lost their lives: men, women, children, for their relatives and for all refugees. Let us unite our efforts so that similar tragedies are not repeated! Only through the concerted collaboration of everyone can we help to prevent them.[49]

Pope Francis in *Evangelii Gaudium* – as well as in earlier and subsequent addresses – has not only given us a social agenda, but through his words and actions he impels those listening to not only "'talk the talk," or read the teaching documents, but to actively engage through entering into a renewed personal encounter with Jesus Christ and those to whom Jesus came to bring the good news, the poor. Pope Francis's social agenda is not new to the Church but it is more simplified, updated, and more practice-based in orientation. It is a breath of fresh air for a Church in need of hope and inspirational for those who have felt marginalized. It could also save the Church from inner turmoil. Finally, and somewhat disappointingly,

---

[48] Address of Pope Francis to participants in a conference sponsored by the Pontifical Council for Justice and Peace celebrating the fiftieth anniversary of *Pacem in Terris* (October 3, 2014), http://w2.vatican.va/content/francesco/en/speeches/2013/october/documents/papa-francesco_20131003_50-pacem-in-terris.html.

[49] Ibid.

Pope Francis's social agenda is not as insightful – at least in *Evangelii Gaudium* – with regard to how women presently experience both Church and poverty. This omission highlights that the agenda outlined in *Evangelii Gaudium* and expressed in actions and Pope Francis's papacy continues to be a work in progress.[50]

---

[50] Admittedly, Pope Francis has addressed both of these issues on a number of subsequent occasions since, but it remains a work in progress nonetheless.

CHAPTER 10

Evangelizing in an Economy of Death

Mary Doak

Evangelii Gaudium, in response to the 2012 Ordinary Assembly of the Synod of Bishops, is, of course, focused on the topic of evangelization. Emphasizing the joy we find in God's infinite love for us, Francis's first major teaching document maintains that mission is at the heart of the church and should be central to the life of each Christian because all are called to share their joy with others.[1] Francis then summons the church to discernment and rejuvenation at all levels, including reform of administrative structures to better serve the church's evangelizing mission.[2]

It may seem odd, then, that this document received so much media attention in the United States for its rejection of trickle-down economics and its criticisms of global capitalism.[3] Some people are surely wondering how a papal exhortation devoted to evangelization came to focus on matters of Catholic social thought. Or was this yet another example of the media seizing on some small comment, perhaps taken out of context, while neglecting the overall thrust of the document?

No, this time the media did not mislead the public about the pope's intentions. Economic injustice is addressed repeatedly in *Evangelii Gaudium*, as Francis maintains that Christian evangelization necessarily includes opposition to the exclusions and inequalities of our global economy. Even

---

[1] "Christians have the duty to proclaim the Gospel without excluding anyone.... [T]hey should appear as people who wish to share their joy, who point to a horizon of beauty and who invite others to a delicious banquet." Francis 1st, Apostolic Exhortation *EG* (November 24, 2013), §15.
[2] On this point, Francis cites John Paul II. See *EG*, §27, and John Paul II, Apostolic Exhortation: *Ecclesia in Oceania* (November 22, 2001), §19: *AAS* 94 (2002), 390.
[3] See, e.g., the *New York Times* article http://www.nytimes.com/2014/01/06/us/politics/popular-voice-in-the-capitol-its-thepopes.html (accessed on September 6, 2014).

though he insists that this exhortation is not intended to be a social document, Francis devotes a major chapter to "the social dimensions of evangelization."[4] Further, as I will argue in the following text, Francis makes a significant contribution to Catholic social thought with his astute analysis of the dire social problems we face as well as with his compelling vision of a countercultural Christian response to these problems.

Until relatively recently, social justice was often described in official Catholic teaching as "pre-evangelization." The idea was that, by caring for people in need and working to reform unjust institutions, Christian evangelizers positively disposed people toward Christianity and thus laid the groundwork for their conversion.[5] In ecclesial documents of the 1970s, however, church leaders agreed that justice is so fundamental to Christian discipleship that the designation of justice as "pre"-evangelization should be rejected. Justice isn't "pre" anything – it is not a preface to Christian life, and it most certainly is not a mere strategy to impress potential converts. To the contrary, justice has intrinsic value and is a constitutive aspect of Christian discipleship and even of evangelization.[6]

Francis fully embraces this development in Catholic social thought, as is evident in his insistence that the task of evangelization cannot proceed apart from a Christian commitment to justice. Our joy in the gospel must be proclaimed in our deeds as well as in words because, as this current pope succinctly states, "to evangelize is to make the kingdom of God present in our world."[7] Evangelization, after all, does not seek merely to change someone's beliefs, but rather intends to share a love that transforms people and societies.

Francis's emphasis on justice is grounded in a concept of the human person as social. That is, humans are by nature so thoroughly relational that we become our true selves only in and through relationships of communion with God, with each other, and with the rest of creation (a theme developed further in Francis's encyclical *Laudato Si'*).[8] This understanding of humans as persons-in-community is the foundation for the long-standing criticism in Catholic social thought both of an individualistic capitalism,

---

[4] EG, chapter 4.
[5] See the succinct discussion of the development from pre-evangelization to evangelization in E. F. Sheridan, S.J., ed., *Do Justice: The Social Teaching of the Canadian Catholic Bishops* (Toronto: Jesuit Centre for Social Faith and Justice, 1987), 28–29.
[6] See especially the World Synod of Catholic Bishops, *Justice in the World*, esp. §6, and Paul VI, Apostolic Exhortation: *Evangelization in the Modern World* (December 8, 1975), esp. §§30 and 31.
[7] EG, §176.
[8] See Pope Francis, Encyclical Letter *Laudato Si'* (May 24, 2015), especially §66.

which neglects social responsibilities, and a collectivist communism, which fails to respect the dignity and rights of persons.[9]

Firmly located within this tradition of a social anthropology, Francis is convinced that the quality of social relations is a fundamental Christian concern, one that should inspire Christian resistance to the undermining of human community and the destruction of the environment by the forces of global capitalism.[10] Francis thus explores in *Evangelii Gaudium* what it means to live as a Christian, confronting the exchange relations of the market with the love of a creative God who empowers communities to value each other and all of creation.

Evangelii Gaudium is a lengthy and rich text that bears study from multiple angles. My focus here is on Francis's contribution to Catholic social thought, especially in terms of the demands of Christian witness today. I will explore Francis's contributions in two major areas: first, his incisive assessment of the ways in which current economic practices distort society, even to the point that the free market economy has become a new idol for many; and, second, Francis's vision of a countercultural ecclesial response in which prayer and an option for the poor become the hallmark of a church engaged in dialogical approaches to peace and justice in the face of the often-violent divisions of our world. Through these two intertwined contributions, Francis not only reiterates the essential insights of Catholic social thought but also includes new and challenging perceptions that intend to shake the church out of its complacency and into a more thoroughly countercultural witness to the joy of God's love.

1. Global Capitalism as Counterevangelization

Even while the title and the tone of this document highlight joy, Francis's assessment of the current extent of social injustice, and particularly of the distortions of our global economic structures, is grave and unflinching. Francis is confident that God is at work in the world and he invites us to "believe the Gospel when it tells us that the kingdom of God is already present in this world and is growing," yet he pulls no punches in describing

---

[9] See, e.g., Leo XIII, Encyclical Letter *Rerum Novarum* (May 15, 1891) and John Paul II, Encyclical Letter *Centesimus Annus* (May 1, 1991).
[10] Francis argues for an integral connection between care for the poor and care for the environment in both *EG* and *Laudato Si'*. The relational anthropology and critique of capitalism is consistent throughout these documents, even while the urgency of environmental concerns is the focus of *Laudato Si'* and so more thoroughly developed in that encyclical.

global capitalism as unjust, unequal, and deadly as it spreads throughout the world and has in many places become deified, a new idol.[11]

One might then expect Francis to adopt a dualism in which the reign of the true God and the reign of the false god divide up the world. However, Francis will allow us no such easy dichotomies, as he recognizes that sin and grace are present and intertwined throughout the world. Francis envisions a Christian response that neither accepts the status quo as the best we can hope for in this world nor withdraws in total condemnation of the evil and injustice of society. Rather, Francis calls for trust in the power of God to transform even these deeply entrenched and unjust structures. In ways that are not often foreseeable in advance, Francis contends, the Holy Spirit "overcomes every conflict by creating a new and promising synthesis."[12]

Despite his energizing and hopeful tone throughout this exhortation, Francis refuses to minimize the extent to which economic inequality distorts our societies as well as our very selves. In contrast to those who claim that inequality should be welcomed as the just outcome of economic competition, Francis argues that a high degree of inequality is intrinsically unjust. "The social function of property and the universal destination of goods are realities which come before private property," Francis maintains, and so "solidarity must be lived as the decision to restore to the poor what belongs to them."[13]

Francis's view is, of course, in considerable tension with much of the public conversation in the United States, where political debates often proceed on the assumption that people deserve whatever they have managed to amass, as long as no laws were broken. Many U.S. discussions of inequality even focus predominantly on whether the poor are to blame (even perhaps to be considered immoral) for not having competed more diligently, or whether the poor face barriers that ought to be eliminated so that they can compete more successfully. There is little consideration of the idea that the possession of excessive wealth is itself immoral; that, as Francis quotes from St. John Chrysostom, "Not to share one's wealth with the poor is to steal from them and to take away their livelihood. It is not our own goods which we hold, but theirs."[14] Not surprisingly, to many American ears, this ancient Christian perspective is not orthodox Christianity but communist heresy.

Moreover, Francis contends that an unequal society is inherently a violent society. Intriguingly, his point is not merely the rather commonplace

---

[11] EG, §278. On economic injustice, see especially §§53–60.
[12] EG, §230.
[13] EG, §189.
[14] EG, §57.

Evangelizing in an Economy of Death

observation that desperately poor people will do desperate things in order to survive. Francis further argues that the obvious injustice of extreme inequality encourages societal violence because, just as good spreads, so also evil tends to spread. Hence political and social structures founded on injustice are inherently unstable.[15]

Reading this document in the context of the currently high level of inequality in the United States, it certainly seems that Francis is on to something significant here. Distrust of US civic institutions is widespread. Indeed, one of the few sentiments shared currently by left and right in US politics is a lack of confidence in our government to secure justice and protection for all, though, of course, views about who is most at risk (poor minority communities or a majority white population of home owners) differ considerably. And there can be no doubt that this mistrust leads to violence, as media images of citizens at shopping malls armed with AK 47s, ranchers aiming assault rifles at federal rangers, and looters emptying shops during protests against police brutality make abundantly clear.[16]

Francis further observes that our global economic system no longer merely oppresses the poor by paying them inadequate and unjust wages: This economy "of exclusion and inequality" is deadly. Indeed, as Francis aptly discerns, "human beings are themselves considered consumer goods to be used and discarded" in a system in which "the powerful feed upon the powerless."[17] Not surprisingly, when the economy becomes a society's central source of shared meaning and value, there is little (including human life) that is not subject to market values. As Francis reminds us, even people are now for sale in an expanding global trade that makes people objects of exchange, bought and sold for their sexual services, their labor, or – especially horrific – their organs.[18]

Consider what it means in a consumer-oriented society to be the object rather than the subject of market exchanges. Increasingly in the United States, we appear in public less as citizens than as consumers. People are publicly marginalized not so much because they are (or are considered to

---

[15] EG, §59.
[16] Such images have been abundantly present in US media in 2014 and 2015, though by no means limited to these particular years. "Open carry" advocates are increasingly carrying weapons while shopping in public stores, Cliven Bundy's armed supporters turned back federal rangers in Nevada, while those protesting the police killing of Michael Brown in Ferguson, Missouri, faced fully militarized police sent to keep what Pope Francis would surely acknowledge is a very unjust peace.
[17] EG, §53.
[18] Francis discusses the trafficking of humans, including children, especially in EG, §211, though he does not mention the trafficking in human organs there.

be) incapable of reasoned argument, but rather because they are unable to act as subjects in market exchanges. Those who do not have the economic power to perform as consumers – or, even worse, those who are trafficked, sold to be consumed by others – cannot join in the behavior that marks one publicly as a capable actor participating in the common (economic) life of this society. And, of course, the natural world is seen as merely an exploitable resource, a point Francis also develops further in *Laudato Si'*.[19]

Francis bluntly informs us that this economy of exclusion and inequality is deadly – it kills bodies and spirits.[20] People are dying of starvation, preventable diseases, lack of medical care, and harsh and unsafe labor conditions: In short, people are dying because they are denied access to an adequate share of society's resources of shelter, food, legal protection, and medical services. Among those who survive physically, this marginalization can be lethal to their spirits when they are excluded from meaningful work and from the community ties that are essential to a fully human and dignified life. This is the situation especially of so many of the homeless, the abandoned mentally ill, and the young girls who are sold for sex on the margins of a society that shuns these people as though they are subhuman and of no concern to the rest of us.[21]

Yet Francis is no less troubled by the effects of this economy on those who are among the privileged of the world: Systems of inequality and exclusion also bring spiritual death to people who become indifferent to the suffering and exclusion of others, who are encouraged to overconsume and waste while others go without. Francis aptly identifies this as the "globalization of indifference": An indifference that harms not only those who suffer and die abandoned by society but also those privileged who, enchained by selfishness and habits of overconsumption, have little regard for the suffering of the poor and marginalized, including the natural environment.[22] As Francis declares, "I am interested ... in helping those who are in thrall to an individualistic, indifferent and self-centered mentality to be freed from those unworthy chains and to attain a way of living and thinking which is more humane, noble, and fruitful and which will bring dignity to their presence on this earth."[23] Insofar as our economic system

[19] *Laudato Si'*, §33.
[20] This economy is deadly not only to humans, of course, but also to the fertility of land and to many species, as Francis mentions in *EG* (see, for example, §215) but develops in *Laudato Si'*, esp. §§32–36.
[21] See especially *EG*, §§192, 210.
[22] *EG*, §§54, 215. That overconsumption renders people indifferent to the environment as well as to the poor is a theme developed thoroughly in *Laudato Si'*, especially §§202–204.
[23] *EG*, §208.

atomizes society, encouraging people to think of themselves as individual consumers primarily interested in maximizing exchange value rather than as members of a community with a responsibility for each other, then all of society is diminished.

This papal criticism of global capitalism thus far, though hard-hitting, is not unprecedented. After all, Catholic social thought has long advocated greater economic equality and deplored the injustice that breaks down social bonds, leaving so many destitute around the world. But Francis sails into less charted waters with his identification of free market capitalism as a "sacralized" system, a false god that is distorting society and culture, as all false gods do.[24] A particular sign of our times, in Francis's view, is the extent to which global capitalism has come to be treated as itself an idol, a deified institution.

What does it mean to make an idol out of an economic system? Is this merely a powerful turn of phrase deployed to shock people out of their complacency about the importance of money and material success in society?

I think not; indeed, Francis seems to intend for his accusation of the sacralization of the global economy to be taken quite literally. He warns of an "idolatry of money" in which money has become our central shared value, and he argues that the economy has become "deified" because it is treated as unquestionable, a force that controls our actions rather than being controlled by us.[25] Considering how much of US politics is focused on doing whatever is necessary to ensure a robust economy, it seems that Francis is on to something here. Has our economic system become a god, indeed the god, demanding our allegiance and service, the predominant source of public (and a good deal of private) meaning and value?

Francis's controversial (and much discussed) criticism of trickle-down economics is particularly relevant here. His point is not simply that unregulated capitalism fails to enrich all, though he does think it has failed, as he notes that the trickle-down theory "has never been supported by facts."[26] His further concern is that adherence to trickle-down economics is indicative of the extent to which the capitalist economy has become a salvific force, one that people dare not question as they cling to "a crude and naïve trust" that the market, if given free rein, will provide all they need.[27] Thus

[24] EG, §§54–56.
[25] EG, §§55, 56, 202. The urgency of challenging the demands of the global economic system in order to protect nature, the poor, and more human ways of life is explored further in *Laudato Si'*, esp. §§43–56.
[26] EG §54.
[27] Ibid.

in the United States we see increasing privatization of governmental functions due to widespread belief that the profit motive is more effective than government agencies or collective political action. Yet Francis maintains, to the contrary, "[A]s long as the problems of the poor are not radically resolved by rejecting the absolute autonomy of markets and financial speculation ... no solution will be found for the world's problems."[28]

An interesting point of comparison emerges here: The former pope, Benedict XVI, contends that Marxism undermines human freedom with its conviction that class struggle will inevitably result in the final perfection of a postcapitalist, classless society.[29] Benedict's criticism is not uncommon, and many today scoff at the naïveté of Marxist optimism about the dialectic of history. Yet is the post-1989 confidence that a capitalist economy will automatically result in the greatest good for all any less naïve? Is there any more room for ethics, responsibility, or basic human freedom in the contention that an unregulated economy inherently leads to the best possible outcome?

Another helpful historical comparison is provided by the American theologian Langdon Gilkey. As Gilkey argues in his assessment of the cultural role of the natural sciences in the mid-twentieth century, science at that time held theology's former position as "queen" of the sciences: Science was widely considered the most important form of knowledge, provided the most lucrative careers, and had become the model of true knowledge.[30] Other disciplines developed empirical approaches to emulate the natural sciences and to justify their claim to be a source of knowledge and thus to deserve a place in the university. Consider not only the rise of empiricism in the social sciences, but also the attempts to provide a rigorous "scientific" method for philosophy, literary criticism, and even theology!

Perhaps most significantly for our purposes here, Gilkey further argues that the natural sciences had become sacred, honored for their ability to save human beings from the powers of nature that threatened human well-being.[31] People at this time were more concerned with having a long, healthy, and secure life in this world than with the dangers of a punitive afterlife so, rather than seeking religious paths to heaven, they revered science as the source of freedom from physical threats and suffering in this life. The considerable mid-century optimism about powers of science led at times to exuberant descriptions of a scientifically based utopia

[28] EG, §202.
[29] Benedict XVI, Encyclical Letter *Spe Salvi* (November 30, 2007), §21.
[30] Langdon Gilkey, "The Creativity and Ambiguity of Science," in his *Society and the Sacred* (New York: Crossroad, 1981), 75–89.
[31] Ibid., esp. 77–78.

Evangelizing in an Economy of Death

that would soon ensure full health and physical well-being in climate-controlled cities.

Gilkey's assessment of the dominant social role played by science in the twentieth century might well engender feelings of nostalgia in readers today, at least in the United States. The results and even the basic presuppositions of the natural sciences are now widely questioned and often dismissed in public debates, where empirical evidence is frequently assumed to be a matter of perspective rather than an objective report on reality (or, worse, a fraud perpetrated on the public by a conspiracy of scientists seeking personal gain). Moreover, is it not indicative of the loss of prestige of the natural sciences that American universities are importing more science graduate students from abroad because American students are less interested in developing expertise in these fields?

Rather than concluding that the throne occupied first by theology and then by science is now empty, I would suggest that the fields of knowledge associated with business have assumed the social and cultural role played by science a few decades ago. Undergraduate students are flocking to majors in marketing and finance, graduate degrees in business are increasingly common, and universities are revising their requirements and offerings to increase their own and their students' marketability.

I would further contend that advertising, not scientific empiricism, currently provides the model of an acceptable public argument. Evidence or objectivity matter much less than a claim's "attractiveness" as measured by its social impact and ability to garner support. That is, if enough people take an argument seriously, that alone justifies its claim to be taken seriously. Further, market values have so colonized our habits of thought that it is common to hear even church leaders talk – without any evident irony – about increasing their market share. If there is a dominant model of knowledge, a new queen of the sciences in the United States, surely the economic sciences hold that position. Now more than ever, "the business of America is business."[32]

Francis is certainly right that the refusal to question the forces of the market is a denial of human freedom and responsibility no less than is the Marxist belief in the inevitability of a classless society. There is also considerable evidence that economics and business sciences are now the fields of study that provide the most widely esteemed knowledge. Still, we might

---

[32] This is a common rephrasing of US President Calvin Coolidge's actual statement "The chief business of the American people is business." See Coolidge, "Address to the American Society of Newspaper Editors, Washington D.C.," January 17, 1925. Available at http://www.presidency.ucsb.edu/ws/?pid=24180 (accessed September 7, 2014).

ask, is the market truly society's new idol? If so, from what fundamental threat does this god promise to save us?

In decades recently passed, as Gilkey's analysis shows, there was a general expectation in the United States that increasing scientific knowledge would provide salvation from nature's power to destroy human beings and their projects. Today, people are preoccupied with the economy because they hope that it will save them from poverty, unemployment, deprivation, and the loss of opportunities for self-development (available to those who can afford them). Neoliberal economists assure us that, if market forces are allowed to function freely, those forces will supply all human needs and material desires, presumably including the desire to be distracted with ever new things to consume. In sum, if people cooperate with the forces of the market, they are told they can hope to inhabit a consumer paradise; by contrast, if people do not sacrifice enough to the economy and serve it well, they fear being subjected to poverty and destitution.

If this analysis is correct, there have been significant cultural changes in those societies that once worshipped God and feared an afterlife in hell, then revered science and feared a lack of control over natural forces, but now focus on the free market, fearing the loss of consumer power brought about by an economic downturn. As Francis has pointed out, while God seeks to unite people in communities of love and justice, the false god of the market dissolves community bonds, insisting that all compete and consume as individuals and without concern for the inequality and injustice, the abuse of people and of nature that result.[33]

There is, then, an inherent conflict between Christian allegiance to the values of God's reign and the profit motive of the capitalist economy. Indeed, Francis explicitly challenges the assumption that seeking profit easily accords with serving the reign of God. Rather, Francis argues, from the perspective of market values, "God can only be seen as uncontrollable, unmanageable, even dangerous, since he calls human beings to their full realization and to freedom from all forms of enslavement."[34]

2. Christian Resistance to the Economy of Death

Francis's purpose with *Evangelii Gaudium* is not, of course, simply to provide yet another diatribe against global capitalism and its demand for the sacrifice of community, relationships, natural resources, and finally

---

[33] *EG*, especially §67. This theme is also developed in *Laudato Si'*, especially in chapters 2 and 3.
[34] *EG*, §57.

even of lives. Francis intends to strengthen the spread of Christian values that challenge the social dominance of capitalism and inspire people to transform the unjust structures and practices that result in so much suffering and death. But what should Christians do? How would Francis have Christians – and the church – evangelize in the context of this death-dealing economy?

In describing the countercultural Christian life, Francis emphasizes three key aspects of witness to the true God and the values of God's reign that are especially needed today if the church is to be engaged in, but decidedly not of, the world. Through a personal and collective spirituality, through political actions, especially to restructure the economy, and through the manner in which religious beliefs are brought to bear in the public realm, Christians cooperate with God's desire to transform a suffering world, both human (as emphasized in *Evangelii Gaudium*) and nonhuman (as developed in *Laudato Si'*).[35]

The first and fundamental component of Christian resistance to the hegemony of the global capitalist system, then, is that each Christian strive to grow in a spirituality of prayer and personal concern for the poor. As Karl Rahner once declared, "the Christian of the future will be a mystic or he [sic] will not exist at all."[36] Francis invites all Christians to seek each day "a renewed personal encounter with Jesus Christ, or at least an openness to letting him encounter them."[37] Certainly if Christians are to resist the power of this false economic god and its demand for worship, they must be fully rooted in a relationship with the true God who makes it possible to value all things rightly (i.e., as of value in itself and not merely in terms of marketability) and who inspires "a communion which heals, promotes, and reinforces personal bonds."[38]

In addition to being a more prayerful people, Francis calls for the church to become a church of and for the poor. We must go first not to our friends or to the wealthy, Francis insists, but to those most alone and in need, notwithstanding the cost to ourselves and to the church.[39] As Francis proclaims, "I prefer a Church which is bruised, hurting and dirty because it

---

[35] For the discussion of spirituality, political engagement, and public religiosity in resistance to climate change and thee abuse of the natural world, see *Laudato Si'*, especially chapter 6.
[36] Karl Rahner, *Concern for the Church* (New York: Crossroad, 1981), 149.
[37] EG, §3.
[38] EG, §67.
[39] EG, §48.

has been out on the streets, rather than a church which is unhealthy from being confined and clinging to its own security."[40]

Papal support for the option for the poor is not new, of course. John Paul II introduced this concept from liberation theology (endorsed by the 1979 3rd Annual CELAM conference in Puebla Mexico) into papal writings, especially in *Centisimus Annus*.[41] Francis cites the writings of Benedict XVI as well as of John Paul II in confirmation that the option for the poor is a well-established tenet of Catholic social thought.[42]

However, Francis adds a new and, I think, profoundly challenging aspect here with his contention that no Christian is so busy or so important that she or he is excused from personal engagement with those who are poor, powerless, or insignificant to society.[43] It is not enough that we have our hearts in the right place, that we are concerned about social problems and fully support those (others) who are engaged with the poor. According to Francis, Christians who are not in some way actively reaching out to include the marginalized or to accompany the vulnerable are only partially living the Christian vocation. A fully Christian life does not "outsource" its option for the poor, hiring others to care for those in need in our stead.[44]

Alas for academics, Francis specifies that talking and writing about the causes of poverty, even holding symposia about the option for the poor, are also insufficient.[45] Those who would follow Jesus of Nazareth must be committed to personal engagement with the marginalized and rejected of society. After all, what else could it mean to follow the One who proclaimed God's reign at hand?

In Francis's vision of the church, then, prayer and some form of a personal option for the poor are the essential elements of a spirituality that forms Christians individually – and the church collectively – to resist the hegemony of the market and its false values.[46] Taking the time for prayer, which can only appear as a waste of time from an economic perspective,

---

[40] EG, §49.
[41] *Centesimus Annus*, §57. See also the discussion in E. F. Sheridan, ed., *Love Kindness: The Social Teaching of the Canadian Catholic Bishops* (Toronto: Jesuit Centre for Social Faith and Justice, 1991), esp. 20–23.
[42] EG, §198.
[43] EG, §§201, 20, 187.
[44] I am indebted to Gary Arps, of St. Paul's Episcopal Cathedral in San Diego California for the application of the term *outsourcing* to the option for the poor.
[45] EG, §207.
[46] This is, of course, drawing on an a well-established understanding of Christianity (as Gustavo Gutiérrez has often said, there is no Christian life without prayer and no Christian life without active concern for the poor). But these two aspects of Christian life are especially significant in countering the market values of contemporary culture.

enables people to be formed by the dangerous values of God's passionate concern for the poor and vulnerable.

Personal engagement with the poor is also, of course, a form of resistance to market values, as it is seldom an efficient way to maximize one's economic power. Indeed, for many (perhaps most) Christians, forming relationships with the abandoned people on the margins of society takes too much time, time that many feel they cannot afford to divert from efforts to advance careers and to increase their economic viability. And so, as Francis notes, people believe themselves too busy to follow Jesus in a thoroughly countercultural way of being in the world. It is much easier to sprinkle a little Christian worship on top of lives that otherwise differ little from the rest of society.

Yet personal engagement with the poor, the marginalized, and the suffering not only challenges the capitalist values that would subject everything to a cost-benefit analysis, but also provides an effective antidote to the globalization of indifference that Francis has drawn our attention to and that, I believe, often covers a deep despair. People who do not take some real action, even a small one, are surely more likely to be overwhelmed by the scope of the problem and more inclined to turn away from thinking about the tremendous and seemingly inevitable suffering in the world.

As Benedict XVI reminds us, especially in his encyclical *Deus Caritas est*, personal involvement is also necessary to resist an overly bureaucratized response to poverty. People need more than material assistance distributed through an impersonal system. In addition to food, shelter, and medical care, human flourishing requires what entitlement programs cannot provide: love and affection, esteem, social relationships, a place in society.[47] As Benedict explains, "Seeing with the eyes of Christ, I can give to others much more than their outward necessities; I can give them the look of love which they crave."[48] A Christian option for the poor must then extend beyond simply funding professional social workers, however important these are; a Christian approach includes personal relationships that reknit the bonds of human community.

Though Francis clearly shares the concern of Benedict XVI (and, perhaps more notably, of Dorothy Day)[49] that Christians not shirk their

---

[47] Benedict XVI, Encyclical Letter *Deus Caritas Est* (December 25, 2005), §§18, 34, 35.
[48] *Deus Caritas Est*, §18.
[49] To whom Pope Francis paid special tribute when addressing both US houses of Congress in 2015, Address of the Holy Father, US Capitol (September 24, 2015), https://w2.vatican.va/content/francesco/en/speeches/2015/september/documents/papa-francesco_20150924_usa-us-congress.html.

personal responsibility to the marginalized and suffering in society, Francis nevertheless refuses to let us off the hook politically, as though we could have an option for the poor that did not respond to the systemic causes of poverty. He reminds his readers that official magisterial teaching affirms that "participation in political life is a moral obligation."[50] Francis is especially concerned that the systemic causes of inequality and poverty be addressed. With considerable urgency, Francis insists that "the need to resolve the structural causes of poverty cannot be delayed ... because society needs to be cured of a sickness which is weakening and frustrating it."[51] This then brings us to a second significant aspect of Francis's call for resistance: Christian responsibility to engage in political action to transform an unjust society and economy.

That we should work to ensure that the economy is more justly structured, so that the goods of the earth serve the good of all people, is nothing new for Catholicism. Catholic social thought has long held that the economy, as well as culture and politics, should be informed by the values of the reign of God. As many will recall, Benedict discussed this at length in his last encyclical, where he finally was able fully to affirm that justice is not merely the task of the state but also a concern of the church, because justice is a necessary requirement – indeed, the necessary institutional path – of love.[52] To be sure, justice and love are not identical; rather, as Paul Tillich argued in his classic text *Love, Power, and Justice*, justice and love are distinct but inseparable because justice preserves what love seeks to unite.[53]

In calling Christians to resist, and ultimately to transform, an idolatrous and unjust capitalist economy, Francis thus stands firmly within the Catholic mainstream, which emphasizes concern for the sociopolitical structures of society. As understood in the Catholic tradition, Christianity is not properly confined to one's private or inner emotional life but rather

---

[50] *EG*, §220, quoting the US Conference of Catholic Bishops' Pastoral Letter, *Forming Consciences for Faithful Citizenship* (November 2007).

[51] *EG*, §202.

[52] Benedict XVI, Encyclical Letter *Caritas in Veritate* (June 29, 2009), esp. §7. See my more developed discussion of the evolution of Benedict's thought on the centrality of justice in Mary Doak, "Love and Justice: Engaging Benedict XVI on Christian Discipleship in a Secular Age," in (*At the Limits of the Secular: Reflections on Faith and Public Life*, ed. William A. Barbieri, Jr (Grand Rapids, MI: Eerdmans Publishing, 2014), 250–272.

[53] Paul Tillich, *Love, Power, and Justice: Ontological Analyses and Ethical Applications* (New York: Oxford University Press, 1954), pp. 25, 67–71. In *Laudato Si'*, Francis clarifies that the loving union of all in God extends to all of creation. See *Laudato Si'*, especially §§89, 92.

engages the full human being and is intended to transform all aspects of life, including social and political relationships.[54]

And yet there is a contemporary – and fairly popular – argument that Christians should focus their energies on providing a communal witness against the injustice of society rather than working to transform governmental policies and structures. John Howard Yoder and Stanley Hauerwas contributed enormously to the development of this perspective in the United States, arguing that the political responsibility of the church is primarily to be the church, showing the world what a truly just, peaceful, and loving community is.[55] Despite a tendency of those schooled in this perspective to produce antigovernment diatribes that have more than a little in common with American libertarianism, this is not finally an individualistic form of Protestant Christianity, but rather one that emphasizes the role of the Christian community.[56]

In brief, contemporary theological arguments against Christian engagement in politics are usually based on some combination of the following tenets: (1) The modern secular state lacks the explicit acknowledgment of God essential for all true justice; (2) Christian churches contribute more to society by providing the countercultural witness of living justly within the Christian community than by engaging in the ultimately futile effort to make a secular state more just; and (3) engaging in efforts to persuade the general public to support more just structures in fact weakens the Christian witness by accepting the secular framework essential to participation in the larger public debate. Because Christian values cannot appear in public life as properly Christian, it follows that any Christian perspective risks distortion when put forth in the secular terms of the public conversation.

There can be no doubt that Christians can and should better witness to true justice through more faithful, just, and loving church communities. Indeed, Francis calls the church to provide a stark contrast to this war-torn and deeply divided world through a witness of ecclesial harmony. Francis writes, "I especially ask Christians in communities throughout the world to

---

[54] EG, §§178, 180.
[55] See especially John Howard Yoder, *The Priestly Kingdom: Social Ethics as Gospel* (Notre Dame, IN: University of Notre Dame Press, 1984) and Stanley Hauerwas, *After Christendom: How the Church is to Behave if Freedom, Justice, and a Christian Nation are Bad Ideas* (Nashville, TN: Abingdon Press, 1991).
[56] See, e.g., the critique of "the state" for monopolizing the right to use violence within a territory as developed by William T. Cavanaugh, "The City: Beyond Secular Parodies," in *Radical Orthodoxy*, ed. John Milbank, Catherine Pickstock, and Graham Ward (London and New York: Routledge, 1999), 182–200.

offer a radiant and attractive witness of fraternal communion. Let everyone admire how you care for one another."[57]

Nevertheless, Catholic social thought does not accept that there is a forced option between providing the witness of a Christian community united in love and justice, on the one hand, and Christian involvement with efforts to create a more justly structured society, on the other hand. Instead of choosing between these two approaches, Catholic social thought insists that both are necessary and, in fact, the two inform each another. This is especially evident in the documents of the Second Vatican Council, in which the Catholic Church defines itself as "like a sacrament, or as a sign *and* instrument both of a closely knit union with God and of the unity of the whole human race."[58] As with any sacrament, according to Catholic thought, the witness (or sign) and the effective transformation (instrument) are not distinct but rather are integrally related.

There is great wisdom in this insistence on combining rather than separating witness and sociopolitical engagement. After all, the church cannot be a credible and successful agent of greater human unity in the world if the church cannot manage to achieve a reasonable degree of community within itself. (In noting the deep divisions and even warring within Christian communities, Francis aptly asks, "Whom are we going to evangelize, if this is the way we act?"[59]) At the same time, to the extent that Christians are transformed by the experience of loving community within the church, will this not result in greater appreciation of human relationships and thus lead to different, more loving engagement with others outside of the church?

Francis's central theme in *Evangelii Gaudium* is that Christians who experience God's love in their own lives should feel compelled to bring the joy of that love to all others in the world. Indeed, Christians have a responsibility especially to those outside of the Christian community, to those who, as Francis says, "are living without a faith community to support them, without meaning and a goal in life."[60] However powerful the witness of a loving Christian community may be, Christian life is not intended to be lived within the comfort of the church. As Francis explains, "my hope is that we will be moved by the fear of remaining shut up within structures which give us a false sense of security ... within habits which make us feel

---

[57] EG, §99.
[58] Emphasis added; Second Vatican Council, Dogmatic Constitution on the Church, *Lumen Gentium* (November 21, 1964), §1.
[59] EG, §100.
[60] EG, §49.

safe, while at our door people are starving" (literally and figuratively).[61] All have a duty to evangelize in word and in deed, and this includes attending to what Francis has called "the social dimensions of evangelization": creating more just and truly human socioeconomic and political structures.[62]

But what about the claim that Christian engagement in the politics of a secular society cannot succeed because any polity that fails explicitly to recognize God is incapable of true justice? This perspective draws on an interpretation of the thought of St. Augustine of Hippo, especially in his *City of God*, where St. Augustine argues that full justice requires that each and all, including God, receive their due. Hence, a society that fails to honor God would be inherently deficient and cannot be made completely just.[63]

Despite the depth of St. Augustine's influence on the Catholic tradition, Catholic sociopolitical thought has not generally supported the conclusion that only governments that explicitly recognize divine authority can achieve the relative justice among people that it is the obligation of the state to provide in this world. To be sure, grace is necessary to overcome sin and to restore the human capacity to do good. However, the Catholic tradition has also maintained that divine grace may well be present in the lives of those who do not believe in God. Further, as the Thomistic tradition has maintained, justice is a natural rather than a theological virtue, so that governments can provide the relative political justice needed in this world regardless of whether the government affirms belief in God.[64]

Again we find Francis consistent with the Catholic tradition on this point. He does not agree with the claim that only theists can achieve political justice. Instead, Francis clearly proclaims that all who seek truth, goodness, and beauty, even those who do not consider themselves religious, are the church's "precious allies in the commitment to defending human dignity, in building peaceful coexistence between peoples and in protecting creation."[65]

Finally, a key argument against Christian engagement in liberal democracies depends on the claim that Christian positions cannot appear as Christian in public life, an argument developed especially by Stanley Hauerwas.[66] However much it may have been the case that some

---

[61] Ibid.
[62] See especially *EG*, §§176–216.
[63] See, e.g., Cavanaugh, "The City," esp. 183.
[64] See especially Thomas Aquinas, *Summa Theologiae*, Pt. I-II, Q 109, art. 2 and Pt. I-II, Q. 62, art. 2 and 3.
[65] *EG*, §257.
[66] See, e.g., his article, "The Church and Liberal Democracy: The Moral Limits of a Secular Polity," in Stanley Hauerwas, *A Community of Character: Toward a Constructive Christian*

mid-century Christian ethicists suppressed specifically Christian insights in their social ethics, Hauerwas engages in his characteristic exaggeration in maintaining that distinctly Christian arguments cannot be inserted in the public discussion. This is simply not true, at least in the United States. Indeed, explicitly Christian positions are so common and at times even expected in American politics that it is mystifying that this allegation has been taken seriously. The attention given publicly to *Evangelii Gaudium* and, more recently, to *Laudato Si'*, is itself evidence that an explicitly and thoroughly Christian criticism of the values of the modern capitalist economy can indeed be a part of the public conversation.

Certainly there are some who cite the "separation of church and state" in opposition to the inclusion of explicitly religious positions in public debates. Yet the idea of such a separation (which is not itself part of the US Constitution) is best understood as appropriately describing the separation of authorities, so that leaders of religious communities have no inherent right to decide political questions for society, and political leaders have no authority to interfere in the internal affairs of the church. And, of course, there is no good reason for non-Christians to accept a Christian position as authoritative simply because Christian authorities (whether Bible or church leaders) declare it to be so. To persuade a non-Christian, one would be well-advised to proffer reasons not dependent solely on Christian authority. Nevertheless, the fact that some religious arguments may not be persuasive or that some people reject them out of hand does not mean that religious arguments are in fact banned from political discourse, at least not in the United States. Rather, those who take seriously the Catholic understanding of reason as a gift from God to lead us to the truth have grounds to hope that religious differences need not be a barrier to reasoning together about politics, as Francis contends.

In broaching the topic of religious argumentation in public life, we have come to the third and (for present purposes) final aspect of Francis's contribution to the social role of Christians in the contemporary world: his defense of the public character of religion and his call for Christian engagement in dialogue. If a key part of Christian discipleship in our times involves political action, as Francis has insisted in this papal exhortation, then it makes sense that we must pay some considerable attention to the

---

Social Ethic (Notre Dame, IN: University of Notre Dame Press, 1981), 72–86. As he asserts there, "All I mean by secular is that our polity and politics gives no special status to any recognizable religious group. Correlatively such a policy requires that public policies be justified on grounds that are not explicitly religious" (72).

role of religion in the public discourse of the many increasingly pluralistic societies.

The previous two popes, John Paul II and Benedict XVI, also defended the public role of religious beliefs, arguing strenuously against the privatization of religion (especially in resistance to atheistic communism and the secularization of Europe). Francis, adding his voice in support of the fundamental religious freedom to give public witness to one's beliefs, clarifies that a religiously pluralistic society must allow all beliefs – and all opposition to belief – in the public conversation.[67] Francis would thus have Christians engage rather than simply criticize secularism and atheism.

Francis further contends that the wisdom of a particular religious tradition is not necessarily inaccessible to those outside of that tradition. He specially mentions religious classics as texts that communicate wisdom from which all might learn, regardless of whether people share the religious presuppositions of the work.[68] In Francis's view, humanity is not condemned to a clash of narratives, to the inherently agonistic stance of seeking "to position" others within one's perspective in order to avoid being "positioned" by an alternative view (as described by John Milbank).[69] Francis instead maintains that people of all backgrounds and beliefs can think together, especially as they seek to determine their common good as the basis for public policy. Because politics must seek the good of all in society, and this good cannot be defined from one perspective or by an elite group, Francis insists that all affected should be involved in the discernment.[70]

Instead of downplaying or suppressing differences, then, Francis encourages dialogue as a means to greater understanding, respect, and peace.[71] Religious (or other) differences need not lead to violence that tears society apart, but should instead be valued as a means of mutual enrichment and community. In fact, Francis calls Christians and others to respond to the pressing social need of "a means for building a consensus and agreement while seeking the goal of a just, responsive and inclusive society."[72]

---

[67] EG, §§255, 257.

[68] EG, §256. Cf. the similar defense of the public role of the religious classic in David Tracy, *The Analogical Imagination: Christian Theology and the Culture of Pluralism* (New York: Crossroad, 1981).

[69] See especially, John Milbank, *Theology and Social Theory: Beyond Secular Reason* (Oxford and Cambridge, MA: Blackwell, 1990), especially 1–6.

[70] EG, §239. Francis further argues in *Laudato Si'* that inclusive public dialogue is our best option for overcoming the dominance of market values that is a barrier to political action in protection of the environment. See *Laudato Si*, especially §§179–181.

[71] EG, §§238–258, esp. 250.

[72] EG, §239.

Francis is thus quite clear that such dialogue, while integral to evangelization in all of its aspects, is not intended solely to convert others. Nor do Catholics engage in dialogue simply to understand others better (though this is one of dialogue's valued results). Francis further expects that all engaged in dialogue can learn from one another, in what he refers to as an "exchange of gifts."[73]

In an approach that is very similar (if not identical) to the mutually critical correlation method in theology, Francis also contends that openness to learning from others ought to be a hallmark of Christian dialogue with culture and science.[74] Even while Christian faith benefits from the developments of culture and the sciences, the "light which faith offers" may contribute insight even to nonbelievers as it "stimulates reason to broaden its perspectives."[75] If we take seriously the Catholic affirmation of an ultimate harmony between reason and faith, as Francis does, then we need not fear that we risk our Christian beliefs by engaging and learning from non-Christian perspectives and religions.[76]

3. Conclusion

In *Evangelii Gaudium*, Francis enriches Catholic social thought with his vision of a church fully engaged in resisting and transforming the economic structures that lead to so much unnecessary suffering, death, and diminishment. As I have argued here, most notable is his account of the evangelizing power of a Christianity marked by a spirituality of personal prayer and active option for the poor, by political action to end the structural causes of poverty, and by engagement in public dialogue leading to greater understanding and peace. As Francis argues, all of this is integral to the Christian task of evangelizing, of spreading the joy of the gospel and the reign of God in a culture of death and indifference to widespread suffering and loss of life.

In a world of individualism, competition, and self-centeredness, Francis challenges us to move beyond preoccupation with personal security, to foster solidarity, and to be dedicated to action with and for others and the natural world. While this affirmation of social engagement in seeking a

---

[73] EG, §246. See, also, the discussion of ecumenical and interreligious engagement in Chapter 12 of this present volume.

[74] See the discussion in David Tracy, *Blessed Rage for Order: The New Pluralism in Theology* (Minneapolis, MN: Seabury Press, 1975), especially 32–34.

[75] EG, §238.

[76] See especially EG, §242.

truly common goodwill appear to some as a threat to the distinctiveness of Catholic identity, it is to be hoped that more will recognize that such openness is a thoroughly countercultural stance rooted in faith in the Triune God who has opened the divine life to embrace the otherness of all of creation. Christians need not – and should not – respond to diversity by turning inward and focusing their energies on maintaining a distinct Christian identity in opposition to others. As Vincent J. Miller has argued, such a strategy is itself a refusal to be truly countercultural as it conforms "to the dominant cultural logic" of fragmentation.[77] Francis calls the church instead to the more profound and evangelical Christian witness of a life risked in open engagement with all others and in commitment to the common good of all in God's creation.

---

[77] Vincent J. Miller, "Media Constructions of Space, the Disciplining of Religious Traditions, and the Hidden Threat of the Post-Secular," in Barbieri, *At the Limits of the Secular*, 162–196.

PART III

Church and World in the Twenty-First Century: The Dialogical Vision of *Evangelii Gaudium*

CHAPTER 11

The Global Vision of *Evangelii Gaudium*

Cultural Diversity as a Road to Peace

Drew Christiansen, S.J.

A postsynodal apostolic exhortation is a special genre of papal teaching. Ordinarily it consists of a pope's presentation of the recommendations of a synod. A commission of bishops elected from among the synod's participants shapes the pope's message from proposals made by the whole assembly. Some, like John Paul II's "Hope for Lebanon" (*Espérance pour le Liban*, 1997), have an exceptionally structured character, laying out the papal agenda. Others, like *Ecclesia in America*, the exhortation after Synod for America (1999) are more straightforward presentation of the proposals voted by the synod.

What distinguishes *Evangelii Gaudium* from earlier apostolic exhortations is that it blends a fulsome report on the synod's conclusions with extended reflections that belong uniquely to Pope Francis, like his advice on homiletics (§§135–159) and his four principles for promoting peace and the common good (§§217–237). In addition, there are extraordinary passages of incisive psychological and spiritual assessment, notably on the failings of the Church's "pastoral workers" (§§76–109). Every time I pick it up I am intellectually and spiritually challenged. For this essay, however, I want to focus on Pope Francis's view of the role of cultural diversity in the structure of peace.

Inculturation

On the question of the legitimate diversity of cultures, Francis could not be more different than his predecessor. Benedict XVI tried to preserve the Christian identity of Western Europe. In my opinion, he was right on the history, and right in pleading that today's Europeans, at a minimum, should recognize the Christian heritage of Western civilization; but for the most part his efforts were rejected. By contrast, Francis's position is that the gospel embraces all cultures and European civilization is not privileged. It turns out that the fact that we have a pope from outside Europe has resulted in a teaching that is truly more universal in its appreciation for non-European cultures.

In his controversial lecture at Regensburg, Benedict privileged Greco-Roman culture and assigned to the Greek language and Hellenistic philosophy a quasirevelatory status. There is a "profound harmony between what is Greek in the best sense of the word," he argued at Regensburg, "and the biblical understanding of faith in God."[1] For Benedict, the inculturation of Christianity into Hellenistic culture is privileged among the cultural expressions of Christianity. "The New Testament was written in Greek and bears the imprint of the Greek spirit, which had already come to maturity as the Old Testament developed," he wrote. Even the Septuagint Greek text, Benedict argued, is more than another translation of the scriptures. It "is an independent textual witness," Benedict wrote, "and a distinct and important step in the history of revelation, one which brought about this encounter in a way that was decisive for the birth and spread of Christianity."[2]

While some aspects of ancient Greek culture may be rejected, Benedict argues Greek reason cannot be. For "the fundamental decisions made about the relationship between faith and the use of human reason," he asserts, "are part of the faith itself; they are developments consonant with the nature of faith itself." Thus, for Benedict, European Christianity holds a primacy not enjoyed by other Christian cultures. "Christianity, despite its origins and some significant developments in the East," he declared, "finally took on its historically decisive character in Europe."[3] That last comment manifests a failure to appreciate the heritage of Oriental Christianity.

---

[1] Pope Benedict XVI, "Faith Reason and the University – Memories and Reflections," September 12, 2006, https://w2.vatican.va/content/benedict-xvi/en/speeches/2006/september/documents/hf_ben-xvi_spe_20060912_university-regensburg.html. All subsequent quotations from the same text.
[2] Ibid.
[3] Elsewhere, in his dialogue with the German philosopher Jurgen Habermas, *The Dialectics of Secularization: On Reason and Religion* (San Francisco: Ignatius, 2006), p. 76, Cardinal Ratzinger conceded that "our secular rationality may seem very obvious to our reason, which has been formed in the West; but *qua* rationality, it comes up against its limitations when it attempts to demonstrate itself. The proof of it is in reality linked to specific cultural contexts, and it must acknowledge that it cannot as such be reproduced in the whole of mankind."

Francis insists, by contrast, that the spirit is at work in all cultures, seeding a *preparatio evangelica* in every culture on par with that of classical Western culture. Francis takes direct aim at the proposition that Western, Hellenistic culture has primacy.

> We cannot demand that peoples of every continent, in expressing their Christian faith, imitate modes of expression which European nations developed at a particular moment of their history, because the faith cannot be constricted to the limits of understanding and expression of any one culture. It is an indisputable fact that no single culture can exhaust the mystery of our redemption in Christ.[4]

Putting a point on his critique, Francis writes, "We in the Church can fall into a needless hallowing of our own culture, and thus show more fanaticism than true evangelical zeal."[5]

As prefect of the Congregation of the Doctrine of the Faith (CDF), Cardinal Ratzinger stressed uniformity in both doctrinal and theological formulations. In *Evangelii Gaudium*, Francis, who believes that the gospel defies any single formulation, supports theologians in their scholarly efforts "to advance dialogue with the world of cultures and the sciences";[6] and in reading the Signs of the Times, Francis foreswears any claim to propose generalized solutions to the world's problems, an ambition both John Paul II and Benedict XVI still shared.[7]

In *Dominus Jesus*, the CDF tried to preserve the Church from syncretism.[8] Francis, instead, invites us to find the spirit's work in strangers of every type; he is confident that the spirit brings us novelty and diversity as well as unity. In his openness to other traditions, Francis is more like Pope Saint John Paul II who, in *Redemptoris Missio*, affirmed that the "Spirit's presence and activity affect not only individuals built also society and history, peoples, cultures and religions."[9] Above all, he affirms that the unity to which God is leading us will preserve every culture's gifts in its uniqueness. In the inculturation of the gospel, therefore, Francis is disposed to see not syncretism, but – and I quote – "new synthesis" initiated by the Holy Spirit.[10]

---

[4] *EG*, §118.
[5] Ibid., §117.
[6] Ibid., §133.
[7] Ibid., §51.
[8] Congregation of the Doctrine of the Faith, *Dominus Iesus*: Declaration on the Unicity and Salvific Universality of Jesus Christ and the Church (Vatican, 2000).
[9] *Redemptoris Missio* (1990), §28.
[10] *EG*, §129. See, also, Chapter 2 of this volume by Dennis Doyle on the notion of synthesis in *EG*.

Please do not take these contrasts the wrong way. I believe Pope Benedict did many forward-looking, progressive things that go unacknowledged because of hasty judgments on the part of academics and journalists, two professions I know from the inside. But on the question of diversity, Benedict had a blind spot; and he particularly lacked feeling for the diversity of cultures, including an explicit dismissal of the ancient Oriental Christian cultures that lay at the basis of the church's claim to universality. Recall his dismissal of Eastern Christianity in the Regensburg Lecture, "Christianity, *despite its origins and some significant developments in the East,* finally took on its historically decisive character in Europe."[11] Pope Francis, by contrast, is attuned to diversity in its multifarious forms.

Part I: A Theology of Diversity

Diversity in the Spirit

Diversity as a constituent gift of God to the Church and to the human family is the most novel and disruptive concept in the exhortation. In support of this position, Francis cites Thomas Aquinas's famous affirmation that the diversity of creation witnesses to the glory of God.[12] In church life, of course, we may think about the diversity of charisms (Eph 4:11) and of the twenty-four Eastern churches in their various cultures. It is not a stretch to say that in *Evangelii Gaudium* "diversity" is almost a transcendental, like the one, the true, the good, and the beautiful in classical and scholastic philosophy. Arguably, not since John "Duns" Scotus and Nicholas of Cusa have diversity and multiplicity been as esteemed in Western theology. Perhaps never before has a reigning pontiff put as much theological justification for change and development in the church's life, for, according to Francis it is the syntheses of diverse cultures with the gospel that constantly renews the church's life.

The emphasis on diversity is an indication of the new pope's sense of the divine creativity working through the particularity and multiplicity of life. Like his namesake Francis, the wandering troubadour, who gave us "The Canticle of the Creatures" or his fellow Jesuit Gerard Manley Hopkins, the author of "Pied Beauty," he finds signs of divine glory in the diversity of creation and of human culture. God is present and active, not just in

---

[11] Benedict XVI, "Faith Reason and the University", emphasis mine.
[12] EG, §40 and n. 44.

rationally organized dimensions of life, but in all its brimming, buzzing multiplicity as well.

William James wrote there are two kinds of intellectual temperaments, monists and pluralists.[13] When you read "The Joy of the Gospel," I am sure you will agree Francis seems a pluralist, though pluralist with a lowercase "p," because the universe is ultimately united in Christ. Diversity is fundamental, among other things, to his strong and novel pneumatology. For the Holy Spirit "alone," he writes, "can raise up diversity, plurality and multiplicity, while at the same time bringing about unity."[14] Diversity is essential, in short, to God's ongoing creativity in the world. In a monistic (rationalist) world, diversity, plurality, and multiplicity are imperfections to be overcome in a move to a unity, frequently in its simulacrum, uniformity. In Francis's pluralist vision, as the spirit works "new synthesis," diversity, plurality, and multiplicity enrich God's creation, and our human and ecclesial experience.[15] Diversity is a form of perfection. Short of ultimate unity in Christ, every other unity is partial and open to further synthesis and novelty.

Diversity in the One Church

The Church is a prime example of this pluralism. "In the diversity of peoples who experience the gift of God," Francis writes, "each in accordance with its own culture, the Church expresses her genuine catholicity and shows forth the 'beauty of her varied face.'"[16] When it treats Christianity as a "monocultural and monotonous" entity, he believes, the Church falls short of its call to teach all nations.[17] The gospel, Francis firmly believes, is "transcultural."[18] In a vivid contrast to the intellectual temper of his predecessor, he writes, that in spreading the Word of God it is "not essential to impose a specific cultural form, no matter how ancient or how beautiful it may be, together with the Gospel."[19]

Thus, *Evangelii Gaudium* adamantly refuses to reduce evangelization to conversion to *Roman* Catholicism. Rather Pope Francis advances a literal

---

[13] See William James, *Pragmatism: A New Name for Some Old Ways of Thinking* (Cambridge, MA: Harvard University Press, 1975), ch. 1, "The Present Dilemma in Philosophy".
[14] EG, §131.
[15] Ibid., §129.
[16] Ibid., §116 (citing John Paul II, Apostolic Letter, *Novo Millennio Ineunte* (6 January 2001), AAS 93 (2001), §40.
[17] Ibid., §117.
[18] Ibid.
[19] Ibid. The comment "no matter how ancient or how beautiful" suggests a subtle critique of the Ratzinger/Benedict position.

interpretation of the Dominical commission as proclaiming the gospel "to all nations" (Matt 28:28). Citing John Paul II's *Tertio Millennio Ineunte*, the exhortation reads:

> The history of the Church shows that Christianity does not have simply one cultural expression, but rather, "remaining completely true to itself, with unswerving fidelity to the proclamation of the Gospel and the tradition of the Church, it will also reflect the different faces of the cultures and peoples in which it is received and takes root."[20]

It is through its varied cultural expressions, Pope Francis contends, that the Church fully "expresses her genuine catholicity."[21] Catholicity without diversity is an imposter. Every culture provides values and forms of life, he insists, that enrich the way the gospel is "preached, understood and lived."[22] This is an ecclesiology of communion, reminiscent of Walter Kasper's vision of the Church as a communion of local churches as contrasted with Joseph Ratzinger's ecclesiology of a single Mother Church in which the local churches participate.[23]

Part II: Peace in the Encounter of Cultures

Pope Francis's theology of culture opens new approaches to peacemaking through the encounter of cultures. He proposes an approach to relations between peoples that is more fundamental than the Westphalian interstate system. It appeals to our rootedness in place and time and to our embeddedness in family, language, religion, and culture, even as it invites encounters between people of different cultures. These encounters, he argues, grow through mutual respect, appreciation, and acceptance.

Strong Multiculturalism

Francis's is a strong conception of multiculturalism, far more affirmative of the "other" than Enlightenment tradition of toleration, and far more tangible and embodied than Martin Buber's mystical I-Thou encounter. It embraces both an exchange of values between cultures and the emergence of new values from their mixing. It also addresses the differences, like ethnicity and religion, that have been the source of conflict in the post–Cold War era.

---

[20] *EG*, §116. Again citing from John Paul II, *Tertio Millennio Ineunte*, §40.
[21] *EG*, §116.
[22] Ibid.
[23] See Walter Kasper, "On the Church," *America* (April 23, 2001), 8–14; and Joseph Ratzinger, "The Local Church and the Universal Church," *America* (November 19, 2001), 7–11.

The Westphalian system and the liberal international order that emerged from it suppressed cultural identities within the unitary state. But globalization has fostered reassertion of religious and ethnic identities in unexpected ways, leading in some cases to partial or full devolution (e.g., Scotland and Wales, respectively), in others to ethnic and religious conflicts (the former Yugoslavia), and in still others to religious and cultural oppression (Sri Lanka and Tibet). Two decades ago Samuel Huntington offered an antagonistic interpretation of these developments in his *Clash of Civilizations*.[24] Pope Francis's approach, by contrast, invites positive, peaceable encounters between cultures.

Huntington's theory projects cultural warfare across the great religious divides: between Eastern Orthodox and Western Christianity, between Islam and Christianity, between Confucian China and the West, and between Hindu India and Islam. While the three-way contest between Orthodox, Catholics, and Bosniac Muslims seems behind us, one rift lies today along the tenth parallel between militant Muslims, like Nigeria's Boka Haram, and Christians across Africa.[25] There are obvious subconflicts, above all that between Sunni and Shia Islam across a wide arc from Pakistan to Lebanon. China continues a struggle with its religious minorities, especially Tibetan Buddhists and Uighur Muslims. In Southeast Asia, there are Muslim-Buddhist tensions especially between the Muslim Rohingya peoples and the dominant Buddhists in Myanmar.

Francis does not address the Huntington thesis directly. His thinking about diversity derives more from the missionary experience of attempts to enculturate the gospel rather than with the religio-cultural conflicts on the international scene. (I will, however, have more to say on this later.) His focus is rather on the resolution of conflict through a dialogue of encounter. His thinking can be drawn from his treatment of the four principles of peace.[26] The best way to approach conflict, he writes, "is the willingness to face conflict head on, to resolve it, and to link it to a change in a new process."[27] Even in disagreement, there can be communion, provided that actors "see others in their deepest dignity."[28] The message of peace is not about "a negotiated settlement," he writes, "but rather about

---

[24] Samuel P. Huntington, *The Clash of Civilization and the Remaking of World Order* (New York: Simon and Schuster, 1996).
[25] See Eliza Griswold, *The Tenth Parallel: Dispatches from the Faultline between Christianity and Islam* (New York: Farrar, Straus and Giroux, 2011).
[26] See §217 ff.
[27] EG, §227.
[28] Ibid., §228.

the conviction that the unity brought about by the Spirit can harmonize every diversity."[29]

Francis's problematic is not a political one. Rather, it is a pastoral, theological, and ecclesiological one. Pastorally, he is concerned with reaching out to believers in their own cultural contexts, with generating wider appreciation within the church of the cultural diversity of Christianity, and with encouraging encounters among people of different cultures. Even in times of crisis, as in the US threat to bomb Syrian chemical weapon sites in 2013 and resisting the horrors of the Islamic State (ISIS) in 2014, he objected to the use of force and resorted instead to public prayer.

Theologically, Francis wants to reject the Constantinian imposition of an artificial order within a Latinized church and r-appropriate the diversity of a communion of churches embedded in and exemplified by the different cultures found in the church's early centuries. Symbolically he rejected the Constantinian heritage the night of his election when he rejected the red mozetta and shoes, vestiges of imperial Rome, and spoke of himself not as pope, but as bishop of Rome. Theologically, Pope Francis is raising pneumatology to a new prominence in official theology, where some degree of discontinuity and variation is possible in evangelization, as opposed to the regularizing tendencies of Pope Benedict's Logos Christology with its insistence on historical continuity.[30] In accepting the discontinuity and variety of history as a work of the spirit, Francis is carrying out the agenda of Pope Paul VI, who in *Evangelii Nuntiandi*, testifying to the experience of the spirit by Catholics in the Vatican II era, called for development of a theology of the spirit.[31] Ecclesiologically, Francis is about returning the church to itself, through the synod of bishops, through allowing greater freedom to local churches and encouraging popular Christianity. "Genuine forms of popular religiosity are incarnate," he writes, "since they are born of the incarnation of Christian faith in popular culture."[32] In his respect for popular Christianity, he embodies in an orthodox way Leonardo Boff's notion that symbol making should not be a monopoly of the clergy. This turn to the people is reflected as well in his insistence that the whole church, people and bishops together, possess the *sensus fidei*, a proposition advanced

---

[29] Ibid., §230.
[30] On continuity in Pope Benedict's view doctrinal development and his rejection of periodicity, see *Caritas in Veritate*, §§10 and 12.
[31] See *Evangelii Nuntiandi* ("Evangelization in the Modern World,"), §75. N.B., Pope Paul writes of "the unity in variety which evangelization wishes to achieve within the Christian community."
[32] EG, §90, and also see *passim*.

A Polyhedron

Francis's vision of God's world, as he explains in *Evangelii Gaudium*, is not that of a unitary sphere, but rather of a polyhedron, where each culture, while in relationship to other cultures and to the whole, retains its unique characteristics. Think of a paneled soccer ball. "Pastoral and political activity alike," he asserts, "seek to gather into a polyhedron the best of each."[34] The unity-in-diversity within the Church, which existed in the first centuries and which Francis believes expresses the Church's true nature – a communion of churches rather than a unitary institution, can be a model for the peaceful unity among the world's peoples. One place where this theory of cultural diversity may contribute to peace is the Western encounter with China.

The Case of China

For some years China has explored interaction with the West on a cultural or civilizational basis. Since 2007 the Chinese officials and Chinese organizations have proposed that more productive relations with the West and the world community may be nourished through civilizational dialogue than through standard international relations on the Cold War, state-to-state, strategic model. Under Pope Benedict, Vatican representatives resisted "civilizational dialogue" because it overlooked direct relations between religious communities and most often involved government control.

Francis's theology of cultural encounter opens a way toward the kind of mutually respectful and reciprocally appreciative relations that, at one level at least, China has been seeking from the West. Dialogue can take place today, as it did between Jesuits and the Chinese in the seventeenth-century, at the level of what Pierre Hadot has called "philosophy as a way of life."[35] For, as Francis writes,

---

[33] International Theological Commission, "Theology Today: Perspectives, Principles and Criteria" (March 2012), http://www.vatican.va/roman_curia/congregations/cfaith/cti_documents/rc_cti_doc_20111129_teologia-oggi_en.html.

[34] EG, §236.

[35] Pierre Hadot, *Philosophy as a Way of Life: Spiritual Exercises from Socrates to Foucault* (Oxford: Blackwell, 1995). On other versions of way-of-life philosophies and the potential they offer for dialogue with Christians, see my review essay, "The Unbelievers," *America*, (February 2, 2015), http://www.americamagazine.org/issue/unbelievers. A similar spirit is found in the International Theological Commission's document "In Search of a Universal Ethic" (2009), http://www.vatican.va/roman_curia/congregations/cfaith/cti_documents/rc_con_cfaith_doc_20090520_legge-naturale_en.html, which speaks with appreciation of the world's wisdom traditions.

as well by the International Theological Commission in its 2012 document, "Theology Today."[33]

> The same Spirit everywhere brings forth various forms of practical wisdom which help people to bear suffering and to live in greater peace and harmony. As Christians, we can also benefit from these treasures built up over the centuries, which can help us better to live our own beliefs.[36]

Intercultural dialogue in the field of practical wisdom is the new pope's path to intercultural peace.[37] It is particularly appropriate to high cultures of a nontheistic sort, like China, but perhaps as well to post-Christian societies in the West.[38]

In such encounters, each side must be especially ready to listen to others in-depth, in unfiltered communication. Pope Francis writes,

> We need to practice the art of listening, which is more than simply hearing. Listening, in communication, is an openness of heart which makes possible that closeness without which genuine spiritual encounter cannot occur. Listening helps us to find the right gesture and word which shows that we are more than simply bystanders.[39]

In *Evangelii Gaudium*, Francis has provided a theology for dialogue as a foundation for peacemaking, for diplomatic peacemaking, to be sure, but also for people-to-people encounters where cultural gifts are freely exchanged and reverently accepted.

Strengths and Points of Tension

Peace-through-reconciled-diversity takes Western-Chinese and particularly Chinese-Vatican relations, as Chinese strategic thinkers will recognize, back to a time before the Chinese Rites Controversy, when the Jesuit mission found its success because it recognized the dignity and worth of Chinese culture. For China, the sixteenth- and seventeenth-century Jesuit mission still stands as a model for encounter with the West. The graves of the early Jesuit missioners are guarded and maintained to this day as a tribute to the achievement of that encounter. That the newfound respect for other cultures comes from a Jesuit pope cannot escape Chinese analysts. The promise that the Church is turning the page on the Rites Controversy and has adopted something akin to the early Jesuit approach to cultural encounter could be a great incentive to improved relations between China

---

[36] *EG*, §254.
[37] On practical wisdom, see International Theological Commission, "In Search of a Universal Ethic: A New Look at the Natural Law" (Vatican, 2009), §12.
[38] On the post-Christian West, see my "The Unbelievers," where I suggest that "philosophy as a way of life" is a possible topic between Catholics and the new generation of "religious atheists."
[39] *EG*, §171.

and the Holy See. Pope Francis has already sent a number of signals to China, including his messages when he overflew China on his pilgrimage to South Korea.

More generally, intercultural dialogue has peace-building potential because it bonds persons and groups at a level of depth neither politics nor economics alone is capable of reaching. By placing cultural differences within a dynamic of appreciation, moreover, it also is capable of defusing hostility and righting misplaced competition.

At the same time, intercultural dialogue, when it becomes a general approach to peacemaking, not limited to a single relationship, has the potential for increasing tensions between dialogue partners. For example, Francis's teaching on diversity applies in principle to minorities, like China's own religious and ethnic minorities including the Tibetans. The Church's acceptance of the Western human rights tradition suggests another potential field of difficulty in relations, especially in the treatment of dissidents and protestors. Since *Pacem in Terris* in 1963, human rights has been at the heart of the Church's social mission. In the Second Vatican Council, moreover, the Church named the promotion of human rights as one of the primary ways in which the Church serves the world.[40]

Of course, on this count, the Church has much internal reform to do as well, in the full acceptance of the eastern churches, for example, in the conduct of dialogue with its own dissenters and in the definition and implementation of the rights of the faithful in the Church. So, peace through diversity holds within it challenges to reform on all sides.

We cannot deny, however, that the Church's teaching on human rights will at times be an obstacle to easy dialogue with civilizations that value the group, and especially political authority as the embodiment of the group, to the detriment of the human person. In upholding the dignity of persons, the Church will find itself at odds with repressive governments as the representatives of other cultures. While Francis has proven himself inventive in finding ways around obstacles that blocked others, his inventiveness may find greater obstacles to overcome where human rights are at issue.

As Francis writes in *Evangelii Gaudium*: "The dignity of the human person and the common good rank higher than the comfort of those who refuse to renounce their privileges. When these values are threatened a prophetic voice must be raised."[41]

---

[40] *Gaudium et Spes*, "The Pastoral Constitution on the Church in the Modern World," §41.
[41] §218.

Where cultural differences are part of encounter, neither theoretical nor policy differences are destined to become blockages on the path to peace. If peace arises from personal encounters, then genuine openness will lead to mutual esteem, and mutual esteem to peaceful relations. *Cor ad cor loquitur*, wrote Cardinal Newman, "heart speaks to heart." Interpersonal encounter is at the heart of Francis's theology of evangelization.[42] *Evangelii Gaudium* reminds us that at root peace between people of different cultures will be the fruit of genuine encounters across cultures.

Part III: Maxims for Peacemakers

In *Pacem in Terris*, Pope Saint John XXIII gave us a vision of peace as the promotion and defense of human rights. In *Populorum Progressio*, Pope Paul VI widened that vision to include integral human development and bequeathed us the maxim, "Development, the new name for peace." Being a pragmatic man, Pope Francis gives us four rules for peacemaking in the "Joy of the Gospel":[43]

(1) Time is greater than space.
(2) Unity prevails over conflict.
(3) Realities are more important than ideas.
(4) The whole is greater than the parts.

While Francis invests these maxims with the authority of Catholic social teaching, especially their "permanence" and "universality," I have nowhere found an explicit textual basis for his claim.[44] The four principles instead appear to be his own contribution, generated out of his social praxis. They are related to the conflictual tensions found in social life, and are intended to "guide the development of life in society and the building of a people where differences are harmonized within a shared pursuit."[45]

They are, if you will, the maxims of a priest practitioner to the next generation who may be impatient to build a better society, but must assume their part "in a slow and arduous effort calling for a desire of integration and the willingness to achieve this through a peaceful and multifaceted

---

[42] Ibid., *passim*, especially §§87–88, 91 and above all, §272.
[43] Ibid., §222–237.
[44] Pope Francis appeals to the *Compendium of the Social Doctrine of the Church* Washington, DC: (USCCB, 2004), §161, but that text applies to Catholic Social Teaching in general and not any specific principles.
[45] EG, §221.

culture of encounter."[46] The temporal nature of this effort, not just its historical character, but its gradual, effortful development over time is the subject of the first principle: *Time is greater than space*. It is a counsel against impatience and for (selfless) generativity.

Time Is Greater Than Space

Pope Francis's pragmatism is evident in all four principles, but especially in this first axiom. One of the faults in social processes and social ministry, he argues, is the focus on short-term objectives and overinvestment in short- and mid-term goals. Pope Francis objects to an obsession with closure and attainment. What matters he believes is "initiating processes, not possessing spaces," that is, the static achievements of the past. One sees in this rule Francis's own leadership style, where, whether in grand deeds like calling a synod or small gestures of kindness, he is constantly seizing the initiative. Peacemakers, like Papa Bergoglio, should be alert to seize the moment to take initiatives for peace, whether it means offering a small kindness, creating a public symbol in a liturgy or rally, or undertaking peace-building initiatives in a zone of conflict.

"Sometimes," he writes, "I wonder whether there are people in today's world who are really concerned about generating processes of people building, as opposed to attaining immediate results, which yield easy, quick, short-term political gains, but do not enhance human fullness."[47] This is the worry of a priest who worked steadily for the poor without notice, but also experienced the loss of impatient co-workers too eager for the excitement of quick, radical change. For religious peacemakers, the first maxim is a reminder "to set their hand to the plough and not look back" (Luke 9:62), not to trust in political victories, but to invest their energies in their own peacemaking projects.

I am reminded of John Paul II's praise of the nonviolent commitment of the Polish activists "who ... succeeded time after time in bearing witness to the truth" against their Communist rulers in the 1980s.[48] The same can be said of grassroots Christian peacemakers all over the world today. In face-to-face encounters, they take initiatives that elude the world's power brokers but steadily prepare the path to peace.

Of course, one cannot always be initiating new programs. Paul planted, Apollo did the watering, God gave the increase. There is a place, too, for

---

[46] Ibid., §220.
[47] Ibid., §224.
[48] *Centesimus Annus*, §23.

those who nurture the work begun by others. Those who teach love, forgiveness, and reconciliation in Catholic schools are as necessary as those promoting reconciliation in zones of conflict. Innovators who fail to provide for the continuation of their labors are as much as fault as those who are wedded to an existing work when something else needs to be done.

Francis reminds us that we can become overinvested in our own institutions and our own work to the neglect of present challenges that need to be met. When it comes to peacemaking, he reminds us that new initiatives are always needed, and the needed initiatives will always be evident to those who have given themselves to encounter the needy and people at risk in zones of conflict. A culture of encounter keeps keen the sensibility for innovation in response to human suffering.

Finally, the priority of time over space builds patient characters who will persist in doing good without attaching themselves too closely with any achievement. "It helps us patiently endure difficult and adverse situations or inevitable changes in our plans," he writes. "It invites us to accept the tension between fullness and limitation."[49] Reluctance to accept that tension is a basic temptation of peacemakers. In holy impatience, they desire to make the kingdom come – today. Just as there are temptations for pastoral workers, so too there are temptations for peacemakers.[50] While religious peacemakers are drawn by "the greater, brighter horizon of the utopian future" (§117.6), they must live with the limited achievements in time. In that time, they are charged with building a people "to the point where they can bear fruit in significant historical events."[51] The pope's hope is to cultivate a generative people capable of the kind of human encounter that, under the inspiration of the spirit, establishes that "new synthesis" of the gospel and culture. In the end, they must remember that it is God who mysteriously gives the increase.[52]

Unity Prevails over Conflict

Unity in this maxim points to a specific range of meanings. As noted in the preceding text, Francis does not think of unity as a shallow conformity to one dominant outlook.[53] Rather, in keeping with the model of the polyhedron, it is the result of a diverse unity, "the communion and harmony of the people of God." It means, as we face the conflict, we build

[49] EG, §222.
[50] On the temptations of pastoral workers, see ibid., §§76–109;
[51] Ibid., §222.
[52] Ibid., §223.
[53] Ibid., §118.

communion out of disagreement by responding to the essential dignity of those we encounter where the unity of the human family can be found.[54] That profound unity keeps Christian peacemaking realistic, immune to naïve utopianism. It is our common humanity, not any single historical achievement or even a set of such achievements, that gives assurance that unity will prevail over conflict. With the eyes of faith we can see that conflict is only a passing phenomenon. Building friendship in a conflicted society depends on confidence in this underlying reality. Where conflict arises, it is possible to preserve values on both sides.[55] In so doing, Christian peacemaking not only helps resolve conflict; and it prevents future conflict from springing into life from simmering grievances generated in a one-sided peace.

Realities Are More Important Than Ideas

With this maxim Pope Francis's pragmatism comes decisively into play. It is on this point that the philosophy implicit in his pastoral approach to human problems becomes most evident, and his distance from Pope Benedict is clearest. He "calls for rejecting the various ways of masking reality: angelic forms of purity, dictatorships of relativism, empty rhetoric, objectives more ideal than real, brands of ahistorical fundamentalism, ethical systems bereft of kindness, intellectual discourse bereft of wisdom."[56] Ideas, he explains, "are at the service of communication, understanding and praxis."[57] "What calls us to action," he points out, "are realities illuminated by reason." His approach, in that sense, is rhetorical rather than metaphysical. It is speech aimed at bringing about change in society. It is forensic in the sense that speeches in the Roman forum or the Athenian agora were intended to lead others to take action. But with a difference: They are words intended to change hearts, nourish the church community, and then, in turn, to change society. As distinct from theology as the exposition of doctrine, the pastoral language of the Church calls us to action. Like Maurice Blondel, Pope Francis believes action embraces all. Like William James, he believes the test of a truth is its practical outcome.[58]

Realities are a test of ideas in another sense. They are challenges to our preconceptions; lead us to question our assumptions; open up new lines of inquiry; and, in the end, result in us qualifying and reformulating our

---

[54] Ibid., §117.
[55] Ibid.
[56] EG, §231.
[57] EG, §232.
[58] See n. 14, above.

ideas.[59] In that sense, Pope Francis's pastoral theology is experimental. It learns from experience and adapts appropriately. Consider, for example, the pope's insistence on the primacy of the Gospel of God's Mercy over secondary moral precepts. It is a pastoral conviction drawn from his experience in the slums where so many more people were estranged from the Church because of irregular marriage situations.[60] In this respect, he is much like the Jesuit founder Saint Ignatius Loyola, who would discard even carefully thought out plans because experience showed they were unproductive. *Experientia docuit*, he would say, "Experience has taught." Like Ignatius what matters to Francis is the fruitfulness of a principle in practice, and for both of them fruitfulness is measured in closeness to Christ.

The Whole Is Greater Than the Parts

The fourth principle brings together three related ideas of the relation of the whole-part ensemble. The first is what some call *glocalism*, summarized in the slogan, "Think globally, work locally." "We can work on a small scale in our own neighborhood, but in a larger perspective."[61] As a churchman and as social minister, Francis knows the importance of global dynamics on the church and the political economy. But as a pastor, attuned to the rootedness of his people, particularly in their local culture, he understands that men and women face the forces of globalization out of the culture that has formed them and in which they share; and for him, the cultures of the poor and underprivileged are of special importance. But, whatever our social situation, what matters is that we make "new syntheses" between our received (Christian) culture and the wider world in which we live.

The fourth maxim concerns the diversity in unity. The whole Francis has in mind, as I noted, is not a sphere in which all points are equidistant from the center, but rather the polyhedron – think again of a soccer ball made up of many triangles. In the polyhedron, all the parts converge, but each preserves its distinctiveness.[62] This is a principle of pluralism, both in the church and in the world. For Francis writes, "Pastoral and political

---

[59] See Drew Christiansen, SJ, "On the Slope with Teilhard: Lessons on Matter and Spirit," *America* (December 10, 2010), http://americamagazine.org/issue/759/article/slope-teilhard. For Teilhard, these are the lessons of empirical scientific research. For Francis, they are the lessons experience renders pastoral service and especially Christian peacemaking.
[60] See chapter 5, "The Bishop of the Slums," in Paul Vallely, *Pope Francis: Untying the Knots* (London and New York: Bloomsbury, 2013).
[61] EG, §235.
[62] Ibid., §235.

activity alike seek to gather in this polyhedron the best of each."[63] Francis is reviving the sense of multiplicity the Church possessed in the conciliar period. Both the Council and Pope Paul VI insisted on the variety of ways in which Christians could live out their gospel commitment in the world bound together in charity. In the last forty years, that sense of members of one community pursuing different paths to the common end was forgotten, even to the point for some of rejecting the rights of conscience.[64] Francis, by contrast, makes room even for "people who can be considered dubious on account of their errors" because "they have something to offer which must not be overlooked."[65] Another way to think about the fourth principle is that it is a principle of inclusion. The gospel in its fullness embraces all people: "scholars and workers, businessmen and artists, in a word, everyone."[66]

Finally, the principle of wholeness points to the goal of evangelization. The gospel will always remain good news until it has been proclaimed to all people, until it has healed and strengthened every aspect of humanity, until it has brought all men and women together at the one table in God's kingdom.

Part IV: Pope Francis as Peacemaker

Pope Francis has shown the same initiative in peacemaking that he shows in other areas of his ministry. He has taken daring initiatives, calling, on short notice, for a day of prayer in advance of the announced US bombing of Syria in the controversy over chemical weapons, employing personal acquaintances as emissaries to Israel and China, and finding the perfect symbol to recognize Palestinian suffering by stopping to pray on the Palestinian side of Israel's Separation Wall. He has made exceptional use of the Vatican diplomatic corps, consulting with them on world crises, and sending them forth to plead for peaceful resolution of conflicts. As much as President Putin's agreement to join in disarming Syria, Pope Francis's intervention may have stayed President Obama's hand from bombing Syrian chemical weapons sites. His invitation to Mahmoud Abbas and Shimon Peres to join him in prayer for peace had no immediate result, but it demonstrated his authority to bring world leaders together in the cause of peace.

---

[63] Ibid.
[64] See *Gaudium et Spes*, §43 and *Octogesima Adveniens*, §50, http://w2.vatican.va/content/paul-vi/en/apost_letters/documents/hf_p-vi_apl_19710514_octogesima-adveniens.html.
[65] *EG*, §236.
[66] *EG*, §237.

His solicitude for the Middle East has been unparalleled. In 2014, he met with nuncios to the Middle East and the United Nations just prior to the Synod on the Family, and immediately following the 2014 round of that synod he convoked a consistory of cardinals and patriarchs to discuss the fighting in Iraq and Syria and its impact on their Christian populations further. Through Cardinal Parollin he issued a challenge to moderate Muslims and their authorities to speak out against the barbarities of ISIS. He has also repeatedly argued for the alternative means to force in resolving that conflict. On that count, as I have written elsewhere, it is important for the church to further develop its convictions on the nonviolent themes in its teaching and diplomacy, and, in particular, on the place of the use of force in exercise of the Responsibility to Protect.

Lastly, given Francis's vision of the church as a culturally diverse body, the crises facing Middle Eastern Christians on many fronts point to the need of a new synod on the Middle East that will focus on the future of the Oriental Catholic churches, especially the resettlement of Christians as refugees and their continued presence in the diaspora. If the war with ISIS is a generational struggle, then, realistically, refugees need to be resettled. To have millions of refugees in camps for a decade or more will present a threat to international security. The move to the diaspora may provide obstacles to preserving the cultural diversity of the Oriental churches. One function of a future synod would be to explore how to preserve that heritage outside their historic homelands. In his theology of diversity and his belief in the spirit working in history, Francis provides tools for coping even with this existential challenge to the Church.

CHAPTER 12

The Dialogue of Fraternity

Evangelii Gaudium and the Renewal of Ecumenical and Interreligious Dialogue

John Borelli

1. "Fraternity"

On that memorable occasion when the crowds in Piazza San Pietro met the newly elected Pope Francis for the first time, Jorge Mario Bergoglio spoke only a few lines. He quickly surprised everyone when he asked a favor of his audience: "[B]efore the Bishop blesses his people, I ask you to pray to the Lord that he will bless me: the prayer of the people asking the blessing for their Bishop." He called for silence so they could pray over him, and then startled everyone by kneeing down and bowing his head. This occasion called for a few brief but well-chosen words. Something lengthier and well-prepared would have been unseemly and even disingenuous. Rather, Pope Francis spoke and acted from the heart. Hindsight allows us to judge how truly important those remarks were: Here are just a few:

> And now, we take up this journey: Bishop and People. This journey of the Church of Rome which presides in charity over all the Churches. A journey of fraternity, of love, of trust among us. Let us always pray for one another. Let us pray for the whole world, that there may be a great spirit of fraternity.[1]

Pope Francis described the journey ahead as a "journey of fraternity of love" and "of trust" and called for prayers for the whole world that there may be "a great spirit of fraternity."

---

[1] http://w2.vatican.va/content/francesco/en/speeches/2013/march/documents/papa-francesco_20130313_benedizione-urbi-et-orbi.html (accessed July 16, 2015).

Seven days later and after the official inauguration of his ministry as Bishop of Rome, Pope Francis met with ecumenical and interreligious guests who had attended the ceremonies. He first addressed the Christian representatives, beginning with Patriarch Bartholomew of Constantinople, whom he had addressed as "my brother Andrew," speaking symbolically of himself as Peter. By the sixth sentence he had mentioned the Second Vatican Ecumenical Council, and in two more sentences, he was quoting John XXIII, the beloved pope who had called the Council (and whom Francis would later canonize): "The Catholic Church considers it her duty to work actively for the fulfilment of the great mystery of that unity for which Jesus Christ prayed so earnestly to his heavenly Father on the eve of his great sacrifice; the knowledge that she is so intimately associated with that prayer is for her an occasion of ineffable peace and joy" (AAS 54 [1962], 793). Pope Francis assured the Christians present that he would pursue the path of ecumenical dialogue, continuing with the new era of Catholic teaching on Christian unity inaugurated by the Council and its *Decree on Ecumenism* (*Unitatis Redintegratio*).

He then turned to the Jews present, cited the Council's *Declaration on the Relation of the Church to Non-Christian Religions* (*Nostra Aetate*), and expressed his trust "that, with the help of the Most High, we can make greater progress in that fraternal dialogue which the Council wished to encourage." By referring to fraternal dialogue (*fraternis colloquiis*), Pope Francis was using *Nostra Aetate*'s actual words. The Council fathers through *Nostra Aetate* exhorted the sons and daughters of the church to "conversations and collaboration" (*colloquia et collaborationem*) with the followers of other religions and specifically to "friendly conversations" (*fraternis colloquiis*) with Jews to promote mutual understanding and esteem. After greeting Muslims and the followers of other religions, the new pope underscored "the importance of promoting friendship and respect between men and women of different religious traditions."

Pope Francis then spoke to the whole group of Christians and other leaders and listed a number of common concerns for creation; for the poor and needy; for ending violence and promoting peace; and for how much harm and violence comes from the attempt to eliminate God and the divine from the horizon of humanity. He then spoke of the closeness we must feel with those who, though not "identifying themselves as followers of any religious tradition, are nonetheless searching for truth, goodness and beauty, the truth, goodness and beauty of God." He called these unaffiliated, well-intentioned people "our valued allies in the commitment to defending human dignity, in building a peaceful coexistence between peoples and in safeguarding and caring for creation." With that, he thanked everyone for being present and offered all his "heartfelt, fraternal good wishes."[2]

A note needs to be added, perhaps, on translation and the term *fraternity*. As the passages cited throughout this chapter will indicate, Pope Francis applies *fraternity* and *fraternal* in the broadest possible sense to include women and men and girls and boys. It functions like the words in the conciliar declaration *Nostra Aetate* of 1965 regarding the encouragement of conversations and collaboration, *Filios suos igitur hortatur*. The words are best translated into English, "[The Church] therefore exhorts her sons and daughters," taking the subject from the foregoing sentences and translating *filios*, which can mean specifically "sons" but more broadly "sons and daughters". Pope Francis intends "fraternity" for all human relationships as he similarly applies "solidarity." He entitled his first World Day of Peace Message, for January 1, 2014, "Fraternity: The Foundation and Pathway to Peace." Pointing to the great malaise that has overcome humanity, he used both terms in a single sentence: "The many situations of inequality, poverty and injustice, are signs not only of a profound lack of fraternity, but also of the absence of a culture of solidarity." Later in the message and quoting John Paul II,[3] Pope Francis puts the two terms together: "Christian solidarity presumes that our neighbor is loved not only as 'a human being with his or her own rights and a fundamental equality with everyone else, but as the living image of God the Father, redeemed by the blood of Jesus Christ and placed under the permanent action of the Holy Spirit,' [*Sollicitudo Rei Socialis* (December 30, 1987), 40] as another brother or sister."[4]

Pope Francis is truly committed to implementing Vatican II and has absorbed in a personal way its concepts and commitments. *Dialogue* and *fraternity* and variations of these terms are often in his public vocabulary as they are in the acts of Vatican II. So too are *pilgrim* and *pilgrimage*, especially when these terms refer to Christians and to the church or to efforts toward unity of Christians. Similarly, he uses words such as *accompaniment* and *companion* in reference to the common journey of all peoples.

---

[2] http://w2.vatican.va/content/francesco/en/speeches/2013/march/documents/papa-francesco_20130320_delegati-fraterni.html (accessed July 16, 2015).
[3] Another predecessor whom Francis would come to canonize.
[4] https://w2.vatican.va/content/francesco/en/messages/peace/documents/papa-francesco_20131208_messaggio-xlvii-giornata-mondiale-pace-2014.html (accessed February 5, 2014); the passage from the encyclical of John Paul II can also be found in *Acta Apostolicae Sedis* [AAS] 80 (1988), 566–568, as well as online, http://w2.vatican.va/content/john-paul-ii/en/encyclicals/documents/hf_jp-ii_enc_30121987_sollicitudo-rei-socialis.html (accessed July 22, 2015).

The conciliar draft entitled "On Ecumenism," when presented for the first time in the council hall of Vatican II for general discussion on November 18, 1963, was the first significantly important church document to use the term *dialogue* (*dialogus*) in reference to Catholic relations with others, in this case other Christians. The fourth chapter of that draft decree, entitled "On the Relation of Catholics with Non-Christians and Especially with Jews," referred to fraternal conversations (*colloquiis fraternis*). This fourth chapter would eventually become the separate aforementioned declaration (NA) while the first three chapters of the draft would become previously referenced promulgated decree (UR). There was a fifth chapter in the draft decree that became the separate declaration on religious liberty (*Dignitatis humanae*). The final version of the *Decree on Ecumenism* (UR) would use the term *dialogue* twelve times and variations of fraternal eleven times, including "mutual fraternity" (*mutuam fraternitatem*) when referring to how all the faithful promote Christian unity by striving to live holier lives according to the gospel and thus more deeply and easily growing in mutual fraternity (UR 7).[5]

In his apostolic exhortation *Evangelii Gaudium*, Francis uses *fraternity* numerous times, often in conjunction with solidarity, justice, and peace. He employs *pilgrim* or *pilgrimage* thirteen times, twice in passages from the 1987 encyclical of John Paul II, *Redemptoris Mater*, and once in a passage quoted from the *Decree on Ecumenism*, the one passage where the *Unitatis Redintegratio* uses *reformation* (UR 6). In all cases, *pilgrimage* refers to a sacred journey and *pilgrim* to those on a sacred journey. He uses *companions* only once in *Evangelii Gaudium*, but *accompany* or *accompaniment* occur many times. Pope Francis explains that believers should not flee the company of others and "flit from one place to another or from one task to another, without creating deep and stable bonds." Such a practice would be the opposite of pilgrimage. Rather, he urges believers "to help others to realize that the only way forward is to learn how to encounter others with the right attitude, which is to accept and esteem them as companions along the way, without interior resistance" (EG 91). With these variations of *to accompany* he reiterates that we are not companionless on this journey of faith. God is always present, and we are joined by a great diversity of pilgrims.

[5] See the translation of *The Decree on Ecumenism* by Thomas F. Stransky, C.S.P. (Glen Rock, NJ: Paulist Press, 1965), 61, which provides the first historical account of the *Decree* and its terminology, as well as being the first official English translation with commentary of the text. Stransky was one of the original staff members of the Secretariat for Promoting Christian Unity.

In *Evangelii Gaudium*, *journey* appears fifteen times; *path*, twenty-three times; and in Spanish, the pope's native tongue, *camino* occurs fifty-three times. Pope Francis uses *encounter* or *"encuentro"* more than thirty times aside from titles and headings. *Dialogue* appears forty-nine times, apart from headings and subheadings. Those two early communications of Francis, his initial *urbe et orbi* blessing on March 13, 2013 and his address at the reception for ecumenical and interreligious guests on March 20 offered the first significant signs of the overall message of his papacy thus far and the central themes of *Evangelii Gaudium*.

2. Before His Election

Pope Francis's election took place during the jubilee celebrations of Vatican II. Though he is the first pope elected since the Council who was nowhere near it when it met (1962–1965), Francis is thoroughly steeped in its trajectories, including a life of dialogue fostered by the Vatican II church. While he may remind us in many ways of St. John XXIII who convoked Vatican II, he personally draws inspiration from Blessed Pope Paul VI who gave direction to the Council and brought it to a successful conclusion. In fact, *Evangelii Gaudium* takes its name from two apostolic exhortations of Paul VI, *Evangelii Nuntiandi*, which closed the 1974 synod on evangelization,[6] and *Gaudete in Domino*, issued a few months earlier than *Evangelii Nuntiandi*, on Christian joy.[7] The initial citation Pope Francis makes in *Evangelii Gaudium* is to *Gaudete in Domino*, "no one is excluded from the joy brought by the Lord." Both texts of Paul VI are cited twice in the first nine citations. Similar to *Evangelii Nuntiandi*, *Evangelii Gaudium* closes a synod on evangelization, the XIII Ordinary Assembly of the Synod of Bishops on the theme of the new evangelization that was called by Pope Francis's predecessor and intended by Pope Benedict XVI to be a celebration of the fiftieth anniversary of the opening of the Second Vatican Council.

Cardinal Bergoglio came to the papacy already with deep friendships with other Christian and with interreligious friendships. His long-standing relationship with Rabbi Abraham Skorka, rector of the Seminario Rabínico Latinoamericano in Buenos Aires and chief rabbi of Benei Tikva congregation in the Belgrano district of the same city, became quickly known.

---

[6] (Dec. 8 1975), http://w2.vatican.va/content/paul-vi/en/apost_exhortations/documents/hf_p-vi_exh_19751208_evangelii-nuntiandi.html.

[7] (May 9 1974), http://w2.vatican.va/content/paul-vi/en/apost_exhortations/documents/hf_p-vi_exh_19750509_gaudete-in-domino.html.

Their collection of dialogues, *Sobre el Cielo and la Tierra*,[8] was one of the few lengthy sources easily available after Bergoglio was elected pope. In 2004, Cardinal Bergoglio paid the first visit ever of a bishop to the Islamic Center of the Argentine Republic. He began to meet regularly with its president, Abel Made, and this was also the case in his friendship with Rabbi Skorka. Made passed away, and the cardinal returned to the center for his wake. Omar Abboud took over as director of the Islamic Center and continued the ongoing relationship with the cardinal. Abboud, who with Skorka would accompany Pope Francis on his visit to the Holy Land in May 2014, has taken Bergoglio's four civic principles, reiterated by the pope in *Evangelii Gaudium*, and has rendered them into Islamic concepts: the whole is greater than the part, unity is superior to conflict, reality is superior to the idea, and time prevails over space.[9]

Bergoglio's approach to dialogue in Argentina focused on friendship and action. Indeed, friendship and trust are all-important first accomplishments of dialogue and make other achievements easier – ongoing discussions for mutual understanding, effective cooperation, joint statements, responses to crises, and sharing on a level of spiritual practice and insight. At times, Pope Francis has chided those engaged in theological conversation for taking so much time and worrying over too many nuances. He did this on an all-important day for celebrating ecumenical sharing at the Basilica of St. Paul Outside the Walls on January 25, 2015. Traditionally this date, the Feast of the Conversion of St. Paul, closes the Week of Prayer for Christian Unity. After that service in 1959, John XXIII disclosed in a private reception for the cardinals in attendance, that he intended to call a universal council of the whole church. Subsequently, popes have presided at Vespers on this day at the basilica, often with ecumenical guests and marking important occasions in an ecumenical manner. In his homily at Vespers in 2015, Pope Francis urged the ecumenical guests and their Catholic companions to make something of their theological dialogue:

> Christian unity – we are convinced – will not be the fruit of subtle theoretical discussions in which each party tries to convince the other of the soundness of their opinions. When the Son of Man comes, he will find us still discussing! We need to realize that, to plumb the depths of the mystery of God, we need one another, we need to encounter one another

---

[8] Originally published in 2010 by Editorial Sudamericana, the English translation appeared about a month after the papal election, *On Heaven and Earth*, translated by Alejandro Bermudez and Howard Goodman (New York: Image, 2013).

[9] See Austen Ivereigh, *The Great Reformer: Francis and the Making of a Radical Pope* (New York: Henry Holt and Company, 2014), 321–322.

and to challenge one another under the guidance of the Holy Spirit, who harmonizes diversities, overcomes conflicts, reconciles differences.[10]

When he met with the Pontifical Council for Interreligious Dialogue for the first time at their plenary meeting on November 28, 2013, Pope Francis described a deep conviction that encounter with someone different from us can be an occasion for growth in a spirit of fraternity and mutual witness: "We do not impose anything, we do not employ any subtle strategies for attracting believers; rather, we bear witness to what we believe and who we are with joy and simplicity." Pope Francis identified as "false fraternity" the setting aside of our beliefs or pretending that we not believe something essential to our faith. He encourages and endorses acknowledging diversity and living with it respectfully to ward of the narrow-mindedness of the past: "The future lies in the respectful coexistence of diversity, not in homologation to a single theoretically neutral way of thought."[11]

Pope Francis is also famous for his ecumenical friends. His eight-year relationship with the Pentecostal Bishop Tony Palmer, until his untimely death in a motorcycle accident, is widely known. His relationships with Pentecostals and Evangelicals, those often on the fringes of the ecumenical movement, have been groundbreaking.[12] Journalists have repeated the account of the testimony of the Primate of the Southern Cone province of the Anglican Communion, which includes Argentina, about Cardinal Bergoglio's negative views of the establishment by Pope Benedict XVI of an Anglican Ordinariate in the Catholic Church to receive Anglican communities fleeing the Anglican Communion and seeking union with Rome. His words to Archbishop Gregory Venables in this regard were not different from what he had also said to Tony Palmer – we need you for who you are.[13]

In a lecture at the Catholic University of America on November 6, 2014, Cardinal Walter Kasper, who had served many years as Secretary and then as President of the Pontifical Council for Promoting Christian

---

[10] http://w2.vatican.va/content/francesco/en/homilies/2015/documents/papa-francesco_20150125_vespri-conversione-san-paolo.html (accessed July 17, 2015).

[11] http://w2.vatican.va/content/francesco/en/speeches/2013/november/documents/papa-francesco_20131128_pc-dialogo-interreligioso.html (accessed July 17, 2015). I wish to acknowledge the important article by James L. Fredericks, "Francis's Interreligious Friendships: Soccer and Lunch, Followed by Dialogue," *Commonweal* (August 15, 2014): 13–16.

[12] I refer here to the video message of Pope Francis that Tony Palmer taped in January 2014 and took with him to a meeting of Pentecostals a few weeks later, the surprising visit of Pope Francis to the Pentecostal Church of Reconciliation, Caserta, Italy, on July 28, 2014, and the visit to the Waldensian Temple in Torina, Italy, on June 22, 2015, to name just a few.

[13] See Ivereigh, *Great Reformer*, 327.

Unity, outlined a series of frustrations many Protestants and Catholic had felt in more than a dozen years before the election of Pope Francis. He then observed:

> A new stimulus and a new vision were necessary. Pope Francis gave them in his totally personal way. He is a man of encounter.[14]

One of Francis's first ecumenical guests was the newly appointed Archbishop of Canterbury Justin Welby on June 14, 2013. Already Francis was articulating his dual emphasis on theological dialogue and fraternity:

> Recent decades, however, have been marked by a journey of rapprochement and fraternity, and for this we give heartfelt thanks to God. This journey has been brought about both via theological dialogue, through the work of the Anglican-Roman Catholic International Commission, and via the growth of cordial relations at every level through shared daily lives in a spirit of profound mutual respect and sincere cooperation.[15]

When he received a delegation from the Lutheran World Federation, Pope Francis expressed gratitude for "many advances made in relations between Lutherans and Catholics in these past decades, not only through theological dialogue, but also through fraternal cooperation in a variety of pastoral settings, and above all, in the commitment to progress in spiritual ecumenism."[16]

Pope Francis acknowledges ecumenical and interreligious achievements through dialogue. He knows that theological dialogue is necessary, but he joins that venerable approach, the one that the documents of Vatican II encouraged and opened for Catholics, with the fundamental element of friendship or fraternity and with that often-neglected or passed over joint activity, spiritual ecumenism. It is not either/or, but it is not exactly both/and. Fraternity and spiritual sharing are primary; otherwise, theological agreements are almost pointless.

This is not something new at all. In fact, the *Decree on Ecumenism* speaks of the "fraternal harmony" or concord (*fraterna concordia*) (UR 2) of the church as the one family of God and of accepting members of separated Christian communities with brotherly love and affection (*fraterna*

---

[14] Walter Kasper, *Pope Francis' Revolution of Tenderness and Love* (New York: Paulist Press, 2015), 54. Cardinal Kasper's lecture, Chapter 8 in this volume, is an excellent summary of the ecumenical vision of Pope Francis.

[15] http://w2.vatican.va/content/francesco/en/speeches/2013/june/documents/papa-francesco_20130614_welby-canterbury.html (accessed on June 14, 2013).

[16] http://www.vatican.va/holy_father/francesco/speeches/2013/october/documents/papa-francesco_20131021_delegazione-luterana_en.html (accessed October 22, 2013).

reverentia et dilectione) (*UR* 3) before introducing the notion of "dialogue" that takes place between competent experts. Dialogue in its technical sense is the second feature of the ecumenical movement, following "every effort to avoid expressions, judgments and actions which do not represent the condition of our separated brothers with truth and fairness and so make mutual relations with them more difficult" (*UR* 4). By his renewal of the element of fraternity, Pope Francis is urging a more merciful and pastoral policy for widespread ecumenical sharing and not waiting for the theological experts to solve all the major obstacles for celebrating full unity. Unanticipated in the conciliar decree and not mentioned by Pope Francis fifty years later is how much time is need for "official reception" by the churches involved in formal agreements. Fraternity and spiritual sharing are lived experiences of ecumenical reception.

3. *Evangelii Gaudium* as a Basis

The apostolic exhortation *Evangelii Gaudium* is the seminal text of the papacy of Jorge Mario Bergoglio. Dated November 24, 2013 and released two days later, a little more than eight months after his election. It was his first major unalloyed writing and remains the major text for understanding the mind of the Argentinian Pope Francis behind the remarkable and refreshing period that he has opened up in the church. At this point *Evangelii Gaudium* is still his only apostolic exhortation while he has issued two encyclicals, one on faith and a second on the environment. Hindsight confirms that the apostolic letter is the foundational text of Francis's papacy, and not his first encyclical, which preceded it by several months.

By Francis own admission, two weeks before the appearance of *Lumen Fidei*, this yet-to-be-released first encyclical was the work "of four hands."[17] Once the text appeared, one could read, in the pope's own words, that Benedict "himself had almost completed a first draft of an encyclical on faith" (*LF* 7). We can reasonably assume that Benedict continued to work on the draft at the urging of his successor. Indeed, Pope Francis was quite generous allowing his predecessor to establish the conceptual framework of the encyclical. The further that we move into Francis's papacy, the

---

[17] See, e.g., *Vatican Insider* (June 13, 2013), http://vaticaninsider.lastampa.it/en/news/detail/articolo/papa-el-papa-pope-vaticano-vatican-25611/ (accessed June 27, 2015), "Now, Francis himself has said the 'cross-pontificate' encyclical is the work 'of four hands,' of two men that is, Ratzinger and Bergoglio. Francis has also stated that he intends to give his predecessor recognition for his contribution and put this in writing."

easier it becomes to distinguish two distinct languages and orientations in *Lumen Fidei*.

The term *dialogue*, for example, appearing thirteen times in English translation of *Lumen Fidei*, is employed in several ways: to describe the classical relationship between scripture and its Hellenistic context, the relationship between theology and philosophy, the relationship of communion within God and through faith with all believers, and a kind of literature belonging to the ancients. Only two of the thirteen instances, referring to interreligious dialogue and how believers witness their faith to others (par. 34 and 35), are descriptions that contemporary readers will find relevant to their present lives. As one commentator noted at the time of *Lumen Fidei*'s release, "Much of the encyclical shows the thinking of Benedict who had completed most of the text before his resignation: extensive appeal to the doctors of the church, a sacralizing of Hellenistic philosophy and a preoccupation with 19th-century atheism."[18]

Curiously, those two numbered paragraphs (34 and 35) seem to reflect Francis's own thinking and language. After observing that faith leads to a truth born of love that can penetrate "to the personal core of each man and woman," the encyclical declares, "Clearly, then, faith is not intransigent, but grows in respectful coexistence with others." The next section begins with this sentence, "The light of faith in Jesus also illumines the path of all those who seek God, and makes a specifically Christian contribution to dialogue with the followers of the different religions" (35).

Path is a key term in *Evangelii Gaudium*, connoting one of Pope Francis's favored images of the church, a people of faith on pilgrimage. Drawing on the biblical image of the magi, *Lumen Fidei* refers in this same section to "religious man" as "a wayfarer," "ready to let himself be led, to come out of himself and to find the God of perpetual surprises" (35). We are back to the language of Pope Benedict, which is confirmed by reference in a few sentences to *Dominus Iesus*, the declaration issued by him in 2000 while he was still President of the Congregation for the Doctrine of the Faith. *Dominus Iesus* was one of the causes of frustration, even consternation, among the ecumenical and interreligious friends of the Catholic Church to which Cardinal Kasper was referring. The passage in *Lumen Fidei* underscores how Jesus is the unique Savior, and the encyclical concludes that "no journey of man to God, which cannot be taken up, illumined and purified by this light." Pope Francis does not cite

---

[18] Drew Chrisitansen, S.J., "Knowing the One Whom We Love," *America* (July 4, 2013), http://americamagazine.org/light-faith (accessed June 27, 2015).

Dominus Iesus in his major writings, but the reference in *Lumen Fidei* is followed by this sentence: "The more Christians immerse themselves in the circle of Christ's light, the more capable they become of understanding and accompanying the path of every man and woman towards God" (35). This sentence seems to echo something Cardinal Bergoglio said in conversation with his friend Rabbi Skorka: "I do not approach the relationship in order to proselytize, or convert the atheist; I respect him and I show myself as I am. Where there is knowledge, there begins to appear esteem affection, and friendship."[19] Two ways of presenting the same thought on interfaith accompaniment implicitly seem to suggest two different views of dialogue.

4. *Evangelii Gaudium* on Dialogue

What does *Evangelii Gaudium* say about dialogue specifically, especially in light of the expanded concept of fraternity? "Dialogue" occurs at least three times as often as *fraternity* or *fraternal* combined in *Evangelii Gaudium*. The first instance is among the activities of parish life (28) where Pope Francis, appropriate to his pastoral emphasis of local over universal and peripheral over central, begins his reflection on "An Ecclesial Renewal That Cannot Be Deferred." Kasper's "new vision" and "new stimulus" were needed broadly in the Catholic Church. The next paragraph refers to other phenomena of the local church, such as basic communities and movements that "bring a new evangelizing fervor and a new capacity for dialogue with the world whereby the Church is renewed" (29). Local church in the technical parlance of Vatican II refers to dioceses where the one bishop presides in unity with his clergy and the faithful and in the communion of the one church where bishops collegially govern, teach, and administer the sacraments with the help of their clergy and people. Francis specifically mentions that each bishop must foster "this missionary communion in his diocesan Church" (31). Reading the references to dialogue carefully in *Evangelii Gaudium*, one realizes that Francis is speaking of dialogue as necessary for both the internal life of the Catholic Church one encounters locally, as well as relations with Christians, Jews, Muslims, and others. Bishops are to employ various "forms of pastoral dialogue, out of a desire to listen to everyone and not simply to those who would tell him what he would like to hear" (31).

---

[19] Jorge Mario Bergoglio and Abraham Skorka, *On Heaven and Earth*, trans. Alejandro Bermudez and Howard Goodman (New York: Image, 2013), 12.

Under "Challenges from Urban Cultures," Pope Francis introduces the concept *fraternity* and also mentions *dialogue*. He begins with the image of the New Jerusalem of *Revelation*, where the fullness of humanity and of history will be realized. He urges us to contemplate our current cities and those who live with us there and look for the presence of God that "dwells among them, fostering solidarity, fraternity, and the desire for goodness, truth and justice" (71). He calls for careful discernment of the present situation so that we may be able to enter into a "dialogue," as Jesus did with the Samaritan woman (John 4) (72). That gospel dialogue is an emblematic interreligious dialogue in the gospel narrative and obviously one that is important to Pope Francis. This narrative on Samaritan-Jewish tensions is appropriate because Francis describes cities as multicultural networks of imagination, creativity, and dreams, and places where "various subcultures exist side by side, and often practice segregation and violence." Into these situations of diversity, hopes and dreams, and exclusion and violence, Francis says that "the Church is called to be at the service of a difficult dialogue" (74). Diversity and exclusion mark relations among religions, immigrant nationalities, and economic classes.

Thus, well before the latter sections of the apostolic exhortation where Pope Francis gets around to addressing ecumenical and interreligious dialogue in a formal way, he has already delved deeply into the needs, dynamics, and importance of the various forms of dialogue. Significantly, those later sections on ecumenical and interreligious dialogue appear in chapter 4, "The Social Dimension of Evangelization," and under the subheading "Social Dialogue as a Contribution to Peace." They follow from the subheading "The Common Good and Peace in Society." In that prior section on the common good and civic and political relations, Pope Francis offers his aforementioned four principles for "building a people in peace, justice and fraternity" (221). These again are time is greater than space, unity prevails over conflict, realities are more important than ideas, and the whole is greater than the part.

Outlining and discussing these four principles just prior to the sections on ecumenical and interreligious dialogue keeps them applicable to religious relations. I make a distinction between dialogue on social and public issues for the common good and ecumenical and interreligious dialogue that share goals of mutual understanding, reconciliation, joint social action, friendship, and spiritual engagement. Ecumenical dialogue stands apart with the specific goal of the restoration of unity among Christians, whose disunity is a scandal to evangelization. Christian unity should be a sign for the world to believe (John 17:21). That major purpose of ecumenically oriented theological dialogue is a gospel purpose. It is one of the more noble aspects of evangelization as a whole. Interreligious dialogue, like ecumenical dialogue, shares the noble purpose of spiritual companionship.

The major difference between public dialogues for the common good, which the four principles of Pope Francis should guide, and ecumenical and interreligious dialogues, which jointly are "theological" in character, is that in public dialogues divergent faith traditions are respected, equal before the law, and set aside as much as is possible for pursing the common good of society while a religious or spiritual dimension pervades ecumenical and interreligious dialogues and relationships. "Theological" may seem a burdensome qualification to distinguish these relationships from "public" dialogues on the day-to-day issues that all citizens of a community face. Still, when a Muslim and a Christian become friends, share leisurely activities, live and explain their faith in one another's company, and discuss those same public issues, they may not feel that they are speaking "theologically" to one another, but they are to a degree. When religious groups band together to assist the poor in their communities, they do so out of respect for how each of their faiths urge them to this joint activity. That is a theological point; yet, these religious groups would not describe their joint activity as theological. Their friendships and cooperation flow out of their faith traditions, and they do not avoid being the members of their respective religious communities. These two hands of dialogue, the theological hand and public hand, remind us that such distinctions do not hold up neatly as realities. Dialogue in both senses is needed. The approaches complement rather than compete. Some persons emphasize theological dialogue; some emphasize public dialogue.

My perception is that Pope Francis speaks of both kinds of dialogue too, but tends to emphasize public dialogues as embodied in the principle "realities are more important than ideas." Thus, Pope Francis uses *fraternity* primarily for addressing social ills – poverty, injustice, oppression, the ecological crisis, the elements that needs to be added to the slow progress of ecumenical theological dialogue. He also uses fraternity in a religious sense as spiritual accompaniment. Time being greater than space also demonstrates his preference for contemplation in action over the more nuanced discussion of contemplation that can take place in interreligious theological dialogues. Still, he has referred to *The Cloud of Unknowing*, a fourteenth-century mystical text by an anonymous English author who feels harassed by actives to justify himself as a contemplative. That text, he says, "attempts again and again to describe God and always finishes pointing to what He is not."[20] Francis knows about pure contemplation. I heard him preach on the "Jesus prayer," a formula used by hermits seeking the solitude of prayer.[21] Aware as he is of these practices, Pope Francis favors action over ideas, time with others in social action over creating space for institutions, like hermitages, and promotes the unity to counter conflicts. He chides those in theological conversation not to lose sight of present needs, pastoral as well as social, because theological differences and nuances will be with us until the end.

Let us look more closely at *Evangelii Gaudium* to see what Pope Francis says specifically about ecumenical and interreligious dialogue. These reflections fall within the fourth and final part of chapter 4, "The Social Dimension of Evangelization" with the subtitle "Social Dialogue as a Contribution to Peace." He spends several paragraphs (238–241) discussing the social dimension of dialogue aimed toward peace. He draws from the *Letter to the Ephesians* referring to the gospel of peace (6:15) and Christ our peace (2:14) and then urges every Christian to be a peacemaker. The second reference to the *Ephesians* is also a passage used in the Vatican II declaration *Nostra Aetate* (4) in reference to relations with Jews for Christ "has made the two into one." Pope Francis believes that all forms of dialogue should promote human dignity, reconciliation, justice, and peace. This is not dialogue for a privileged few or for a highly educated and skill class but for everyone.

Chapter 4 has five subheadings with the first on the dialogue between faith, reason, and science (242–243). Despite "between" being a problematic translation in English for a relationship among three elements because reason could join with either faith or science, it is clear that Francis is speaking of "dialogue" in its public dimension. Pope Francis then devotes three numbered paragraphs to ecumenical dialogue, citing first a key passage in Vatican *Unitatis Redintegratio* reiterating one of the Council's major contributions – the notion of real but imperfect communion that Catholics share with all the baptized in varying degrees. Pope Francis universalizes the relationship by using a favored image of the church, "We must never forget that we are pilgrims journeying alongside one another." Ecumenism

[20] Ibid., 14–15.
[21] This occurred at morning liturgy January 22, 2015 at Santa Marta. He mentioned the prayer, "Lord Jesus Christ have mercy on me," and alters it a little based on the scripture readings of the day, Mark 3: 1–12 and Heb 7:25; 8:6, "Lord Jesus Christ, have mercy on me, intercede for me." http://www.news.va/en/news/mass-at-santa-marta-the-one-who-intercedes-on-our (accessed July 17, 2015).

is the pilgrimage of Christian peoples to that full unity for which Christ prayed on the night before he died. He then urges us to have "sincere trust in our fellow pilgrims" and quickly couples trust with peacemaking citing the beatitude or "peacemakers" from Matthew (5:9) and Isaiah's vision of swords into plowshares (2:4).

After recalling the contributions of Greek Orthodox Patriarch Bartholomew and of Archbishop Rowan Williams of Canterbury to the synod on the new evangelization, for which *Evangelii Gaudium* was written as a summation and exhortation, he devotes an entire paragraph to the scandal of division. What is his focus? It is not on the work to be done to resolve the differences among Christians. He urges doing something now: "If we concentrate on the convictions we share, and if we keep in mind the principle of the hierarchy of truths, we will be able to progress decidedly towards common expressions of proclamation, service and witness" (246). This is an immediate goal. He continues in this practical line:

> If we really believe in the abundantly free working of the Holy Spirit, we can learn so much from one another! It is not just about being better informed about others, but rather about reaping what the Spirit has sown in them, which is also meant to be a gift for us. (246)

Indeed, this has been Francis's own practice and why he is a celebrity among so many worldwide. He has knelt down for blessings from Evangelical and Pentecostal Christians. He was washed the feet of Muslims. He has met with Christian leaders who are generally outside the formal ecumenical movement, whose communities have expressed little interest in being one with the Catholic Church, and has offered words of consolation and reconciliation. In his treatment of ecumenism in *Evangelii Gaudium*, Pope Francis does not talk specifically about the progress in the formal dialogues and their accomplishments. Earlier in the encyclical (32 and 41), he cites *Ut Unum Sint*, the 1995 encyclical of John Paul II, particularly its striking paragraphs where his predecessor invited all Christians to reflect with him on the role of papacy in the service of unity (95) and, in keeping with the spirit of his own encyclical, where John Paul II reiterates in a conciliatory way "that the expression of truth can take different forms" (19). Both of these references serve Pope Francis's point that what is most important is the gospel, and we need the diversity of Christian voices for enhancing its message today. While, for example, the 1999 *Joint Declaration on the Doctrine of Justification* between the Holy See and the Lutheran World Federation was a remarkable achievement and one to be celebrated, Pope

Francis is pressing home how much unity we already have that allows effective evangelization now.[22] His concerns are for immediate needs.

Pope Francis then offers three numbered paragraphs on relations with Jews (247–249). Rather than citing the conciliar declaration *Nostra Aetate*, he quotes the key passage from St. Paul's *Letter to the Romans* that *Nostra Aetate* restores as a basis for Christian-Jewish relations. It is this New Testament letter that reminds the followers of Jesus that God's covenant with the Jews has not been surpassed nor replaced: "the gifts and the call of God are irrevocable" (Rom 11:29). That covenant, the history of salvation, and the Jewish people are collectively the roots of the Christian community (11:16–18). Pope Francis makes a further point that had become obscured in the aftermath of discussions and arguments generated by *Dominus Iesus*, the declaration of the Vatican's Congregation for the Doctrine of the Faith mentioned earlier. Pope Francis declares, "We cannot consider Judaism as a foreign religion; nor do we include the Jews among those called to turn from idols and to serve the true God (cf. *1 Thes* 1:9)."[23]

In a brief paragraph, Pope Francis acknowledges how the more our friendship with Jews increases the more we "bitterly and sincerely regret the terrible persecutions" that we Christians have perpetrated against them. Then, he testifies to the rich cooperation available despite the fact that major Christian beliefs are not acceptable to Jews and that Christians must always proclaim Jesus as Lord and Messiah. For example, he singles out "a rich complementarity which allows us to read the texts of the Hebrew Scriptures together and to help one another to mine the riches of God's

---

[22] On December 18, 2014, Pope Francis received a delegation of Lutherans from the Evangelical Lutheran Church in Germany. On that occasion he said: "Joint texts, such as the 'Joint Declaration on the Doctrine of Justification' – to which you referred – between the Lutheran World Federation and the Pontifical Council for Promoting Christian Unity, officially signed 15 years ago in Augsburg, are important milestones, which allow us to proceed with trust on the path undertaken." http://w2.vatican.va/content/francesco/en/speeches/2014/december/documents/papa-francesco_20141218_chiesa-evangelica-luterana.html (accessed December 20, 2014). When he met a year earlier (October 21, 2013) with a delegation from the Lutheran World Federation, he cited John Paul II's *Ut Unum Sint* on reconciliation: "How can we proclaim the Gospel of reconciliation without at the same time being committed to working for reconciliation between Christians?" http://www.vatican.va/holy_father/francesco/speeches/2013/october/documents/papa-francesco_20131021_delegazione-luterana_en.html (accessed October 22, 2013).

[23] For a discussion of Cardinal Bergoglio's reaction to *Dominus Iesus* see Fredericks, "Francis's Interreligious Friendships," 14. See also, John R. Donahue, "Trouble Ahead? The Future of Catholic-Jewish Relations," *Commonweal* (March 13, 2009) and John Borelli, "Troubled Waters: Catholic-Jewish Relations in the United States Have Grown Strained," *America* (February 22, 2010).

word" and that we "share many ethical convictions and a common concern for justice and the development of peoples."

Pope Francis proceeds by a traditional route from the conciliar documents of Vatican II, first mentioning Christians with whom we share a real but imperfect sacramental communion, then Jews with whom we share a scripture and much more from a common tradition, and then to relations with the followers all the other religions with whom we have varying commonalities and many differences. He devotes the most space to interreligious relations. The architecture is important because he begins this chapter with an opening section on peace and closes it with section on religious freedom. These sections apply to relations with all people of goodwill.

Beginning with an interesting reference to "forms of fundamentalism on both sides," Pope Francis declares that "interreligious dialogue is a necessary condition for peace in the world, and so it is a duty for Christians as well as other religious communities" (250). The approach of Pope Francis in most matters involves both humility and balance. Before he points a finger, he admits his own flaws. Recall how he opened his interview with Antonio Spadaro, S.J., in August 2013, "I do not know what might be the most fitting description.... I am a sinner. This is the most accurate definition. It is not a figure of speech, a literary genre. I am a sinner." As the interview proceeded, he offered harsh criticisms, not to any specific person by name but to general groups, especially church leaders. For example, when he explained what he meant by "thinking with the church," he criticized those who live with the status quo: "We must not reduce the bosom of the universal church to a nest protecting our mediocrity." In exploring the image of the church as a field hospital he offers this popular criticism: "The people of God want pastors, not clergy acting like bureaucrats or government officials."[24] Rather than blaming other religious groups for "fundamentalism," Pope Francis acknowledges problems on both sides.[25] Dialogue is necessary for peace, a duty for all, and an opportunity for honesty and discernment.

Almost naturally, then, Pope Francis presents interreligious dialogue in *Evangelii Gaudium* in its most ordinary and humble form: "This dialogue is in first place a conversation about human existence or simply, as the bishops of India have put it, a matter of 'being open to them, sharing their

---

[24] "The Exclusive Interview with Pope Francis: A Big Heart Open to God," *America* (September 30, 2015) 16, 22, and 24.

[25] A point reiterated in his in-flight press conference on departing from his visit to Africa in December 2015.

joys and sorrows'" (250). The reference is to a text of the Indian Bishops' Conference, a final declaration of their Thirtieth Assembly, entitled *The Role of the Church for a Better India* (March 8, 2013). Citations to regional and national conferences of bishops were a surprising and refreshing feature of *Evangelii Gaudium*. None are cited in *Lumen Fidei*.

The Pontifical Council for Interreligious Dialogue, known as the Secretariat for Non-Christians for the first twenty-two years of its history, has gathered the expertise from Catholics around the world to summarize the lessons and insights gained. Their first major summary appeared in 1984 under the title *The Attitude of the Church toward Followers of Other Religions: Reflections and Orientations on Dialogue and Mission*.[26] That text for the first time laid out a fourfold form for interreligious dialogue: the dialogue of life, the dialogue of deeds, the dialogue of specialists, and the dialogue of religious experience. Later, in 1991, the Pontifical Council for Interreligious Dialogue in the text is coproduced with the Congregation for the Evangelization of Peoples, *Dialogue and Proclamation: Reflections and Orientations on Interreligious Dialogue and the Proclamation of the Gospel of Jesus Christ*, slightly renamed these: the dialogue of life, the dialogue of action, the dialogue of theological exchange, and the dialogue of religious experience.[27] Both lists begin with the dialogue of life. Pope Francis shows his awareness of this in two ways. First, he suggests that the dialogue of life provides a basis for the dialogue of action, "We can then join one another in taking up the duty of serving justice and peace, which should become a basic principle of all our exchanges." Commitment to action raises ethical questions, provides opportunity for mutual listening, and orientates the participants with a love for truth (250). Second, Pope Francis turns to the title of the 1991 joint text, "Dialogue and Proclamation," in the next paragraph.

Pope Francis agrees that there is an "essential bond between dialogue and proclamation" (251). Discussion of the relationship between the two has not been fully satisfying. Not entirely pleased by the effort of the

---

[26] The text can be found in several places. There is a website: http://www.pcinterreligious.org/dialogue-and-mission_75.html (accessed July 20, 2015). It is included in *Interreligious Dialogue the Official Teaching of the Catholic Church from the Second Vatican Council to John Paul II (1963–2005)*, ed. Francesco Gioia (Boston: Pauline Books and Media, 2006), 1116–1129. The Secretariat for Non-Christians published it in *Bulletin* 56 (1984-XIX/2) in several languages.

[27] *Dialogue and Proclamation* is far easier to find. E.g., http://www.vatican.va/roman_curia/pontifical_councils/interelg/documents/rc_pc_interelg_doc_19051991_dialogue-and-proclamatio_en.html (accessed July 20, 2015), in Gioia, *Interreligious Dialogue*, 1156–1189, and in *Origins, Catholic News Service Documentary Service* 21(8) (July 4, 1991).

The Dialogue of Fraternity

Secretariat for Non-Christians to explain the relationship in its own text in 1984, Pope John Paul II asked the Secretariat to do it again but jointly with the Congregation for the Evangelization of Peoples. Eventually, this process involved a third Vatican office, the Congregation for the Doctrine of the Faith, and the text, "Dialogue and Proclamation" was issued in 1991, six months after Pope John Paul II's encyclical on mission, *Redemptoris Missio*.[28] Pope Francis also cites this encyclical as well as some 2006 remarks by Pope Benedict XVI on the same topic. Francis's point is not one of rigidity and requirements but of authenticity urging avoidance of an inauthentic facile syncretism, a totalitarian gesture, and "diplomatic openness." Citing John Paul II, he urges a confident openness based on steadfast convictions as well as a desire to hear and understand others for mutual enrichment and for each to share the good that they have been given. *Desire* is an important word. It implies more than giving lip service to a need to listen to others. Pope Francis is speaking not of formal exchanges but of friendship. Personal relationships of respect and friends are the lens for interpreting the complementarity of evangelization and dialogue, for example, in the remarks of Pope Benedict XVI in his final summary speech to the Roman Curia (251).[29]

Pope Francis then devotes two paragraphs to relations with Muslims. What he writes is not new about the Catholic Church's esteem for Muslims, but his tone is encouragingly a revival of the approach of the Council. While John Paul II was well-received and publicly thanked by Muslim leaders on several public occasions, Pope Benedict's relationship with Muslim leaders was rocky.[30] Francis devotes a paragraph to repeating the teaching of the Second Vatican Council and cites the *Dogmatic Constitution on the Church (Lumen Gentium)* (16) for strength (252). In the next paragraph, he observes that "suitable training is essential for all involved," presumably in Christian-Muslim dialogue, especially to "acknowledge the values of others, appreciate the concerns underlying their demands and shed light

---

[28] The best commentary on the process was written by Jacques Dupuis, S.J., "A Theological Commentary: *Dialogue and Proclamation*," in *Redemption and Dialogue: Reading Redemptoris Missio and Dialogue and Proclamation*, ed. William Burrows (Maryknoll, NY: Orbis Books, 1993), 119–160.

[29] The citation in *EG* is: Cf. Benedict XVI, Address to the Roman Curia (December 21, 2012): AAS 105 (2006), 51; Second Vatican Ecumenical Council, Decree on the Missionary Activity of the Church *Ad Gentes*, 9; *Catechism of the Catholic Church*, 856.

[30] See John Borelli, "Judgment at Regensburg," *New Theology Review* 20(3) (August 2007), 44–54; John Borelli, "Of a Different Order," *The Tablet* (August 21, 2010), 9–10; Marco Politi, "The Pope and Islam: Is There Anything Benedict XVI Would Like to Discuss?," *The New Yorker* (April 2, 2007).

on shared beliefs." Pope Francis is making equal demands of Catholics and involved in dialogue. He tells Christians that they should "embrace with affection and respect Muslim immigrants" and entreats countries with Muslim majorities "to grant Christians freedom to worship and to practice their faith." While upset as all are with "disconcerting episodes of violent fundamentalism," nevertheless Pope Francis warns Christians against "hateful generalizations" for he knows that Muslims and their scriptures oppose every form of violence (253). His words and tone are courageous because there has been a tendency to blame Muslims as a whole for the persecution and killing of Christians.

Pope Francis concludes the section on interreligious dialogue with one more paragraph of general reflections. Here he draws mainly from a report of the International Theological Commission, "Christianity and the World Religions" (1996).[31] While not providing the richest set of theological reflections on religious pluralism, the report does not give a negative interpretation. *Dominus Iesus*, the 2000 declaration issued by the Congregation for the Doctrine of the Faith while Pope Benedict XVI was still its prefect, did give a negative interpretation, embodied best in this passage: "If it is true that the followers of other religions can receive divine grace, it is also certain that objectively speaking they are in a gravely deficient situation in comparison with those who, in the Church, have the fullness of the means of salvation." There followed a citation to the encyclical of Pope Pius XII *Mystici Corporis*.[32] I have always felt that the citation was inappropriate because it was a reference to all who are separated from the Roman Catholic Church, including those Christians who very nearly agree doctrinally with Catholics.

The statement in *Dominus Iesus* follows a paragraph of reluctant acknowledgment of the efficacy of other religions. The text admits that other religions have elements from God and give evidence of the Holy Spirit working in the hearts of their followers, but even their prayers and rituals are occasions when their hearts might need be "to be open to the action of God." It is as though "those elements from God" in the hearts of other believers are twice removed from their divine origin. This then allows *Dominus Iesus* to judge that "these," presumably the prayers and rituals of the other religions that may assume a role of preparation of individual hearts and minds for the gospel, are not of divine origin and lack salvific

---

[31] http://www.vatican.va/roman_curia/congregations/cfaith/cti_documents/rc_cti_1997_cristianesimo-religioni_en.html.

[32] *DI* 22. http://www.vatican.va/roman_curia/congregations/cfaith/documents/rc_con_cfaith_doc_20000806_dominus-iesus_en.html (accessed July 21, 2015).

efficacy, which *Dominus Iesus* then qualifies, "is proper to the Christian sacraments."[33] Pope Francis's tone is far more conciliatory, "While these lack the meaning and efficacy of the sacraments instituted by Christ, they can be channels which the Holy Spirit raises up in order to liberate non-Christians from atheistic immanentism or from purely individual religious experiences" (*EG* 254).[34] He then declares that the same spirit brings wisdom, strength, and other benefits to all and opportunities for mutual learning. The tone is more welcoming and the message is more positive and appreciative of religious diversity than conveyed in *Dominus Iesus* and often in the messages its sponsor, Cardinal Ratzinger, when he became Pope Benedict.

5. Conclusion

Enormously important as *Evangelii Gaudium* is as the bedrock text for understanding the core beliefs and values of Pope Francis, it still offers little explicitly on exactly what difference Francis will make in the long run on ecumenical, interreligious, and other forms of Catholic outreach through dialogue. When he spoke in January 2015 to an interreligious gathering in Colombo, Sri Lanka, he called for fraternal solidarity among a population that had suffered through decades of civil strife: "How many are the needs that must be tended to with the healing balm of fraternal solidarity!" He then offered this significant qualification: "I think in particular of the material and spiritual needs of the poor, the destitute, those who yearn for a word of consolation and hope."[35] A few months earlier in September 2014, speaking to an assembly of religious leaders in Tirana, Albania, he raised the topic of interreligious dialogue in the context of providing for those in need:

> Let us look around us: there are so many poor and needy people, so many societies that try to find a more inclusive way of social justice and path of economic development! How great is the need for the human heart to be firmly fixed on the deepest meaning of experiences in life and rooted in a rediscovery of hope! Men and women, inspired in these areas by the values of their respective religious traditions, can offer an important, and

---

[33] *DI* 21.
[34] See Fredericks, "Francis's Interreligious Friendships," 14.
[35] "Interreligious and Ecumenical Gather," Bandaranaike Memorial International Conference Hall, Colombo (January 13, 2015), http://w2.vatican.va/content/francesco/en/speeches/2015/january/documents/papa-francesco_20150113_srilanka-filippine-incontro-interreligioso.html (accessed July 20, 2015).

even unique, contribution. This is truly a fertile land offering much fruit, also in the field of interreligious dialogue.[36]

Turning to ecumenical relations, when Pope Francis became the first pope ever to visit a Waldensian church on June 22, 2015, he spoke of fraternity. The tiny Waldensian Evangelical Church, original to Italy, has roots in the earliest phase of the Protestant Reformation and has not always been interested in an ecumenical outreach, especially with the huge Catholic Church of its native land. For Waldensians of the reformed tradition, the message of fraternity was just right:

> One of the principal fruits which the ecumenical movement has already allowed to be harvested in these years is the rediscovery of the fraternity which unites all those who believe in Jesus Christ and have been baptized in his name. This bond is not based on simply human criteria, but on the radical sharing of the foundational experience of Christian life: encountering the love of God which is revealed to us in Jesus Christ and the transforming action of the Holy Spirit who assists us in the journey of life. The rediscovery of this fraternity allows us to perceive the profound bond which already unites us, despite our differences. It is a communion still in progress – unity is achieved while walking – a communion which, with prayer, with constant personal and communitarian conversion and with the help of theologians, we hope, faithful in the work of the Holy Spirit, it may become a full and visible communion in truth and in charity.[37]

Pope Francis offered two examples of how this communion-while-walking might grow – through evangelization and through service to the humanity that is suffering, to the poor, to the sick, to migrants. And, when he made a return visit to Evangelical pastors, because they had visited him in Buenos Aires, he accepted an invitation to a Pentecostal church in Caserta, Italy. There he told the audience, "We are on this path of unity, between brothers and sisters." This was his reiteration of a point made earlier in his address: "Christians standing still: this harms, because what is still, what does not walk, spoils."[38] The longtime staff member of the Pontifical Council for the Promotion of Christian Unity who has staffed

---

[36] "Meeting with Leaders of Other Religions and Other Christian Denominations" (September 21, 2014), http://w2.vatican.va/content/francesco/en/speeches/2014/september/documents/papa-francesco_20140921_albania-leaders-altre-religioni.html (accessed October 9, 2014).

[37] http://w2.vatican.va/content/francesco/en/speeches/2015/june/documents/papa-francesco_20150622_torino-chiesa-valdese.html (accessed June 30, 2015).

[38] http://w2.vatican.va/content/francesco/en/speeches/2014/july/documents/papa-francesco_20140728_caserta-pastore-traettino.html (accessed July 28, 2014).

relations with Pentecostals and Evangelicals, Monsignor Juan Usma Gomez, told Vatican Radio in advance that Pope Francis teaches that "to work for Christian unity you need brotherhood, [fraternity]" and this is why he nurtures the friendships he had in Argentina, and why he gave special attention to Pentecostal Bishop Tony Palmer.[39]

The conciliar *Decree on Ecumenism* (UR) makes the point that "there can be no ecumenism worthy of the name without a change of heart" (7). From the moment Francis knelt down on the balcony of St. Peter's basilica and asked for everyone's blessing and prayers, he has signaled such a change of heart. Speaking as a shepherd, teacher, and retreat master, Pope Francis guides everyone wishing to join this pilgrimage from inner discernment, through acknowledgment of imperfections and conversion, to resolution to follow the example of Christ, toward serving a world in great need.[40] In this context, Pope Francis has embraced the ecumenical and interreligious trajectories of Vatican II. His apostolic exhortation *Evangelii Gaudium* can be read, along with other evidence from Francis's life, as a call to renew the dialogue initiatives of council in the spirit that the council intended them. One of the great prophets of reform at Vatican II, Yves Congar, O.P., observed in his monumental volume, *True and False Reform in the Church*, "The true prophet, the prophet according to the Spirit that gives life to the church, finds a way to do what must be done and to be listened to. For there is a certain tone that does not deceive and that the church can discern as authentic."[41] In conveying the joy of the gospel while rallying Catholics to a pilgrimage and accompaniment with others toward discernment, reform and action, Pope Francis is fulfilling the role of Congar's true prophet.

---

[39] Cindy Wooden, "Meeting 200 Pentecostals, Pope Renews Friendship, Talks Unity," Catholic News Service (July 28, 2014).
[40] John Borelli, "Evangelii Gaudium: Meaning and Impact – Power to the People of God," *The Tablet* (December 5, 2013).
[41] Yves Congar, O.P., *True and False Reform in the Church*, trans. and with an introduction by Paul Philibert, O.P. (Collegeville, MN: Liturgical Press, 2011), 283.

Index

Abboud, Omar, 226
Accompaniment, 223, 224, 231, 233, 243
Acedia of White Supremacy, 17, 144, 156, 157
Acta Apostolica Sedis, xvii
Ad Gentes, xvii, 39, 47, 47n15, 87n29, 239n29
Aggiornamento, 43n8, 55, 106
Albania, 241
American Academy of Religion, 95
Anglicanism, 227, 228
Apostolicam Actuositatem, xvii
Argentina, 6, 24, 70, 98, 99, 105, 110, 111n49, 117, 136, 145, 146, 146n14, 146n16, 157, 163, 166, 168, 225, 226, 227, 242, 243
Augustine of Hippo, 49, 57n15, 134, 195
Australia, viii, xii, 169

Bartholomew, Patriarch, 222, 235
Beinert, Wolfgang, 58, 59, 59n6, 64n15, 65
Benedict XVI, Pope, 1, 3, 10, 17, 18, 25, 26, 27, 29, 30, 30n18, 31, 32, 33, 34, 36, 49, 59n7, 65, 95n11, 96, 98, 109, 128, 128n9, 153, 162, 162n2, 163, 170, 172, 173, 174, 186, 186n29, 190, 191, 191n47, 192n52, 197, 203, 204n1, 205, 225, 227, 239, 239n29, 239n30, 240
Bernanos, Georges, 49
Blondel, Maurice, 217
Boff, Leonardo, 107, 107n37, 109n46, 110, 116, 210
Boston College, vii, viii, xi, xii, 14, 17
Brazil, 48, 105
Buber, Martin, 208
Buddhism, ix, 209

C9. *See* Council of Global Cardinals
Caritas in veritate, 29, 192n52, 210n30

Catholic Social Teaching, xii, 16, 143, 179, 180, 181, 185, 190, 192, 194, 198, 214n44
Centesimus Annus, xviii, 18n19, 190n41
China, 18, 209, 211, 212, 213, 219
Christus Dominus, xvii, 39, 42
Civilizational Dialogue, 18, 211
Columbia, xii, 110, 146n16
Comblin, José, 118, 118n74, 118n77
Common Good, 45n13, 47, 104, 126, 127, 128, 129, 139, 140, 141, 142, 153, 197, 199, 203, 213, 232, 233
Conclave of Cardinals, 163, 164, 166
Congar, Yves, 51, 77, 84, 90, 243
Congregation for the Doctrine of the Faith, xvii, xviii, 27, 27n14, 31, 97, 106, 109, 109n46, 205, 230, 236, 239, 240
Consumerism, 29, 171
Council of Global Cardinals, 98, 108
Council of Trent, 51
Critical Race Theory, 144, 149, 156
Cuba, 7

Day, Dorothy, 191
de Lubac, Henri, 24, 49, 165
Dei Verbum, xviii, 39, 44, 165
Dignitatis Humanae, xvii, 48
Dignity of Work, 29
Diplomacy, 212, 219, 239
Doak, Mary, viii, x, 17, 109n44, 179, 192
Dolan, Cardinal Timothy, 175
Dominus Iesus, xviii, 106, 205n8, 230, 236, 236n23, 240, 240n32, 241n33
Donum Veritatis, xviii
Dulles, Avery, 149, 150

Index

Eastern Orthodoxy, ix, 209, 235
Ecclesial Renewal, 83–85
Ecclesial Structures, 75–83, 85, 92
Ecclesiam suam, xviii, 77
Ecclesiological Decentralization, 15, 33, 52, 76, 85, 90, 92, 100, 116, 119, 119n82
Ecclesiological Pluralism, 115–17
Ecclesiological Realism, 117–21
Ecclesiology of Liberation, 109–17
Ecology, 8, 52
Economic Justice For All, 127, 127n6, 129, 130n19
Economy of Death, viii, 179, 188
Ecumenical Dialogue, 91, 96, 222, 233, 234
Environmentalism, 4, 42, 132, 138, 139, 140, 181n10
European Union, 168
Evangelicalism, 227, 243
Evangelii Nuntiandi, xviii, 38, 47, 102, 102n19, 137, 137n36, 225
Evangelization as Kenosis, 65–74

France, 48, 87
Francis of Assisi, 5, 36, 98, 107n37, 163, 166
Fundamentalism, 140, 217, 237, 240

Gaudet Mater Ecclesia, 24n8, 39, 40, 40n4, 41, 54, 82n14
Gaudete in Domino, 225
Gaudium et Spes, xviii, 19, 34, 35, 36n23, 38, 39, 45, 45n13, 46n14, 48, 50, 57, 57n15, 57n15, 65, 67n21, 68, 82n13, 101, 101n16, 102, 126, 213n40, 219n64
Georgetown University, i, vii, viii, ix, xi, xii, xiv, 12, 16, 17, 18, 111n51, 155n52
Global Capitalism, 67, 179, 181, 182, 185, 188
Global Church, 1, 51, 90–92
Global South, 7, 9
Globalization, 141, 142, 143, 169, 170, 175, 184, 191, 209, 218
Globalization of Indifference, xvi, 32, 132, 143, 156, 157, 165, 169, 170, 175, 184, 191, 198
Gomez, Msgr. Juan Usma, 243
Gravissimum Educationis, xviii
Guardini, Romano, 49
Gutiérrez, Gustavo, 110, 110n48, 112, 112n54, 115, 116, 116n71

Hadot, Pierre, 211
Hauerwas, Stanley, 193, 195, 196

Hellenism, 58, 65, 66, 204, 205, 230
Hopkins, Gerard Manley, 206
Huntington, Samuel, 209

Ignatius of Loyola, 133, 218
Inculturation, 11, 51, 53, 71, 76, 81, 104n26, 111n50, 148, 149, 154, 155, 204, 205
India, 48, 209, 237
Inter Mirifica, xviii, 39
Intercultural Dialogue, 212
International Theological Commission, xvii, 211, 211n33, 211n35, 212n37, 240
Interreligious Dialogue, i, ix, 14, 18, 39, 47, 52, 96, 102n18, 103, 104, 106, 145n11, 173, 173n34, 198n73, 222, 225, 228, 230, 232, 233, 234, 237, 238, 240, 241, 242, 243
Islam, ix, 105, 167, 173, 209, 209n25, 210, 220, 222, 226, 231, 233, 235, 239, 239n30, 240
Italy, xii, xiii, 120, 227n12, 242

James, William, 207, 217
Jesuits, viii, ix, xi, xii, 9, 17, 18, 23, 54, 98, 110, 111n50, 111n50, 116, 133, 136, 146, 147, 147n19, 163, 170, 180n15, 190n41, 206, 211, 212, 218
Jesuit Refugee Service, xi, xii, 17
Jesus Prayer, 234
John Chrysostom, 182

John "Duns" Scotus, 206
John XXIII, Pope, i, x, xi, 2, 7, 8, 15, 18, 19, 24, 31, 39, 40, 40n4, 41, 49, 51, 54, 54n29, 71, 82n14, 97, 101, 103, 106n35, 108, 119, 126, 126n3, 214, 222, 225, 226
Judaism, 2, 48, 58, 65, 66n19, 145, 222, 224, 231, 232, 234, 236, 236n23, 237

John Paul II, Pope, x, xviii, 3, 25, 26, 26n13, 27, 28, 29, 29n17, 30, 31, 32, 34, 36, 40, 43, 51, 82n15, 85, 91, 95, 96, 96n2, 108, 108n42, 109n46, 120, 127, 128, 129n17, 153, 179n2, 181n9, 190, 197, 203, 205, 208, 208n20, 215, 223, 223n4, 224, 235, 236n22, 238n26, 239

Kasper, Cardinal Walter, 14, 33, 34, 34n21, 35, 76, 76n2, 76n3, 90, 91n43, 208, 208n23, 227, 228, 228n14, 230, 231
Keenan, James F., 158, 159

Index

Laborem Exercens, xviii, 129n17
Latin America, 4, 7, 8, 16, 48, 51, 52, 95, 99, 109, 110, 110n48, 111n49, 111n50, 112, 113, 114, 116n70, 146n16
Liberation Theology, 16, 94, 109, 110, 110n48, 111, 111n49, 111n51, , 112, 113, 115, 116, 117, 121, 122, 190
Localization, 141, 142
Lumen Gentium, xviii, 38, 38n3, 43, 44, 45, 45n11, 46, 57, 194n58, 239
Lutheran World Federation, 235
Lutheranism, 104, 228, 235, 236n22, 236n22

Magaña, Alvaro Quiroz, 113, 114
Mali, 168
Marxism, 186, 187
Massingale, Bryan, 143, 153, 153n45, 156
McCartin, Joseph, 155
Mexico, 110, 110n48, 113, 190
Milbank, John, 193, 197
Miller, Vincent J., 199
Multiculturalism, 149, 208
Muslim. *See* Islam
Myanmar, 209
Mystici Corporis, 25, 25n11

Neoliberalism, 188
Newman, Cardinal John Henry, 49, 63, 65, 214
Nicholas of Cusa, 206
Niebuhr, Reinhold, xiv, 141, 142
Nilles, Bernd, 171
Non-Believers, 39, 149, 197, 198, 230, 231
Nostra Aetate, xviii, 48

Optatam Totius, xviii
Option for the Poor, 35, 110, 128, 129, 131, 132, 133, 135, 136, 137, 142, 172, 176, 181, 190, 190n44, 191, 192, 198
Oriental Christianity, 204, 206, 220
Orientalium Ecclesiarum, xviii
Orsy, Ladislas, 24
Ortega y Alamino, Cardinal Jaime Lucas, 166

Pacem in Terris, 39, 42, 126, 176, 177n48, 213, 214
Palmer, Tony, 227, 227n12, 243
Paul VI, Pope, xviii, 24, 29, 31, 34, 38, 42, 42n7, 47, 49, 51, 77, 96, 96n12, 97, 102, 102n19, 122n88, 137, 137n36, 164, 180n6, 210, 214, 219, 225

Peacemaking, 18, 208, 212, 213, 214, 215, 216, 217, 218n59, 219, 235
Pentecostalism, 120, 227, 227n12, 235, 242, 243, 243n39
Perfectae Caritatis, xviii
Philippines, xii, 48
Pius XII, Pope, 25, 40, 97, 240
Pluralism, 18, 70, 73, 82, 84, 85, 86, 87, 104, 115, 116, 117, 159, 197, 207, 218, 240
Pontifical Council for Interreligious Dialogue, ix, 227, 238
Pontifical Council for Promoting Christian Unity, 228, 236n22
Porta Fidei, 162, 162n2, 163, 170
Presbyterorum Ordinis, xviii

Rahner, Karl, 24, 54, 189
Ratzinger, Joseph. *See* Benedict XVI, Pope
Reconciled Diversity, 104–06
Redemptor Hominis, xviii
Redemptoris Missio, xviii, 239n28
Rerum Novarum, 16, 125, 181n9
Ressourcement, 54, 56
Roncalli, Angelo. *See* John XXIII, Pope

Sacrosanctum concilium, xviii
Secretariat for Non-Christians. *See* Pontifical Council for Interreligious Dialogue
Secularism, xv, 26, 58, 65, 193, 195, 196n66, 197, 204n13
Segundo, Juan Luis, 114, 114n61, 115, 115n62, 115n63
Semmelroth, Otto, 24
Skorka, Rabbi Abraham, 225, 226, 231
Sobrino, Jon, 24, 114, 116
Society of St. Pius X, 59
Sollicitudo Rei Socialis, xviii, 223
Spadaro, Antonio, 75, 111n50, 237
Sri Lanka, 209, 241
Stransky, Thomas, 224n5
Syria, xii, 7, 168, 219, 220

Tauran, Cardinal Jean-Louis, 5
Teel, Karen, 145, 148, 148n23
Teilhard de Chardin, Pierre, 24
Tertio Millennio Ineunte, 208, 208n20
The Cloud of Unknowing, 233
The Decree on Ecumenism, 224n5
Theological Dialogue, 226, 228, 233
Thomas Aquinas, 49, 57n15, 101, 195, 195n64, 206

Tibet, 209, 213
Tillich, Paul, 192

Unitatis Redintegratio, xviii, 34, 39, 42, 44, 44n10, 47, 90n39
United Nations, 8, 175
United States of America, 48
Ut Unum Sint, xviii, 40, 43, 235, 236n22

Waldensians, 120, 242
Williams, Archbishop Rowan, 235
Wise, Tim, 144

Yancy, George, 145, 147, 148, 155, 155n54, 158, 160, 160n72
Year of Faith, 17, 162–64